KU-175-230

PETER ALLISS
MY LIFE

PETER ALLISS

MY LIFE

HODDER &
STOUGHTON

Copyright © 2004 by Peter Alliss

First published in Great Britain in 2004 by Hodder and Stoughton
A division of Hodder Headline
This edition published in 2005

The right of Peter Alliss to be identified as the Author
of the Work has been asserted by him in accordance
with the Copyright, Designs and Patents Act 1988

A Hodder and Stoughton paperback

1

All rights reserved. No part of this publication may be reproduced,
stored in a retrieval system, or transmitted, in any form or by any
means without the prior written permission of the publisher,
nor be otherwise circulated in any form of binding or cover other
than that in which it is published and without a similar condition
being imposed on the subsequent purchaser

A CIP catalogue record for this title
is available from the British Library

ISBN 0 340 83400 5

Typeset in Galliard by Hewer Text UK Ltd, Edinburgh
Printed and bound by Mackays of Chatham Ltd, Chatham, Kent

Hodder Headline's policy is to use papers that are natural, renewable
and recyclable products and made from wood grown in sustainable forests.
The logging and manufacturing processes are expected to conform to
the environmental regulations of the country of origin

Hodder and Stoughton Ltd
A division of Hodder Headline
338 Euston Road
London NW1 3BH

*To Jackie and to all my family, who have
been so supportive over the years, through thick
and thin, good and bad, my love and
thanks always*

Contents

Contents

ACKNOWLEDGEMENTS

My sincere thanks to Marilyn Cooper, who carried on helping me with this book after the tragic death of my secretary and family friend Helen Cameron. Many thanks also to Marilyn's husband Roy, who has been a tower of strength.

Thanks, too, to all at Hodder & Stoughton and particularly Roddy Bloomfield, for all the hard work he put into this project despite being seriously ill for a month during the last stages of the book's construction. Happily he is now back at his desk.

Photographic Acknowledgements

The author and publisher would like to thank the following for permission to reproduce photographs:

Allsport Hulton Archive/Getty Images, Central Press/Getty Images, Clear Water Images Limited, Adam Cooper, Empics, Bob Gomel/Time Life Pictures/Getty Images, Jeff Haynes/AFP/Getty Images, Michael Joy, Andy Lyons/Getty Images, Brian Morgan Golf Photography, Popperfoto.com, Phil Sheldon Golf Picture Library, Rick Stewart/Getty Images, Tim Wood of Classic Folios.

All other photographs are from private collections.

IN THE BEGINNING

'Just before Hitler closed the banks in 1932, mother managed to extract some money which, on leaving the country, she stuffed in her bloomers'

Life began for me on a spring evening in May 1930.

It was getting on towards the end of May and my father, Percy, had had a busy day at the Wannsee Golf Club teaching many of the local dignitaries and, as he made his way home through the course to the rather substantial bungalow the Alliss family lived in at that time, he was looking forward to a good supper and an evening's relaxation. Remember this was 1930 – no television, I'm not too sure he even had a radio, so what would the evening's festivities consist of? Conversation? Tiddlywinks? Cards? You name it . . . but it wasn't to be an evening like that. Supper came and went, suddenly it was time for bed. Mother was looking particularly attractive in her long Winceyette nightgown with a little pink jacket to keep her shoulders warm. She had decided that this was a night of loving passion. What happened after that I don't know but on 28 February 1931 I appeared at 14lb 11oz, a European record which stood for many years, and not only was I such a substantial baby, but I was one of twins. It was perhaps fortunate that my twin never fully developed. Poor mother weighed about 9 stone, so delivering two heavyweights could well have proved too much for her. As it was, she had to spend several months in bed recovering from my birth.

'Manners maketh man' say the Wykehamists. Hmmm, I'm not sure that's quite enough and I'm not exactly certain what their manners meant in that context. My feeling is that many elements make a man as he strives towards maturity – parents, education, environment, events, happenings, personalities, luck, good or bad, relationships, but perhaps most of all, people.

We all have our time on this planet. Someone once said that two weeks after a funeral, apart from the immediate family, it seems as though the deceased never existed. Life moves on. There is a generation, indeed generations, to whom the name Percy Alliss means nothing. Some old men may remember the name, for Percy Alliss won the Matchplay Championship twice, the Italian Open twice and the German Open Championship five times, once when the whole of the American Ryder Cup team was on parade. He played in three Ryder Cup matches, losing only one single, and in the Open Championship finished in the top six no fewer than seven times. In 1931 at Carnoustie, he finished third, two shots behind the winner, Tommy Armour. Perhaps if he had been a little more ruthless he would have been a truly great player. He was blessed with an even temperament and a relaxed repeating swing. As Henry Cotton told me once, 'Your father has one of the neatest swings I have ever seen.' Certainly he was one of the few outstanding players of his time but, to me, he was Percy Alliss, my father, whose main mission in life was to make a living for his family. The fact that he played golf at the highest level and was successful was the added icing on the cake.

He was one of the first British professionals to take up a post in Europe and from 1926 to1932 he was the professional at the Wannsee Golf Club on the outskirts of Berlin. Wannsee was a new golf club and very smart indeed, as many of the continental clubs were, as golf was a new and growing game. Father was paid the stunning retainer of £800 per year. He gave lessons from morn till night and yet still had time to win the German Open Championship four years in a row, which was quite amazing for he sometimes went weeks on end without hitting a ball in anger.

Among the famous people who came out for lessons were Marlene Dietrich and Marion Davies, Richard Tauber and Fritz Kreisler. My father refused unconditionally to teach Kreisler or to encourage him to play golf in any way. He was afraid that the famous violinist would damage his hands and my father simply would not have that on his conscience. But Kreisler was so interested that he would come out to the club and stand watching father teaching, or hitting balls, for an hour at a time. Von Ribbentrop was another regular visitor and keen supporter of the club.

The Nazi party was growing in strength and influence at this time, and life became progressively more difficult. When I was eight months old, my father decided we should come back to England.

Getting out of the country was increasingly hard; taking out capital was very difficult indeed. Just before Hitler closed the banks in 1932, mother managed to extract some money which, on leaving the country, she stuffed into her bloomers. Mother always said it was her way of saying, 'Knickers to Hitler!' She wouldn't have been able to get much in her knickers today, judging by the size of most on display! You might get a couple of £50 notes down the side of a thong but that's about all. How much better it was, in that sort of emergency, to have a good stout pair of bloomers! Jordan, eat your heart out!

As far as I can recall, mother managed to conceal perhaps £2,000 or £3,000 out of a total of £15,000–£18,000 that had been on deposit. That's where it remained for the best part of twenty years until, under the war reparation scheme, father was awarded compensation, which amounted to some £3,000 – better than nothing but a long way off the amount he'd managed to save over his six years hard work in Berlin.

The fact that father lived and worked outside the British Isles meant he was unable to play in the Ryder Cup matches. This ruling by the PGA looks ludicrous now but it clearly said in the original documents drawing up the rules and regulations for Ryder Cup play that the participants had to be born and resident in the United Kingdom.

Of course, the same rules applied to Henry Cotton and Aubrey Boomer, so in 1931 the Ryder Cup team set sail to do battle with the Americans without three of their best players. 'The three musketeers' went anyway. Father got a job reporting the matches for one of the daily newspapers, I think the *Express*. The three of them agreed there were exhibition matches they could play, plus a few tournaments, so perhaps they could come home showing a profit, and they would share any winnings. Well, it didn't work out that way. Aubrey Boomer fell totally, utterly and completely in love during the six-day trip to New York, was totally besotted, couldn't hit his hat, and went home. Henry Cotton was struck down by a plague of boils. Father, like the trooper he was in the Argyll & Sutherland Highlanders in the

Great War, soldiered on and did very well. He tied with the mighty Walter Hagen for the Canadian Open Championship that year but lost at the 37th play-off hole. They were tied after a 36-hole play-off and went to sudden death, Hagen winning with a birdie on the first hole. Of course, it never crossed Dad's mind not to share his winnings with the invalid and the absentee.

Back in the UK from Germany, father played in the Ryder Cup matches of 1933, 1935 and 1937, losing only one singles and that was to Gene Sarazen in the matches at Southport & Ainsdale in 1937. Thereby hangs one of those tales that persist in the golf reference books under the heading 'Odd Happenings'. Father was nicely on the 34th green when Sarazen's approach went fizzing through the back but landed in the lap of a woman spectator, who rather nervously jumped up, spilling the ball back on to the green. It stopped four yards from the hole, laying father a dead stymie. This was a time when balls on the greens could not be picked up and marked. Sarazen won the hole and the match 1 up.

After the war, in 1945 and at the age of forty-eight, father found himself in the final of the Matchplay Championship, or, as it was called then, the Victory Championship, which was played at Walton Heath, a superb golf course just inside the present M25 and not a million miles from Reigate. He was playing the unknown professional Reg Horne. Father was sure to win, but no, he lost by 4 and 3. He came home and decided his tournament career was over. He would concentrate on his club job at Ferndown, try to get the shop back on an even keel and spend the rest of his time playing with the members or giving lessons.

He'd started at Ferndown in 1939 – the previous seven or eight years had been very nomadic. He'd returned from Berlin, gone to the Beaconsfield Golf Club for a couple of years before going to a large golfing complex on the outskirts of Leeds called Temple Newsam.

Originally from Sheffield, father came from a large family who had a market garden business. In fact, their smallholding of about ten or twelve acres was where the Hallam Towers Hotel was built a good number of years later. He used to do a bit of caddying at the Hallamshire Golf Club and this possibly opened his eyes to the wonders and some of the mysteries of the game of golf. His first job after the First World War was as the assistant professional at the Stanmore Golf Club in Middlesex. Then he moved on to the famous Royal Porthcawl Golf Club situated halfway between Cardiff and Swansea. After a short spell at the club he was offered the full professional's job at the Clyne Golf Club.

By this time he had met his future wife, Dorothy, who was also from Yorkshire, Hull in fact, her father being Captain Joseph Rust, the owner of two deep-sea trawlers. Captain Rust had left Hull to explore the possibility of other fishing grounds off the southwest coast of Ireland. With a couple of others, he turned north and became one of the early pioneers of the great Icelandic fishing grounds.

The Rust family lived in a little village called the Mumbles. Mother played the organ at a church in Sketty. She was an artistic type with a fine mezzo-soprano voice and I suspect she would really have loved a career in music or showbusiness. In fact, she went on to run a very successful concert party during the war called the Black Dominoes. Among her early discoveries was a certain young comedian from Bournemouth called Tony Hancock. Both my parents worked hard and kept my brother Alec and me warm, well fed, clothed and cosy, in the best traditions, I suppose, of a lower middle-class family.

These then were my parents. Father was a meticulous man,

neat, tidy, tweedy, favouring plus-fours. His shoes were always shined and he had clean finger nails. A Liberal voter, when that party faded into oblivion, he turned to conservatism. I suppose today he would have been called a Tory wet. Mother was outgoing, occasionally tempestuous, sometimes moody and a scratch golfer with the sweetest of swings. They both had a tremendous influence on me but I didn't think about that at the time. Of course, my brother and I grew up somewhat in father's shadow but we were at the delightful, leafy Ferndown Golf Club on the edge of Dorset and Hampshire. It's much changed now but it's still a delight, heather and pine and sandy subsoil. I found myself in the most mellow of environments and I love it still to this day.

When war came in September 1939 my father was off and running; he couldn't wait to join up. The Dorsetshire Regiment let him in at the age of forty-two but he didn't last long. He was invalided out because of lumbago, which seemed a little namby-pamby at the time. In fact, his condition rapidly worsened and he spent long spells in a wheelchair during the war and all the treatment had little effect. Then a new member joined Ferndown, a Major Mason. Some of you may remember Mason's famous 'OK' sauce for fish. It was very popular at the time. The Major took a shine to father and sent him to see Sir John Weir, one of the king's physicians. He had all sorts of X-rays and it was discovered there was a displacement at the base of his spine. They tracked down the cause to an incident that had happened many years ago when on a chilly night he was jogging across the course on his way home after a busy day's teaching and turned his ankle in a rabbit hole. He thought nothing of it but it caught up with him all those years later. It took eight months of Weir's treatment before he was able to walk properly and a year to get back to full throttle at the club.

My brother Alec, who was seven years older than me, became a wireless operator on a minesweeper in the Royal Navy, spending most of his war in the North Atlantic and Mediterranean zones, not the best places to be with the shipping lanes being pounded by Hitler's U-boats for months on end.

My wartime school days were relatively pleasant. I first went to the Queen Elizabeth Grammar School in Wimborne, one of the oldest in England, but after a run-in with a sadistic headmaster by the name of Airey, I was taken away and ended up at Crosby House School on the north side of Bournemouth, some five miles from where we lived.

To me, the war years were interesting. We were only five or six miles from Poole Harbour, which was very shallow, so the powers that be didn't think a German landing force would come there in any great numbers; they were more likely to attack Southampton or Portsmouth. Schools were very mindful of air raids, so children were not out playing cricket in the summer and football and rugby in the winter, and people didn't often ride horses, certainly not people at my level of society. Then there was the black-out, not a light to be seen for five months of the year from 3.30 in the afternoon to 8.30 the following morning. It was about this time that I learned to be frugal, conserving electricity and heat. Oh those expeditions across to the golf course at Ferndown, coming home with sacks full of fir cones, which we used to put on the fire to supplement the meagre ration of coal. How quickly they burnt but what a joy they were when they burst into flame and sent out a wonderful heat that was all too quickly gone.

From the very start it was pre-ordained that I would become a golf professional. After school in the summer I would head over to the golf course and seek out Jim Dean, the head greenkeeper, and Jim Bracher, his assistant. They let me ride on the tractor and rake a bunker or two. I spent hours in the greenkeepers' sheds, which were crude, to say the least, but with a wonderful smell – a mixture of paraffin and oil. The greenkeepers were proud of their machinery and looked after it brilliantly. None of them had a motor car. They used to arrive at the club, six of them, all well over fifty years of age, on bicycles. Nowadays most golf clubs need a car park just for the staff!

Ferndown was surprisingly busy during the war. There was a large American army base at St Leonards on the way to Ringwood. I got friendly with one or two of the GIs and used to go up there occasionally for Sunday lunch – fried chicken, sweetcorn and baked potatoes. They complained bitterly that the food was rubbish but I thought it was heaven.

Things got busier and busier. We didn't realise it at the time, of course, but they were building up for the Normandy invasion of 1944. They put an anti-aircraft battery on the golf course. You can still see some of the remains between the 3rd and the 4th holes.

We got bombed twice – German planes missing Southampton suddenly realised they were in the wrong place and, heading for home, just jettisoned their bombs – but Bournemouth had one crippling raid. It was lunchtime in the summer, a Sunday, the planes scuttled overhead and dropped half a dozen bombs. One hit a busy pub at the Lansdowne, a church and a hotel. A large number of Canadian Air Force personnel died in that hit and run.

I was a formidable player as I reached my teens and by the age of fifteen I was playing off scratch. There were a number of members of the club who took me under their collective wing and for that I will be eternally grateful. Of course, there were no new golf balls to be had and, if you had a golf tee, you got grandma to make a woolly tassel to tie on to it in the hope you'd never lose or break it.

My special friends formed a very interesting group. Ralph Close, a retired dental surgeon, had served in the army and reached the rank of major. He was known as Joe for some reason and he and his wife, who was a very good player, had a house at the bottom of the 18th fairway. He asked me one day if I'd like to play nine holes – I jumped at the opportunity. He gave me half-a-crown (that's an eighth of a pound for you late starters – 12½ p). Then later on that reached 5 shillings (25p). Joe was fiery, a stickler for etiquette and the rules of the game.

Mr Longmore, better known as 'Daddy', would give me sixpence (2½p) for every hole I beat him on, which I could do most of the time. Steve Prentice was a rare survivor of the *Titanic*, and Ted Chubb, tobacconist and newsagent, told me how lucky he was to have been allowed to become a member because most of the others were professional men. God forbid there should be a butcher, a baker, a candlestick-maker.

Then there were the Wakefield brothers, Willie and Harold. Their family owned the Wakefield Oil Company which, long ago, was swallowed up by one of the other major oil concerns. Willie, it turned out, was a 'stage door Johnny', a term I didn't understand at the time. I now know that it means he was attracted to showbusiness and many a time went round to the stage door of a theatre with a bouquet of flowers or a bottle of champagne, as a way of introduction to someone from the cast of the show. I'm not sure whether he ever drank champagne out of a chorus girl's shoe or slipper, but that's what a stage door Johnny was! Harold's great love was motorbike scrambling; he had a team of young riders who went across southern England participating in this new sport of riding a motorbike as fast as you could over terrain not built for the job. We played at least once a week and they always gave me a 10 shilling note each!

Major Ruttle from the Gresham Trust was another member. He seemed to have so many irons in the fire and was one of the prime movers in creating London's Planetarium. He had a daughter, Maureen, who was a year or two older than me and a fine golfer. She went on, as Maureen Garrett, to captain the Curtis Cup team in 1960. She became President of the Ladies' Golf Union from 1982 to 1985 and in 1983 took the Bobby Jones Award for her outstanding services to the game of golf.

I can't leave the old boys without mentioning Ralph Langton whose family owned a brewery on the Isle of Wight. He was the epitome of an English toff. About 6ft 4in, he'd served in the Guards during the war and had a great eye for the ladies. He loved to play golf and, although slightly impoverished, some-how always managed to find a little something for me.

Simply listening to these people taught me so many things about life, business, money, the big world beyond Ferndown, gamesmanship, and how to hold a knife and fork, which is more important than some of you may think.

I didn't play much golf with my father; he certainly never gave me many lessons. We'd talk about the game from time to time, particularly if I was having a problem. We would walk to the side of the 18th fairway and he'd watch me hit ten or twelve balls and say, 'That's it, now you work on that.' Or, if I was chipping badly or not able to get out of a bunker, he'd select a member of the club, irrespective of his handicap, and say, 'You know Mr so and so, now he's a very good chipper with a little 7-iron from just off the green. You just watch him and then come and tell me what he does. Try to copy him. Learn, use your own brains. If you don't, when you come under pressure, you'll collapse and your mind will go out of gear and you'll fail.' Wise words.

In 1946 he took me to play in the Boys Championship at the

Bruntsfield Golf Course on the west side of Edinburgh. Preceding it was an international match, England v. Scotland. The England team had some very interesting characters including Guy Wolstenholme, father of our 2003 Amateur Champion, Gary, and Arthur Perowne, who came from a farming family in Norfolk, Michael Pearson, Sandy Bethell and a number of other players who went on to become home internationals and county champions. I reached the semi-final and the newspapers of the day, led by Leonard Crawley, announced that 'Here was the winner, Peter Alliss, even though he has a slightly dodgy grip'. But it wasn't to be, a little fellow called Donald Dunsdon saw me off. He, in turn, was beaten in the final by A.F.D. McGregor, the biggest young man I've ever seen in my life, with legs like oak trees and a barrel chest. It truly was a Little and Large contest. We got home and father said, 'Well, I don't think you're going on to great academic things and you have a good eye for a ball. You can become an unpaid assistant at the Ferndown Golf Club.'

Aged sixteen and a half, I made my first appearance in the Open Championship in 1947. It was played at Hoylake and won by Fred Daly. I didn't make a great showing, scoring 79 and 86. I was on my way home before my feet had really touched the ground and back at Ferndown, playing with my various mentors. This continued until I was seventeen and father gave my brother Alec and me £50. Alec was to be my chaperone. I was to compete in the *Yorkshire Evening News* tournament at the Moortown Golf Club in Leeds, travel up for the Spalding event at St Andrews and then back to Manchester or, more correctly, the Mere Golf Club just south of Manchester for the *Manchester Evening Chronicle* tournament. Fifty pounds, can you imagine it, to last two people for three weeks. If I won money, well so be it.

'Just see what you can do. I'm not expecting great things. Be sensible and let's see what you've got in you,' my father said.

I failed in the *Yorkshire Evening News*, so early business was not good, but found St Andrews to be absolutely magical. I got round the Old Course twice in 153 strokes and qualified by 1 for the final 36. I'm not sure if I managed to win any money; if I did, it was certainly no more than £3. Then we travelled down to Mere, the home of George Duncan, and, wonder of wonders, I finished fifth and also won the Assistants' Prize. The two prizes together totalled £57.10s (or £57.50p). Father was delighted, and why not, he had invested £50 and I'd come home with a profit. He said there was a chance I could make a living from tournaments, local events, alliances and so on. Suddenly, out of nowhere, I was a tournament professional.

That didn't last. In June of 1949 I was summoned for National Service – eighteen months that ended up being two years with the RAF Regiment, first at West Kirby and later at the RAF Regiment Depot at Catterick. In October/November the wind blew raw and the River Swale, which we had to wade through at regular intervals while some idiots threw thunder flashes at us to simulate battle action, was very cold and uninviting. They asked me if I'd like to stay on to take a course in small firearms and, if I did well, I would end up a corporal. I declined their kind offer, although one of the good things about being at Catterick was that twice a month I would get a bus down to Leeds and play a round of golf with Walter Barnes, son of Ted, the professional at the Sand Moor Golf Club, and fellow assistant Ted Dockray. Just across the road was Bill Green, the pro at the Moortown Golf Club. What great fun we had. On Saturday night Ted Dockray and the other assistants would clean seventy or eighty sets of golf clubs ready for Sunday's play and then there was just time to get up to the Chained Bull pub at Moortown corner for a pint of Black & Tan, or Tetley's best.

After a couple of other excursions I ended up at Watchet, a small village on the north Somerset coast a few miles from Minehead. It was less than 100 miles to Ferndown but it took six hours on the train. At least there were trains that made the cross-country journey. You changed about five times but it cost 'umpence'. Brother Alec, in the meantime, had spent some time at the Brighton & Hove Golf Club. Just after the war it was very quiet with not, seemingly, many prospects. Then he was offered the job as professional at Weston-super-Mare, which was within striking distance of Watchet. Once or twice a month I managed to get out for a weekend and have some golf with some very good players at the club. Jack Poole and George Irlam come readily to mind. They had a wonderful, if slightly eccentric, secretary called Donald Hoodwright, who would liven things up on occasion. There was also a very good golfer called Jack Payne, who might well have played for England but decided that Britain after the war was too austere and cut loose for Canada.

Although I felt at the time I was wasting my life, I'm sure National Service did a lot for me. I learned to live a communal life and I spent much time observing the human condition of other eighteen-year-olds. I learned to keep time, work hard, retain a sense of humour and, above all, look after my own kit and myself but be mindful of the wants of others. In my two years, I don't suppose I managed to play more than thirty rounds of golf.

I was demobbed on 15 June 1951. Ferndown seemed different, a smaller place.

2

CLUB PRO

*'Ah, club life, learning to deal with people, I
wouldn't have missed it for the world'*

In December 1953 I married Joan McGuinness, a fashion
buyer at Beales, a Bournemouth department store, whom I had
met in the summer of 1952. It was a nice ceremony at the very
ancient parish church of West Parley, and the Ferndown members provided us with an archway of clubs as we left the church.
Father had converted his house at Ferndown into two and we
took the top flat for the princely sum of £4 a week, which I
thought was a bit harsh at the time but business was business. In
due course, Gary and Carol, my first family, arrived, Gary in
1954, Carol in 1960.

Already, by the time of my marriage, I was getting slightly
uncomfortable at Ferndown, wanting, I suppose, a bit more
recognition than I was getting. There were people on the
committee at the time who debated whether or not I was to
be allowed to use the clubhouse. One committee member even
suggested that perhaps they should wait to see if I was selected

for the Ryder Cup team of 1953. If I were, somehow that would give me more kudos and I would obviously be able to handle myself better! All these debates became history. My brother Alec had given up his position at Weston-super-Mare and gone off to Northern Rhodesia to take up a position at the N'Changa Golf Club in the middle of the fabled wealthy Copper Belt where he was to spend four years. I had a modicum of success in 1956 and, in the spring of 1957, Alec and I applied for, and got, the job as joint professionals at the Parkstone Club overlooking Poole Harbour. Reggie Whitcombe had been their pro for many years and had won the Open Championship in 1938, so it was a great feather in our caps when Jack Stutt, the chairman, said his committee would like us to become joint professionals.

A whole new world opened up. Parkstone was a different club. It had lots of butchers and bakers and candlestick-makers. It also had a couple of knights, an earl, a couple of rogues, and several flirts – it was tremendous. Ferndown, lovely Ferndown, had been my home, my life since childhood, yet here I was at Parkstone, which was equally lovely with different people and those majestic, ever-changing views across Poole Harbour and Brownsea Island. Alec and I decided we would try to offer an outstanding service to the members. The shop would be open all hours. It was tiny but in a good position. At our own expense we ripped it out, extended, redecorated and filled it with modern golfing equipment. Dammit, we must have had about £2,000-worth of stock. We were very pleased with ourselves. We resolved we would not enter the clubhouse uninvited. Parkstone was progressive and backed us solidly. We actually took up residence on April the first. Two days later I went off to Llandudno to play in the season's first event, the PGA Championship and, lo and behold, I came back the winner. What a wonderful way to begin a relationship with a new club and it all started on April Fool's Day – was this an omen? There remained a bridge back to Ferndown and its members. A certain Paul Coutts-Trotter, a London stockbroker and Ferndown member, came to me and said he'd noticed how much we'd spent on the shop and I should not go off to tournaments with any financial worries in my head. He'd like to make us a loan.

'Pay me back when you can, over three years would be good, with no thought of interest,' he said. I can assure you, that helped a lot.

I had found an R Type Bentley – you remember, the one with the big lift-up boot lid. This caused some consternation at Parkstone Golf Club. The car had done about 45,000 miles and I paid about £800 for it. The club secretary, 'Daddy' Bond, a lovely man, took me quietly to one side and said he thought it might be a little bit iffy for the pro to have a Bentley when some of the members were arriving on bicycles. I assured him they were only doing that to get some exercise and, after all, my car was ten years old and had done 45,000 miles and, being black, it didn't show the many dents that were there if you looked very closely. Eventually, I blew that one up going along the A31 north of Ringwood.

Just imagine being the professional at a substantial club, playing twenty to twenty-five tournaments a year, hoping to become a Ryder Cup player and play in any other international team competition that might be around at the time. In the fifties and sixties, a professional playing a tournament would require cover for the shop for the four, maybe five, days he was away. The tournament pattern then was one round Wednesday and Thursday and two rounds on Friday. After that you would sometimes be facing a long drive home to get back in time for work on Saturday morning, all bright-eyed and bushy-tailed, ready to tend to members' wants. All very well if you had won the tournament – dammit, you might have £300 or £400 tucked away, which many people would have thought a reasonable income for the entire year!

Then there were the general activities of the shop, the banter, getting to know members' traits, working out little deals, sometimes flirting with lady members, particularly those of a certain age who had 'something about them'. You knew very well that thirty, maybe forty, years earlier they had been genuine stars in their own right and there was still a hint of naughtiness in their eyes. Not for them the nonsense of political correctness. If someone dared to say or do something out of place they were very quick with a shaft of acid wit, a bang around the head with a handbag or some derogatory words said in a loud voice for others to hear, making the perpetrator of the saucy deed feel doubly ashamed. Where are such women today? And where are the men, those rakish, raffish men, often in blazers, who set hearts aflutter but weren't 'touchers' and 'bum strokers', just honest-to-God roguish lads with an eye for a well-rounded ankle?

What a wonderful life it's been for me playing tournament golf at the highest level, then returning to the club to look after the needs of the members, seeing the sales reps, giving lessons, shoes re-studded, umbrellas repaired – ah, club life, learning to deal with people. I wouldn't have missed it for the world. I doubt if there's one professional playing at the top level today who would have the faintest idea of what I'm talking about when I say 'club life'.

The role of the club professional has changed dramatically

over the years, probably because the top players are not attached to clubs any more. It's a pity – they miss out on the thrills, the joy and anguish of looking after the members, stocktaking, club repairs. This latter has long since ended, although the pro can still change grips and do a bit of bending to adjust the loft and lie to suit a particular member's needs.

The year 1958 was one of the most exciting and extraordinary periods of my professional life. Alec and I had been doing very well at Parkstone, mainly due to the fact that Jack Stutt was a progressive chairman. A Glaswegian whose company was very prominent in the world of golf-course design and construction, although by this time he'd handed over the reins to his son, Hamilton, Jack was very ambitious for Parkstone, which, at that time, was privately owned. No one can honestly say they enjoy criticism but Jack took it all on board and, if it had merit, he did something about it, which is very commendable and something I've remembered all my life, although sometimes I don't carry it out as well as he did. If Alec and I had any suggestions we thought might benefit Parkstone, he would listen and, if in his eyes they had merit, they were put into effect. He believed that having a successful tournament player contracted to the club, bringing international publicity, was a good thing. And why not? Parkstone was in a tourist area and the club always made visitors very welcome. I remember, when Alec and I went to Parkstone, there were just under 400 members and when we left there were 750. Whether that was good or bad is not for me to say, but I have a feeling the Alliss brothers did something right.

Joan and I had moved house several times during the previous few years. We'd left 40 Hood Crescent and moved into Branksome Wood Road, the slightly cheaper end I hasten to add, and from there to a house called Purbeck Heights, which overlooked Parkstone Golf Club. Then we decided we'd move up the property ladder and took a very swanky house in Leicester Road in an area called Branksome Park. We paid £8,500 for this house, which stood well back from the road on about an acre and a half, maybe two.

Then in the early sixties something very special came along, a gentleman's residence known as Crabb House, sitting proudly on a hill just on the northwest side of Wimborne in the county of Dorset. We looked across the valley towards Canford School, a fabulous view. It was the former home of the Tory MP Sir Richard Glynn and stood in twenty acres. I thought there was no way we could afford it but we found a way. Come to think of it, if parents, friends, events, relationships all combine to form your personality, the sixties did it for me, as it did for many others, no doubt for different reasons.

As I write this in 2004, Parkstone has extended the clubhouse and invited me down. I can't wait to see the end result. I shall always have a soft spot for the Bournemouth district and its golf courses: Ferndown, the Isle of Purbeck, Parkstone, Meyrick and Queens Park; Broadstone and, just along the coast overlooking the Isle of Wight, Barton-on-Sea, which lost a lot of its original course over the years due to sea erosion; also, the tiny 9-hole course at Highcliffe, which looks so easy but is hellishly difficult.

I'm often asked if I've played every golf course in Britain. The quick answer is no. I doubt I've played 200. You see, the circuit used to go round and invariably pop up in the same areas. I wonder if there is anyone who has played all the courses in England? I doubt it. It's a good start if you've had a long amateur career; that way you will have had a chance of playing many courses.

An interesting thing to do if you've got the time and the

wherewithal is to play county by county, but so many courses have sprung up over the years it would be a very expensive exercise today. Talking about expense, at the Open Championship in 2003 I was sent a booklet of the golf courses in Kent with their locations, telephone numbers, the nearest railway stations, hotels and green fees. The booklet was printed in 1935. The Royal Cinque Ports or Deal were the most expensive at a guinea (£1.1s/£1.5p), followed very closely by Royal St George's. The majority of the clubs were between seven and sixpence ($37\frac{1}{2}$ p) and 15 shillings (75p). This gentleman wrote to me saying how it was possible for people on a decent, but still relatively modest, wage to visit and play all the great golf courses before the war, although a £1 green fee was probably an eighth of a week's wages for people with responsible jobs. Now many clubs have green fees of over £100 and in some cases over £200. He made a good but sad point. A large number of courses are now out of reach for many keen players.

So the pleasure of playing and visiting many of the great courses has now been taken away from the rank and file golfer unless they go with a society or on a special company day. Supply and demand, greed, call it what you will, even in this day and age I find £25 enough to pay for a green fee but I wonder how many clubs of any quality have green fees as low as £25 Monday to Friday.

3

TOURNAMENT
PROFESSIONAL

*'The PGA offices comprised a couple of rooms in
Leadenhall Street . . . the whole place was
positively Dickensian'*

Although I was demobilised from the RAF Regiment on 15
June 1951, it wasn't until the Sunningdale Foursomes in 1952
that I set out on my delayed professional career. The Sunningdale Foursomes tournament was a splendid affair, big stuff in
those early days, and heralded the start of the season. It was an
event I always looked forward to and managed to win twice
with the same partner – Jean Donald when she was single and
Jean Anderson when she was a married lady. Played towards
the end of March, it was always a bit of a struggle one way or
other with the course emerging from winter and chilly winds
blowing.

Assistants' Championships were played at Coombe Hill and
Hartsbourne. I won the championship at Hartsbourne that year

and ended the season feeling quite pleased with myself but a number of people said that I should have done better.

I enjoyed tournament golf. The older players took me under their wing – Arthur Lees, who was the professional at Sunningdale, Ken Bousfield, Dai Rees, Max Faulkner, John Jacobs and his cousin Jack, who was the professional at the glorious Lindrick Golf Course near Worksop for so many years. What characters they were! What tales they could tell! Jack Jacobs, for example, could charm the birds out of the trees with his stories of the membership at his club – the steel men, the steel owners, the cutlers, the silversmiths – he had me spellbound for hours.

Long-hitting Harry Weetman appeared on the scene, as did David Thomas who was three or four years younger than me and had just completed his National Service. We struck up an immediate bond, which has stayed through the years. John Panton and Eric Brown, chalk and cheese, represented Scotland on dozens of occasions. John was as gentle a person as you could possibly find but so determined, and dear Eric, flamboyant and wild. Even his friends used to say he could make trouble in an empty 'hoos'. Panton had spent six long years in the army during the war. Some of his stories of driving large army wagons along the precipitous roads of Northern India, Afghanistan and the like were hair-raising, but he came through unscathed; sadly, many didn't. He started winning tournaments soon after he was demobbed in 1945 and it wasn't long before he bought a Triumph Mayflower, a small square car that seemed very reliable. He used to drive through the night from his home at Larbert, east of Glasgow, to be at Moor Park, near Watford in Hertfordshire, ready for a quick practice round and the start of the Silver King competition. No motorways in those far-off days! You had to plan ahead and call the AA to find out where the all-night petrol stations were and which roads were liable to have an all-night café. It was an adventure. John loved the gee-gees and the dogs and went everywhere with numerous newspapers sticking out of his pocket, all folded back so that he could see what was running at Catford or Ascot.

Everyone seemed to get on well. There were very few petty jealousies. A number looked at Henry Cotton with envy because he was in a league above everyone else. He had a wealthy wife; she had a great personality and was a good ally, although you didn't want to upset her! Cotton taught anyone who was prepared to listen and pay a lot. He never overdid his tournament appearances. He never got himself involved in matches if he thought there was a strong possibility of losing. He was very conscious of his image. He won his final Open at Muirfield in 1948 and continued to play tournaments into the mid fifties, but only on special occasions or when he thought he could figure well enough to gain good publicity. You talk of today's players living in fine style; nobody lived better than Henry Cotton. When he was the professional at Ashridge Golf Club in 1932 – he was their first pro – he lived in a fine house just a few hundred yards from the club and had several servants, a butler, chauffeur, gardener, handyman and maid. This lifestyle continued when he moved into a very elegant flat in Eaton Square. None of today's players could better that for sheer style.

I won my first tournament at the delightful Little Aston Club in 1954. It was a happy hunting ground for me. I also won the PGA Championship there some years later. Back then it was a very correct club and totally male-orientated. They had the most wonderful putting green. Not your usual, it had flower-beds and banks of heather running all through it. It must have been the best part of half an acre in size. I remember watching their then professional Charlie Ward, one of our greatest postwar players, chipping and putting there for hours on end. Ah, Charlie Ward. He also befriended me in those early days, as did Fred Daly and Harry Bradshaw. I was very fortunate.

I enjoyed the travel, learning how to find my way round the country, and when I'd become a little better known I was asked to participate in some exhibition matches for the Lord Roberts Workshops and Forces Help Society. We used to play eighteen to twenty matches a year, mostly on Sundays, and were paid £20 in cash as a 'fee' and to cover any expenses we might incur. We were stars and we paid tax!

The format was England v. Wales – Bernard Hunt and Peter Alliss versus David Thomas and Dai Rees. Dai usually arrived just as lunch was starting, one o'clock. At quarter-past-two he'd do a clinic for half an hour or so. Then it was on to the first tee at three o'clock, 18 holes and afterwards a huge auction, some-times over 100 items, which, if they took a minute each to sell, took a few hours. He loved it. Then he'd drive back to his beloved wife Eunice and the girls.

Dai had a nice family house only 150 yards or so from the South Herts clubhouse. Ah, his beloved South Herts! He had a long-time assistant, Steve Thomas, and the Arsenal Football Club used to have lunch there before they played their home matches. Dai used to train with them a bit; I often thought he was fitter than some of the players!

It was around this time one of the most evil 'games' ever instigated came into being, known as 'Find the Noddy'. It all began with two eccentric friends – Hugh Lewis and Alan Gillies – concocting a situation where condoms, or as they were very commonly known in those days 'French letters', were hidden willy nilly to embarrass, to the maximum extent, the people who discovered them.

I was first to be introduced to this evil practice when playing in one of the exhibition matches at the Wilmslow Golf Club. As usual, it was England v. Wales, my good self and Bernard Hunt against Dave Thomas and Dai Rees. The usual pleasantries had taken place – we had arrived at the club at about 12.30, lunch was taken with the captain, lady captain and other dignitaries, Dai Rees had performed his interesting, informative and amusing golf clinic and at three o'clock there we were, shoes polished, clean fingernails, creases in the trousers, standing on the first tee ready for the off. Announcements were made, a coin was spun – England had the honour. One of the young members was carrying my bag. I can remember the situation so clearly. I reached for my driver. In those days I had a set of very impressive sheepskin head covers, beautiful to the touch but slightly bulky. I drew the club out of the bag, withdrew the head cover and, horror of horrors, three very distinctive packets of Durex fell on to the tee in the full gaze of perhaps 250 people. What to do? What to do? My brain went into reverse. I think I tried to stand on them, thereby spearing them with the spikes of my shoes, but failed miserably. I reached down and quickly picked them up hoping that nobody had noticed.

That then was my introduction to 'Find the Noddy'. It progressed to finding them hidden under the sun visor on the passenger side of the car, and you never knew who the passenger might be – a maiden aunt, the local vicar. Sometimes they were there for weeks, months, but when that visor was pulled down it was certainly a moment to remember. They were put in golf bags wrapped up in waterproof trousers so when the moment arrived the trousers were pulled from the golf bag only to have the dreaded 'rubber Johnnies' scattered about. They were put over electric light bulbs, heads of drivers, in an unsuspecting person's dirty laundry – that caused a near divorce or two I can tell you. Nowhere was sacred!

One of the 'terrible twins' – Hugh and Alan – had a dear friend who had a formidable wife, so what did they do? They stretched one over the handle of her vacuum cleaner, so that every time this ice woman did the hoovering she would wonder where that slight smell of rubber came from. It appealed to their somewhat juvenile sense of humour.

Some months after I'd been introduced to this evil game, an exhibition match was staged at the Altrincham Golf Club where Hugh Lewis was the professional. David Thomas and I were to challenge Hugh and Dai Rees. We were the odds-on favourites. Suffice to say they had all the good luck and beat us 2 and 1. There was much celebration. At the end of it all, we went back to Hugh's house, which was only a mile or two from the clubhouse in an area known as Moss Nook. He'd invited some friends round including Altrincham's mayor and mayoress. Drinks were served and everyone was having a jolly time when I had a splendid thought. I noticed the mayor's drink was getting low, so I asked if I could refresh his gin and tonic. 'Yes please,' he said. I took his glass and went into the kitchen, eased a condom out of its packet – I just happened to have one handy – and laid it carefully in the base of one of Hugh's beautiful Waterford goblets. On top of that I laid three large chunks of ice and a generous slice of lemon, added a good pub treble of Gordon's best and topped it up with a drop of fresh tonic. It was a master of disguise. I took it back into Hugh's front room and as I handed it to the mayor, I looked at Hugh and whispered the immortal words, 'Noddy hidden.' An expression of stark horror came over Hugh's face; he was looking, rather wildly, hither and thither, wondering where, what and how. It was a warm evening and, as luck would have it, the ice was melting quickly. Suddenly a small air bubble appeared in the mayor's drink and the teat of the condom started to ease its way through the ice, pushing the lemon to one side – it was rather reminiscent of those old black and white war films of submarines operating in the North Atlantic. I glanced at Hugh and then towards the mayor's glass. 'Noddy hidden,' I whispered again.

Another bubble of air hit the teat and suddenly it was in full view. Hugh spotted it, went as white as a sheet and grabbed the mayor's glass from his hand, saying something quite inane like, 'Oh, I'll have to change that, there's a bluebottle [or did he say pterodactyl?] in your drink.'

After the party I was congratulating myself on this master stroke when Hugh and Alan took me to one side and said it was getting too risky and perhaps we should give the demon game a rest, which we did, and it has certainly never been resurrected – but now you know the story, so do beware if you ever hear the cry, 'Noddy hidden.'

Later, Hugh was the professional at the very well-respected Davyhulme Park Golf Club, six or seven miles southwest of Manchester in a very nice part of the world. I happened to be in that neighbourhood one day and dropped in to see Hugh in his shop. We were standing chatting when he noticed one of the few extravagantly dressed members making his way across the car park. Hugh indicated this fellow was, not to put too fine a touch on it, a bit of a jerk. I didn't need much prompting to see why. He obviously was a devotee of Johnny Miller and was dressed as Miller might have been in the early seventies, i.e. brown and white shoes, Rupert Bear trousers, a diamond patterned sweater and cap with a bobble on the top. He entered the shop, spotted me and said nothing. As he moved towards the counter I heard him say, 'I'd like a trolley please, Hugh,' offering the homespun pro a pound note. From under the counter Hugh lifted out a large cigar box, opened same and gave his member some change. In those days some golf professionals kept the trolley money separate – that was one of their small perks. 'Ciggy or beer money' it was called. Pocketing the change, the member said, 'I would have thought a man of your stature, Hugh, would have had something rather more grand than a cigar box for a till,' to which Hugh replied, quick as a flash, 'For all the business you bring into this shop I could make do with an effing Swan Vesta matchbox.' Exit member in complete silence.

Hugh died a few years ago, much too young. He was, without doubt, one of the funniest, inventive, comedic people I have ever met. If he'd had more discipline, he could have been one of Britain's finest after-dinner speakers but he couldn't do it, which was a great pity. I'll never forget once talking to Hugh about a friend of his who was very much into sex aids – whatever new device appeared on the market he had to buy it. If you've ever seen one of those magazines displaying all the goods it's possible to purchase, you would be amazed at man's ingenuity. This man lived quite close to Ringway, Manchester's airport, and I happened to say to Hugh one day, 'Does so and so really have all these electrical appliances,' to which he replied, 'Indeed he does. In fact, when he's in full flow and switches everything on, the runway lights go out at Ringway!

Tournaments came and went but some sponsors remained staunch – Dunlop and their Masters for instance. We had the Schweppes Tournament and for many years Slazenger were also involved, as were Benson & Hedges. What great sponsors they were to so many sports. Piccadilly, John Player and Martini all played their part. I'll never forget the John Player Championship played at the Notts Golf Club at Hollingwell, won by Christy O'Connor. The first prize was £25,000 – *massive* – and you know what, we talk about players not wanting to come for big money today, i.e. the World Matchplay Championship at Wentworth in October. They didn't come then when £25,000 was the *biggest* first prize in the world of golf and that was thirty-five years ago.

My friendship and Ryder Cup partnership with Christy O'Connor made some team, I can tell you. What battles we had! He was a fantastic partner.

Guy Wolstenholme joined our happy band and more often than not David Thomas, Guy, A.N. Other and I would team up for practice rounds. Bernard Hunt, Peter Butler, Neil Coles and Brian Huggett all seemed to practise regularly together. Tony Grubb and Hugh Boyle were two of the greatest practisers golf has ever seen. Hugh was rewarded with a Ryder Cup cap but didn't get the true rewards for all the hours of practice he put in. It used to annoy me when newspapers wrote that British players didn't practise enough. Bernard Hunt, Brian Huggett, Peter Butler and Neil Coles were all great workers.

After the day's play we often found ourselves dining together. Each person was allowed to go, very quickly, through his round. The others listened sympathetically, at least that's the way we tried to look, and if anyone started talking about golf after that, they had to buy a round of drinks. It worked very well, although some of our fellow competitors never stopped talking about their day on the course. Hour upon hour it was a question of how difficult the bunkers were, how fast or slow the greens.

I enjoyed my playing career. Of course, it was always more satisfactory if you'd had a profitable week. It was nice to go back to the club. In those days you had to be attached to a club to be able to play on the tour. One or two got round it by simply being affiliated to a club. Coombe Hill was a prime mover in that department. They had a 'stable' of some of the best young players, paying them a small retainer so they could use the club's name. Good thinking on their part. Neil Coles, Ken Bousfield, Craig Defoy and many others helped spread the gospel and let the world know of the assistants of Coombe Hill. It was a great stepping-stone for many.

How well I remember my first visit to the Gleneagles Hotel in Perthshire. Henry Cotton had talked Jack Abbott, then the Managing Director of the Saxone Shoe Company, into staging a golf tournament. It was to be a Professional and Amateur foursome knock-out matchplay event played during the third week of October. The hotel was then owned by British Transport Hotels. They thought it was a good idea as it would extend the season by a couple of weeks. In those days the hotel closed in October and didn't open again until Easter. The hotel was splendid, quite different internally from today although it still retains a wonderful magic. How many times I've driven down Glen Devon from the top of which, on a clear day, you can see the hotel stretched out before you, perhaps a couple of miles away – *glorious*. I well remember the characters we met in the hotel – John and Billy, the hall porter and assistant hall porter; Mr Mario, the Maître d'; Jack McLean, the professional, followed by Ian Marchbank, who had been pirated away from the Turnberry Hotel. What a good job he made of it for so many years.

That's one of the things I wonder about today's pros. Those

days have long gone but we thought it was quite something to take along a dinner jacket and tie; wearing a suit in the late fifties was OK but you were the one who looked out of place because all the other diners were in evening clothes! Nowadays, if you put on a dinner jacket, *you* would probably be the odd one out. Is there really any excitement left when you've never had to save up for anything and you've stayed at every posh hotel in the world, all before your twenty-fifth birthday, not caring whether you've got a dinner jacket and tie? But change was on the way in a different guise.

Bernard Hunt, John Jacobs, Harry Weetman, David Thomas and I stormed into the offices of the PGA like revolutionaries, which I suppose we were. We wanted change, we wanted a different set up, we wanted to separate the professional golfers from golf professionals. The PGA offices comprised a couple of rooms in an ancient building in Leadenhall Street in the heart of the City of London, a slightly bizarre residence for a sporting body; the whole place was positively Dickensian. The PGA at that time was run entirely by Commander Charles Roe RN Retd, Miss Cockburn, a splendid loyal secretary, and A.N. Other whose name escapes me. When I say 'entirely', Roe ran all the affairs of the PGA from behind an old roll-top desk. He was a retired sub-mariner who had been cast away, marooned, torpedoed, shipwrecked, the lot. He stood ramrod straight, a short pipe clenched firmly between his teeth. People will say, with good reason, that it was nothing like the business empire the PGA Tour controls today, but there were still cheques to be signed, the organising and administration of all the tournaments, the Ryder Cup and any other international events that might come along to be undertaken plus the administrative requirements of hundreds of club professionals.

A number of people rather pooh-pooh the tournaments that were available for the likes of me forty years ago but, if you took into account the continental events, there were about twenty to twenty-two and that didn't include trips to far-flung places such as Australia, Hong Kong and South Africa. We small band of warriors wanted change, we felt a new structure was needed. Under Charles Roe was a huge committee, getting on for thirty, and in an effort to be democratic, it became silly. The country was divided into sections and if one section, say, had 250 members, they felt that they should have two delegates on the committee, whereas if you came from a less populated area, such as East Anglia, you'd struggle to get one. In many ways, it was a closed shop. Looking back, we were at least ten years ahead of our time but we were the instigators of change, which really started to happen in the seventies when John Jacobs was able to pull together the numerous strands of the Association and build a foundation for the hugely successful PGA European Tour. Again, it has changed much over the last thirty years but it would appear, at least on paper, to be successful. Charles Roe served the PGA from the 1930s well into the sixties and lived a long life, sadly just falling short of receiving a telegram from the Queen on his hundredth birthday.

I won my last tournament in 1969. It was the Piccadilly Medal played at the Prince's Golf Club in Kent. The course had staged the Open Championship many years earlier. Fancy, three courses, Deal, Prince's and Royal St George's, whose boundaries virtually touch each other, all having hosted the Open Championship, J.H. Taylor and George Duncan both winning at Deal, in 1908 and 1920 respectively, and Gene Sarazen in 1932 at Prince's. The Piccadilly was a matchplay medal event. Tony Jacklin was the Open Champion; I beat him in the semifinals to come up against George Will, an excellent player, who was the professional at the Sundridge Park Golf Club in Kent. We had a right royal ding-dong battle, tying at 149 for the 36 holes round a very windy Prince's. I managed to pip him on the first extra hole. My first prize was £750 – a nice figure that took my lifetime earnings to just over £30,000. Yep, £30,000 for a total of twenty-one victories and umpteen placements, but a gin and tonic was only 12p and a Rolls-Royce £1,250.

The amount of goodies handed out in those days intrigued me. You got three balls on the first tee if you were a star player, which were to last you the first two rounds; then, if you qualified for the final 36, you got another three. The Daks Tournament had a first prize of £400, the ninth prize was £30. After that every qualifier got £10. There were one or two long faces at that; after all, if you finished tenth, you'd played quite well. Ten quid was not a fortune – on reflection, perhaps it was £9 – but remember, you were able to buy a pair of their trousers at Lillywhites in Piccadilly for the special price of £3.10s (£3.50)!

I played my last Open Championship in 1974. I was forty-three years of age, had the putting woes and decided that life with the BBC, where I had begun to work, and my friends at Moor Allerton was less stressful. I'd had a wonderful journey, made some great friends, saw the birth of many things. I wouldn't have missed it for anything.

4

THE
INTERNATIONAL
CIRCUIT

*'By now I had a wheelbarrow load of pesetas to
go with a sackful of lire'*

It was in 1954 that I made my first long trip abroad under the
captaincy of Alf Padgham who took a team to play in Argentina
and Uruguay. My teammates were a fine mixture of ancient and
modern. There was Jimmy Adams and Tom Haliburton, Max
Faulkner, who had won the Open Championship only three
years before, Harry Weetman, the long hitter from Shropshire,
Bernard Hunt and myself. We flew from London to Buenos
Aires in a BOAC Argonaut. It took forty-two hours. How can
that be you might ask. Well it was London/Lisbon, Lisbon/
Dakar, Dakar/Recife and then down to Buenos Aires.

We arrived at midnight and found that we had a drive of some
200 miles to Mar del Plata, the famous Argentine resort. At this

time, Peron's dictatorship was showing signs of decay; his rule was growing tougher to ward off the inevitable, and everyone was very tight-lipped when it came to political discussion. When we arrived at the club, we found we were expected to live military-style, in a barracks or dormitory full of cot-beds. This was none too comfortable, but the view next morning made amends. It was quite breathtaking with long white breakers rolling in on wonderful golden sand. Mar del Plata was a beautiful place. The atmosphere of cloak and dagger did not appeal to Max Faulkner who kept tramping around asking loudly, 'Where is this guy, Peron?' much to the discomfort of Tom Haliburton, who always behaved very correctly but particularly so when abroad. Tom hid his face in embarrassment when Max was on parade. The course, although dry, was very attractive and it was while we were out on our first little practice that our dormitory was ransacked and quite a lot of cigarettes, golf balls and money was stolen. An armed guard was promptly posted on the door and ordered to stay there all day long.

We drove back to Buenos Aires, spotting on the way several bursts of firing in the hills, and there were any number of bomb explosions in the city when we arrived. There had been a flare up in Buenos Aires the previous day and I wondered if in fact we were going to be involved in one of those South American revolutions that have made a rich field for fiction writers. The difference was that the explosions did not sound particularly fictitious.

We set off in a Sunderland flying-boat across the river Plate to Uruguay, looking down on the waters where the *Graf Spey* had met her end. We were to play at the resort courses of Punta del Este and Punta Caretta, and very picturesque places they were, with chalets nestling in pine trees behind the most dazzling

My father, Percy Alliss (*far right*), pictured with his four brothers, was one of the outstanding golfers of his generation.

The clubhouse at Wannsee Golf Club in Berlin, where I was born. Dad was the professional from 1925 to 1932.

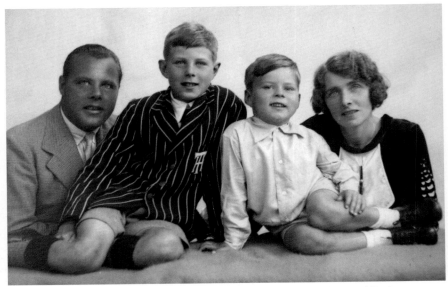

An early family picture of my brother Alec and me, aged three, with Mum and Dad.

Mum and Dad, almost engulfed by the crowd after Dad's victory in the News of the World matchplay.

We came to Ferndown, a delightful place of heather and pine, in 1939. It's much changed now but I love it to this day.

How things change – look at those golf bags, for a start! Flory van Donck, Max Faulkner, Dad and Reggie Whitcombe after a match at Exeter in 1947.

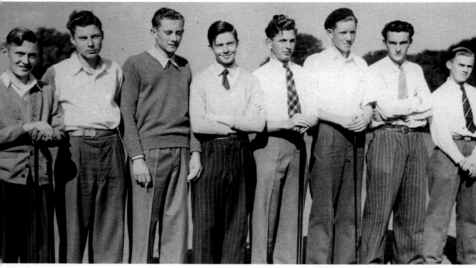

In 1946, England Boys took on Scotland Boys in Edinburgh – the only time I played for England as an amateur. In this group are Arthur Perowne (*on the left*), me, Sandy Bethell (*fourth from left*), Michael Pearson, Guy Wolstenholme and (*far right*) Donald Dunsdon.

Three generations of the Alliss family – Dad (*left*) had a super simple swing, my son Gary (*right*) in full flow and (*opposite*) I'm keeping my eye on the ball. Good position, eh?

Winning the Spanish Open in 1956 changed my life. Here I am (*far left*) in a group including (*from right*) Bob Toski, Al Bessalink and Max Faulkner.

Ben Hogan watches Sam Snead, as do Colonel A.A. Duncan (in uniform) and, next to him, Jeanne Bisgood, twice England ladies champion.

Coombe Hill Golf Club used to pay young players a small retainer so they could use the club's name in order to play on the tour. I was one of the assistants, as the affiliated players were known, in the early fifties and won the championship. *From left:* Tony Fisher, Peter Mills, Arthur De Vulder from Belgium and me, carefully hiding a cigarette.

I played hundreds of rounds with Bobby Locke. He had exceptional talent.

Peter Butler was a great competitor, pictured here in the mid sixties after a tournament in La Moye, Jersey – which I won!

Slazenger signed me up in the early sixties, watched by Buzzer Hadingham (*left*), managing director, and Ian Mitchell, golf manager.

I flew from Buenos Aires to Japan in 1962 to promote a new line of Slazenger clubs. The spectacular Fuji Hagen Golf Club, with the famous mountain in the background, was kind enough to make me an honorary member.

beaches. In meeting a special request to go to Mar del Plata, we left time in Uruguay for only eight holes of practice before we were due to start in the big event, which was won by several shots by the Belgian Flory Van Donck, who tucked away something in the region of $7,000. Flory was a great player 'away from home'. I felt that we had taken on too many commitments, tried to please too many people in giving everyone a chance to see us, and in the end we gave rather less than our best.

In 1955 I took a stab at the US winter circuit along with Tony Harman and John Pritchard (the Sunningdale assistant who was so tragically killed in a car crash with the fine amateur Philip Scrutton on that straight bit of road in Hampshire that passes Blackbushe Airport). John Jacobs was also one of our party and although not with us all the time, so was Peter Thomson with his first wife, Lois, and their new-born baby. All in all, a good learning trip.

Later I was invited to play in the Spanish Open at the new El Prat Club on the outskirts of Barcelona, a few hundred yards from the city's airport. I was experimenting a bit with my swing, trying to make it a little slower. Trying to control the power I had at my disposal, I started to play keeping my left foot firmly on the ground. Come to think of it, this was an idea my father had put to me ten or twelve years earlier. I guess I hadn't listened. El Prat was an immense course over 7,200 yards long, a linksy type through sand dunes. It was suffering a little bit from newness but it had many splendid holes. I was to win the first of my two Spanish championships and won, may I say, in fine style from a good field. I was paid in cash, so I came home with a rather large envelope stuffed with glamorous, if slightly grubby, notes. The season had ended on a high note.

In 1958 I started to play reasonably well and about September I contacted my great friend Ken Bousfield and suggested that we might go and play in the Italian, Spanish and Portuguese Open Championships. Ken had had a particularly good year, winning, I think, two events. Off we went. He suggested we split our prize money. I thought this was more than generous because he was in much better form than me. The first championship was being played at Varese, a new course in northern Italy. Winter was coming early to that part of the world. The course was long and wet and it was cold but, somehow or other, I found a vein of good form and won by 10 shots. A good start for Ken and me. But some signs were not good. Ken had fallen in love with a singer in the band in our hotel. She was a voluptuous Italian dolly who slightly resembled Elizabeth Taylor. The hit song of the day was 'Volare'. He knew all the words, he knew all the movements. I got quite tired of hearing it. *'Volare, ah ah, Volare da da da da, nel blu di pinto di blu, velici lescaro la su'* etc! It was one of those Italian love songs that made the hairs on the back of your neck stand up.

On to Madrid where the championship was being held at the Puerto de Hierro Club three miles or so north of Madrid and the site of one of the last great battles of the Spanish Civil War. The views from the top end of the course across the city were spectacular. This year, 2004, they are celebrating their centenary. Again, everything seemed to go right for me. I'd perfected my swing, I had a few new thoughts, it all worked like clockwork and, once again, I won by 10 shots. By now I had a wheelbarrow load of pesetas to go with a sackful of lire – it was becoming quite a problem especially during working hours.

But it was upward and ever onward to Estoril for the Portuguese Championship. Ah, Estoril, a delightful, small, quirky course, very different now from years ago. I'll always remember the entrance hall at the club. They had lots of free flying birds, finches, canaries, budgies and the like. The extraordinary thing was they never seemed to mess on anybody – very well house-trained. By this time Ken was coming out of his lovesick mode, although the tune 'Volare' was still whistled on occasions when he had a quiet moment. My skills were starting to wane a little but I kept them going long enough to win this championship by 6 strokes. So there I was, aged twenty-seven, having won three Open Championships in three consecutive weeks by 10, 10 and 6 strokes. It was magical and I have doubts whether it'll ever be done again.

Once more we had an envelope full of money, this time escudos – what to do? What to do? Ken's caddy, who spoke English to a handicap of about 18, said we should take our three currencies and go down to the main banking area in Lisbon and get the best rates we could for our loot. We spent about five hours going up and down the street of a thousand bankers, first changing the money into Swiss francs, then converting back into German Deutschmarks, back to US dollars, to pounds, back to French francs etc. At the end of it all I think we showed a loss of about £8 which only showed us that caddies, at that time, were no good at financial matters or giving you the winner of the 2.30 at Ascot.

I hasten to add, we weren't really talking about vast amounts. My total prize money for the three victories was £1,123. Today I suppose it would be close on £500,000, but you could buy a lot for £1,123 back in those far-off days! Incidentally I have a receipt from W.H. Barraclough of Bradford in May 1970 for eight alpaca cardigans. The total, including nine shillings for postage and packing, came to £65 and sixteen shillings. That comes out at around £8 per garment. Now that, in 1970, was expensive. I've still got them but they are a little tight around my chest! Value today, *if* you could find any, perhaps £250 each!

Ken was very meticulous and had kept a list of our outgoings and incomings and, after we'd done the final tot-up and after all expenses for all our hard work over the three-week period, we were down to just over £950, split two ways. But it wasn't the money, it was the taking part and coming home with those three wonderful trophies that made it all so memorable. I was fifty-two under 4s. That's how the scoring was done in those days, par was only for the Americans.

Times have changed. The European tour under the direction of Ken Schofield has done amazingly well over the past five years. It's not easy trying to find employment for several hundred people for ten months in the year. Although it produced many wry smiles when it first happened, taking the Tour to the Caribbean, Australia, Malaysia and the Middle East did create a lot of interest and kept the pot boiling through those miserable early months of the year when golf, at the highest level, is impossible in northern Europe and indeed the courses in southern Spain are nowhere near ready in January, February or March. Schofield must be congratulated, he and his staff have done remarkably well.

5

RYDER CUP PLAYER

*'I had this little putt to win the hole . . . and
leave the Ryder Cup in the balance'*

Memories of the Ryder Cub stay forever – the great moments
of camaraderie, the late nights, the nervous tensions, the flag-
raisings and the anthems, the travel, the grandeur of it all. I was
fortunate, or perhaps I might say successful enough, to play in
no fewer that eight of these great matches. Like anyone who has
played so many times, my memories are a mixture of triumph
and disaster.

In 1953 sixteen players were invited to Wentworth for final
Ryder Cup trials, and I was one of them. Despite the publicity I
had been getting, I felt that I had little chance of winning a
place. Nearly all the others had substantial achievements behind
them and were vastly more experienced. We spent a week at
Wentworth practising and playing various foursomes combina-
tions, and when the final team selection was announced, it was
sensational. To my intense delight and pride I was in. At twenty-
two years and seven months I was one of the youngest ever

Ryder Cup players. Cotton had played at the age of twenty-two and Bernard Hunt, also selected for the team, was a year older than me. Even more important, the Alliss family set another unique record – for the first time, a father and son could boast of being Ryder Cup players.

When the Americans arrived hopes were high, and there was much talk of a new Elizabethan Age. A queen had been crowned, Everest climbed and the Ashes won. Stanley Matthews had got his winner's medal in the FA Cup and Gordon Richards had at last won the Derby. Many thought the Ryder Cup would return that autumn at Wentworth for the first time in twenty years.

Nerves atremble, I was put into the top match of the foursomes, partnered by that mighty hitter Harry Weetman, against Dale Douglas and Ed 'Porky' Oliver. However, nerves or not, I found I was in command of my game and the match was close all the way. Mainly as a result of two putts of indecent length from Oliver, the Americans came to the 35th hole, the 570-yard 17th so well known from TV today, 2 up. Then, glory be, they drove out of bounds. At worst, it looked as if a 5 would give us the hole and the match would go to the last. At this point Harry Weetman hit a very poor tee shot. The best you could say about it was that it was in bounds and straight – but skied only about 150 yards. I followed with a 5-iron safely up the fairway and Harry was left with a longish pitch to the green, which he thinned through the back. The Americans then put their fifth shot about three yards from the hole and I pitched up to about four feet. They got theirs and Harry missed. It was all over by 2 and 1.

Despite those high hopes, the first day continued to go badly for our team. The Irishmen Fred Daly and Harry Bradshaw beat

Walter Burkemo and Cary Middlecoff by one hole, but in between there were two heavy defeats for Great Britain, Eric Brown and John Panton losing 8 and 7 and Jimmy Adams and Bernard Hunt by 7 and 5. How often it had been said that we started off with an in-built advantage because of our supposed greater experience at foursomes play. True, American professionals play no foursomes at all to my knowledge, but we ourselves play very little. Sadly, foursomes are a treasured feature of golf at only a few clubs these days.

Our captain, Henry Cotton, told me that I should have little difficulty in my singles the following day. He considered my opponent, Jim Turnesa, the weakest player on their team and the US captain, Lloyd Mangrum, hadn't picked him for the foursomes, which may have meant he had the same opinion.

At 3 to 1 down we certainly needed a fast start in the eight singles to get ourselves back into the match, and this we got from Fred Daly who, playing second, thrashed Ted Kroll 9 and 7. Remember, they were 36 hole matches in those days. However, Dai Rees lost his match, but this was balanced by Eric Brown beating the formidable Mangrum 2 up. The score stood at 4 to 3 to the Americans.

Then came a miracle. Undoubtedly Sam Snead was the most feared of our opponents, and with six holes to play stood 4 up on Harry Weetman. Unbelievably, he launched into a sequence of wild shots. Harry played steadily, but was more or less handed the match 1 up. The scores stood at USA 5, Great Britain 4, after Max Faulkner had lost to Middlecoff 3 and 2.

Meanwhile, Jim Turnesa had not been proving a weak link in the US team by any means. I was round in 70, which was then 4 under par, yet still went in to lunch 1 down. However, I came to the 16th tee in the afternoon 1 up, and was further encouraged when Turnesa sliced wildly towards the woods. Surely he'd finish out of bounds? Alas, no. His ball struck a woman spectator and left him in play. However, he put his second shot into a bunker short of the green.

My own second shot was straight at the flag but struck a little heavily. I always knew it would be short, and so it was, in the front bunker forty yards from the hole. Turnesa recovered to about ten feet, and my own third shot pulled up about five feet from the hole. He holed his putt. I missed. All square with two to play and the Ryder Cup in the balance – I knew Harry Bradshaw had beaten Fred Haas. It was up to the youngsters, Alliss and Bernard Hunt, to bring the Cup back.

Turnesa drove off safely. My own plan was to hug the out of bounds along the left, then just ten yards off the fairway, with my drive and let my normal fade bring the ball back to the middle of the fairway. Some might think it a risky shot but my driving had this consistent pattern. Alas, the fade didn't take and my straight shot was out of bounds by no more than a couple of feet.

At 1 down with one to play I could no longer win my match (extra holes have never been played in the Ryder Cup). If, however, I could get a half and Bernard Hunt, playing just behind, could win his match we would get the Cup back for the first time in the twenty years since my father had been in that 1933 winning team. The 18th is 500 yards long. If you drive to the centre or left of the fairway, a long iron will probably get you home in 2. As you go right with your tee shot, a faded wooden club second is needed, swinging left to right around the trees. Turnesa, playing first, put his drive way right, some fifty yards into the trees, surely lost or unplayable. I followed with a shot to the perfect position. After much deliberation and with a little luck, Turnesa got his out of the trees and then hit his third shot to some thirty yards short of the green. My second shot with a 2-iron was well struck but pulled a little, about fifteen yards off the green and thirty yards from the flag. Turnesa then pitched up to about five yards.

Many thoughts ran through my mind. For instance, I felt I had to reckon on the American holing out for a 5. I wanted to play a little run-up with my 9-iron up the slope from the small grassy, rather soggy, hollow where my ball lay. That way I'd be sure of my 5, but the run of the ball would be unpredictable. Even a perfect shot could finish ten feet away.

Needing a 4, I decided to pitch with my sand wedge, but negative thoughts were washing into my mind. I caught the ground behind the ball and left it short on the bank of the green. It was still my turn. This time I chipped with a 9-iron, running the ball up to about forty inches.

Turnesa followed by doing the decent thing – he missed. I had this little putt to win the hole and get a half out of my match and leave the Ryder Cup in the balance. I never touched the hole.

It was all made worse fifteen minutes later when Bernard Hunt came to the last green needing to get down in two putts to win his match (which would have made the scores level), but he took three.

The cause of youth didn't benefit and when Ryder Cup time came round in 1955, we weren't picked. Both Hunt and I were back in the team in 1957, the matches this time being played at Lindrick Golf Club. Again hopes were high. After all, we should have won in 1953. Many thought that this was our strongest Ryder Cup team, while the Americans, without Snead, Hogan and Middlecoff, looked a less menacing bunch than usual.

Even so, the foursomes, in which Americans are thought to be at this so-called disadvantage, once more went decisively their way by 3 matches to 1, with Bernard Hunt and I, playing in the first match out, losing by 2 and 1 to Doug Ford and Dow Finsterwald.

Our captain, Dai Rees, was not dismayed and went round his team saying how the singles draw had worked out very well for our side. In my case, he said, I'd have no trouble at all in disposing of Fred Hawkins, 'the weakest man on their team'. That sounded familiar! Max Faulkner asked to be dropped from the singles as he was playing badly, but Harry Weetman was furious to be left out. With certain tempers flaring, it didn't augur well for the morrow.

Yet 5 October 1957 at Lindrick was to be an amazing day. The iron men of America first faltered, then cracked, and finally collapsed altogether. After the first 18 holes almost all of our men were up, and in the afternoon the cheering was particularly loud from around the turn as American after American went down, often by almost unbelievable margins. Dai Rees and Christy O'Connor both won 7 and 6, Bernard Hunt by 6 and 5, Peter Mills 5 and 3 and both Eric Brown and Ken Bousfield 4 and 3. The crowds were running wild, sensing victory.

Meanwhile, I was having a stern battle with Fred Hawkins and was 1 up at lunch, having gone round in 70. In the afternoon, at the 13th, then a par-5 of 470 yards, I looked likely to go further ahead until Hawkins holed a long putt for a half in 4 and birdied the next to draw level. At the 16th, 486 yards, he went ahead with another birdie but faltered at the 17th, a par-4 of 387 yards, when he was short in 2. As I prepared to play my own shot to the green, Rees and Ken Bousfield came running up.

'It doesn't matter,' Dai said, 'we've won, we've won, relax, we've won!'

Of course, I was highly delighted, but the news did nothing for my concentration and I sent my second shot under a hedge to the right of the green. I could do no better than 6 and Hawkins had only to make a 5 to win the hole and the match 2 and 1. Although I was playing number three, only Harry Bradshaw, having a very close match with US Open Champion Dick Mayer, and I were still out on the course. Harry halved his match in fine style.

The Ryder Cup was back in Britain for the first time in twenty-four years, but my own matchplay record read played four, lost four. Nevertheless, I was very proud to be a member of the winning team, and the memory has been warm and bright over the many years that were to pass before we found the men who could do it again.

Although I hadn't won a point, I felt that I had played as well as anyone in the team: in matchplay how your opponent plays is every bit as important. Even so, matchplay seemed to be a problem for me, as it was for Seve Ballesteros in his early years. You can play well but your opponent, perhaps thought to have little chance, raises his game and has all the luck at vital moments.

The 1959 Ryder Cup in California went as many had feared. On home ground the Americans returned to their invincible ways. We won only 2 points, but in this match at the New Eldorado Club in Palm Desert I really arrived as a Ryder Cup player and began a long, wonderful partnership with Christy O'Connor. With him I won my first point when we beat Doug Ford and Art Wall in the foursomes 3 and 2. In the singles I halved my match with Jay Hebert, who was the US PGA

Champion. It was a close contest the whole way, and I came to the last hole one down. Hebert found water with his second shot, thank the Lord, and I managed to put a straight 3-iron plumb in the middle of the green and won the hole.

In 1961 great changes were made in how the Ryder Cup was played. The four foursomes and eight singles, each of 36 holes, were scrapped. Instead, all matches switched to 18 holes, with two lots of four foursomes on the first day and eight singles, morning and afternoon.

Again we began badly in the foursomes, almost putting ourselves out of the contest on the first day. By the close the Americans led 6 matches to 2. O'Connor and I had started the match off well enough, however, by beating Gene Littler and Doug Ford 4 and 3. Even so, the second day resulted in some of my most vivid Ryder Cup memories.

I was drawn to meet Palmer in the morning, a daunting prospect. He was at his very peak, and his famous charges against all the odds had already become legendary. He'd won the Masters twice, the US Open and our own Open a little over two months before at Royal Birkdale. There his performance had included some of the greatest golf ever seen in gale-force winds.

One of his greatest strengths was bold putting. He went firmly for everything, confident that if he ran a few feet past, he could still will the return putt in. Of course, he did miss a few but this went generally unnoticed. He was a little like Tom Watson in his prime, never short, fully prepared to straighten out a borrow by hitting firmly at the back of the hole. His long game won him even more fans. He set himself up to give the ball the biggest crack he could manage. Away the ball fizzed, and the fact that Arnold almost always finished off balance only increased the feeling of power.

I was pleased to find myself in a match that was the morning's main attraction, nervous, but in a positive way. I was playing well and didn't believe there was anyone in the world who could make me look silly on a golf course. I felt he'd have to play well to beat me and it wouldn't be 6 and 5 for sure.

Even though that match took place over forty years ago, I can still remember every shot. You must excuse just one blow by blow account in the story of my life. It is perhaps my favourite.

The 1st at Royal Lytham is a tester, a par-3 of just over 200 yards. After a half in 3s, Palmer went 1 up when we were both short of the 2nd in 2 and he succeeded in getting down with a chip and a putt. However, I was immediately able to come back at him with two wins, the second as the result of a wedge to a couple of feet or so at the 4th. The next two holes were halved. Then we faced the 7th, a long par-5 of 550 yards, unreachable that day into a stiff wind. Just off the green with my third shot, I chipped stone dead. Palmer was a few feet on to the back fringe in 3. Out came his putter; his ball raced at the hole much too hard, I thought, but no. Bang! It hit the hole and plunged in. Match all square – blast him!

However, from through the green at the 8th he was less successful, not hitting his chip clean and I went 1 up again. I was lucky to get a half at the 9th, 162 yards, where Arnold hit the middle of the green, and I bunkered my 7-iron on the right but got down in 2 more, holing a very missable putt.

At the 10th, 334 yards, I looked about to go further ahead when I hit my little pitch to about a yard while he pitched through the green into ankle-deep rough. I thought he had no chance of stopping his chip anywhere near the hole. Instead, he holed it. Blast him again!

The next four holes were halved, and at the par-5 15th we

both drove well. My second shot ended just a few feet short of the green, but Arnold had hooked into a bunker. I chipped close, only two or three feet away. Palmer then played his bunker shot much too hard. It flew out, bounced once and then went straight into the hole on the fly. Well, I thought, this is the kind of crash, bang play I expected from him. Match all square again. Blast him for the third time!

On the next two holes we both had chances, but they were halved in pars. Palmer had the honour on the last, a par-4 of 380 or so yards downwind. He smashed his drive away into the far distance and, although I carried the bunkers on the left, my ball settled in the semi-rough, on a tuft a couple of inches off the ground. Afraid of getting a flier, I decided to hit it as hard as I could with my wedge but got underneath the ball, finishing just short of the green. Palmer played a good pitch, six yards short of the hole.

Dammit, I felt I'd had the edge from the 3rd hole and, but for those three shots holed from off the green . . . Now it looked as if I was going to lose. There he was, just a few yards away and I had some forty yards to the hole. Well, I hated the thought of losing the match to a par on the last hole and steeled myself to get the chip as close as I could.

I took out my 9-iron, the club I trusted most for a running shot, got my hands well forward and struck the ball with exactly the strength and precision I wanted. On and on it went and then, for just a moment, I thought, it's going in! In fact, it caught the edge of the hole and finished less than a couple of feet past.

Palmer settled into his knock-kneed putting stance. The stroke was firm and I held my breath as his ball ran at the hole. No, it wasn't in and stopped a missable distance past, about two-and-a-half feet or so.

I walked up to my putt. 'Pick it up,' Palmer said. Impassively I did so, but I was much relieved. Palmer was looking a little cross. Perhaps he'd expected to hole his first putt and I'm sure he must have expected to win the match. Now he had the two-and-a-half footer to half it.

Unbidden, the words tumbled out. 'That's all right,' I said. 'Pick it up, Arnold.'

It was the most memorable match of my career as a Ryder Cup player. However, two years later came another Alliss versus Palmer Ryder Cup match at Bobby Jones's boyhood course, East Lake, Atlanta, Georgia and my memories of it are nearly as sharp. I was in poor driving form, no width and too much lift on the back swing, followed by a chop across the ball. I was hitting my tee shots little more than 220 yards. Palmer was lacing his about fifty yards past me every time. But this needn't always be a disadvantage if the irons are going well. Mine were, and I was usually inside his shots to the greens on the early holes. In fact, I should have opened up a gap of perhaps three holes, but missed three putts of five feet or less. At the 9th, a par-5 of just over 500 yards, I got a good one away at last and found the green with my second to win it with a 4. I won the 12th as well, holing a putt of three or four yards. I soon lost one of my 2-hole lead when I missed a short putt on the 14th, but Palmer was immediately kind to me on the 15th, a par-5. He hooked his tee shot and bunkered his second so I won it with a par: 2 up with 3 to play.

Par golf should have done it, but I promptly dropped a shot when I missed the green at the 16th and lost the hole. The match seemed more or less mine when I struck a 6-iron twelve feet from the hole at the 410-yard 17th. But Palmer's approach was much better, only a yard away. It was odds on the match going to the last all square. This time my putting worked well. I got mine in to the loudest silence I've ever heard! Palmer had to hole his to stay in the match.

He did, and strode eagerly to the last, a 230-yard par-3. Here he fired his tee shot straight at the flag, but was long by several yards. Nevertheless, it looked a certain par. The first job was to get my ball on the green. This I did, but cut it a little, finishing some twenty yards from the hole with a huge borrow from the right. My putt was one of the best long ones of my entire competitive career, and struck at a moment when it really counted. On and on it rolled, pace and judgment of line always looking good. I began to wonder if it would die into the hole. Well, it nearly did, stopping just inches away. Palmer knocked my ball towards me. He had to hole for a birdie 2 to halve the match.

I was expecting that very bold putter at least to give me a bit of a fright with his putt, to threaten the hole. That he did, but much too hard. I had beaten the hero on his own ground.

Although my memories up to 1963 have mostly been of my singles matches, my best overall Ryder Cup golf was played at Royal Birkdale in 1965, when the O'Connor and Alliss pairing worked very well indeed. In the morning's foursomes we weren't stretched by Don January and Ken Venturi. One under par when the match ended, we won by a very convincing margin of 5 and 4. In the afternoon we shifted up a gear, going to the turn in 31 strokes, but were only 1 up against Billy Casper and Gene Littler. We kept on playing sub-par golf, however, and came through in the end by 2 and 1.

After that first day, we were level at 4 all and Christy O'Connor and I were brimming with confidence on the second morning, facing Dave Marr, that year's US PGA Champion, and, yes, Arnold Palmer. In the event, we played approximate par golf and that isn't often good enough in fourball play. We went down 6 and 4, and after a hurried lunch, were first off in the afternoon, much less confident this time, especially as the luck of the draw had us out against Marr and Palmer again. However, the match was evenly balanced all the way, and we came to the last at Royal Birkdale, a par-5 in those days, all square. Both pairs were several strokes under par. That day the 513 yards really needed two good shots to get home in 2. My tee shot was good, down the right half of the fairway. O'Connor was bunkered, Marr hit a short tee shot and Palmer was in trouble on the right. I was not happy at the thought of having to go with my driver as the lie was tight. A number 4 was the only other wooden club I had in my bag. I decided to play the shot with my hands a little further ahead of the ball than usual and with the club toed in a little, a tip from John Jacobs. Now could I swing freely? It was as sweet a shot as I ever hit. Away it flew towards the right edge of the green. Then a little draw began to take. The ball landed, took one big bounce and rolled on, stopping no more than four yards from the hole.

Neither Dave Marr nor Arnold Palmer could do anything about it, and in the end they didn't even ask me to putt. Christy and I shook hands, winners 1 up. Despite this victory the score was Great Britain and Ireland 6, USA 8 at the end of the second day's play. There were two groups of eight singles left to play so the match was by no means over.

This isn't a blow-by-blow history of the Ryder Cup but just my clearest memories of it, so I won't go too far into the painful details of the third and last day's play. It was very nearly a rout, for the result was hardly in doubt after our first four players all lost in the morning. Overall, the Americans won the singles by 10 points to 5.

However, it was a good day for me because I beat two US Open Champions, Billy Casper, one of America's best who went on to become a considerable force on the US Senior Tour, and Ken Venturi, former US Open Champion who recently retired from being one of the lead commentators with the CBS network. He retired, in fact, in 2002. In the morning I went to the turn in 32 against Casper's 33, and the inward nine was equally closely contested. I had a putt of some five feet for the match on the final green – not my best distance – but I banged it in, much to the crowd's and my delight.

In the afternoon I found Ken Venturi a steady opponent, especially over the first nine, but I was able to pull away later, winning 3 and 1.

With 5 points from my six matches I had enjoyed my best Ryder Cup, being involved in nearly half of our points total. One reward was my only invitation to play in the World Matchplay Championship at Wentworth.

There were a few more great days for Peter Alliss in the Ryder Cup. In 1967, however, I vividly remember we all felt 1 down before any of us so much as reached the first tee. At the pre-Ryder Cup flag-raising ceremony, Dai Rees, called to the colours once again as captain, introduced his team one by one, singling out our greatest achievements. In some cases these were rather slim. To be honest, it was a little embarrassing. Ben Hogan, captaining the USA, topped Dai's remarks very effectively, asking his team to rise to their feet and saying, 'Ladies and gentlemen, the finest golfers in the world.' What an introduction!

We went on to lose 21–6, and the team of O'Connor and Alliss were eclipsed in both the foursomes and fourballs. In the singles I lost a close match to Billy Casper 2 and 1, but beat Gay

Brewer, US Masters Champion that year, 2 and 1. Hogan's statement had become hard fact.

When Ryder Cup time came round again in 1969, memories of our Lindrick triumph twelve years before were growing dim. The Americans had certainly re-established their supremacy on both sides of the Atlantic in the years that followed. However, in Eric Brown we had a very competitive captain, so much so that he forbade us to look for US balls in the rough in case we incurred a penalty stroke by treading on one and moving it.

Our team was very much a mixture of young players and long-established warriors, with O'Connor, Bernard Hunt and I having the most years of Ryder Cup experience. The key figures of our team were to be Tony Jacklin, our recent Open Champion, and Peter Townsend, at that time equally the coming man of British golf.

On the first morning, with hardly a breath of wind, conditions surely favoured the American team. But no, there was a euphoric start as our foursomes pairings of Coles/Huggett, Gallacher/Bembridge and Jacklin/Townsend all won without needing to play the 18th. I saw none of this, being involved with Christy O'Connor in a hard battle with Billy Casper and Frank Beard, two prolific money-winners on the US Tour.

With a birdie at the 1st we jumped straight into the lead, but then lost both the 3rd and 4th holes to pars to go 1 down. We then had birdies at the 6th and 7th to take the lead. The match was all square at the turn. At the 13th, then 517 yards, an American birdie put us behind but we immediately squared with a 2 on the 202-yard 14th. The remaining holes were all halved. I had a putt of about eighteen feet to win the match at the last and I thought I had it, but the ball flicked around the rim and that was that.

In the afternoon I was an observer, commentating with Henry Longhurst and Harry Carpenter for the BBC. It did not go well for Great Britain and Ireland. Sam Snead, the American captain, having used ripe language on his team at lunch, had his men raring to go. Our first two foursomes pairings both lost close matches, but Tony Jacklin and Peter Townsend birdied the last two holes to beat Billy Casper and Frank Beard 1 up.

In the final foursome Jack Nicklaus made his first Ryder Cup appearance no fewer than seven years after he had won his first major professional championship, the 1962 US Open. (Yes, there've been many arguments over first the British and later the European selection procedures for the Ryder Cup. The American notion that you had to serve out a number of years as a member of the US Professional Golfers' Association before becoming eligible was just as controversial as anything contrived by committees this side of the Atlantic! Only after the near defeat of 1983 in Florida were they to produce a more logical system, though still not ideal.)

This final match, between Nicklaus and Dan Sikes and Bernard Hunt and Peter Butler, produced nothing in the way of scoring but plenty of excitement. With the match all square on the 510-yard 17th, both pairs took 6 and Nicklaus hooked his tee shot into the rough on the last hole. Minutes later, however, he played a match-winning shot to this par-5 when he wedged the Americans' third shot to a couple of feet, leaving Bernard Hunt with a long putt to halve the hole in 4s. It missed.

The day ended with Great Britain having a 1-point lead, but some of the momentum was gone. Even so, Great Britain proved to have the better morning golfers on the second day when the two sets of fourballs began. Eric Brown made the possibly risky decision to split the successful pairing of Peter Townsend and Tony Jacklin to 'spread the inspiration around'. One result was that I'd played my last match with Christy O'Connor. He went out first with Townsend and won, while the new combination of Jacklin and Neil Coles, playing at number four, beat Nicklaus and Sikes. In between, Brian Huggett and Alex Caygill halved their match with Ray Floyd and Miller Barber.

My new partner was Brian Barnes. We faced Lee Trevino and Gene Littler, a rather idiosyncratic American pairing. Trevino 'looks wrong' but is perfect through the ball, while Littler is perfect in everything he does except that his tournament results, despite one US Amateur Championship and one US Open, are below what his genius for the game might have achieved.

Brian and I were 1 under par over the first seven holes and 3 down, but birdies on the 9th and 10th brought us back into the match. On the 15th we got the match back to all square, but Trevino holed a long putt at the 17th to take the Americans into the lead once again. Both sides birdied the last, so Barnes and Alliss, though 6 under par at the finish, lost by one hole.

Overall, however, the match was looking good for the home team. We went into the afternoon series of fourballs with a 2-point lead.

In the first match Peter Townsend and Peter Butler were 5 under par at the finish, but that wasn't good enough to beat Billy Casper and Frank Beard, who won by 2 up. There followed perhaps the most ill-tempered match in the history of the Ryder Cup. It was between Brian Huggett and Bernard Gallacher and Dave Hill and Ken Still.

All was peace until the match reached the 7th green, with the

American pair 2 up. Here, Dave Hill putted out of turn and Huggett mentioned this to the match referee. Under the rules of golf, Hill should have replaced his ball and waited his turn, but Ken Still swept towards the 8th tee declaring, 'If you want to win that badly, you can have the hole.'

As the match went down the 8th fairway, Huggett and Still exchanged unfriendly words and the crowd became aware of the ill feeling. There was a little booing and one spectator was restrained from throwing a bottle.

It was definitely time for a pause to let the heart beats slow down. Unfortunately, events on the 8th green quickened them even more. Ken Still, with a putt for a birdie, charged it past the hole and then prepared to putt out, intent on giving his partner, Dave Hill, a 'free putt' from about four feet. Bernard Gallacher, thinking that the borrow of Still's second putt might give his American partner a little useful information, picked up Still's ball and tossed it to him, conceding the par-4. Still was very cross and claimed that Great Britain had conceded the hole because his own ball had been touched. An international incident was in the making, perhaps inflamed when Dave Hill holed his short putt for a birdie and bowed ironically to the crowd. Officials from both the British and US PGA began to move towards the trouble spot to have a word here and there to the effect that it was really just a game – wasn't it?

A few holes later, two policemen arrived on the scene, followed by a few of the US team to urge and counsel their men.

There were no more incidents, and despite the clamour the golf remained of a high standard, typified by Dave Hill hitting the 510-yard 17th green in 2 and then holing his putt for an eagle 3 and a 2 and 1 victory. 'That'll teach 'em,' he seemed to be saying.

All in all, I suppose this match saw the most heated tempers in the whole long Ryder Cup saga. Even so, it amounted to little more than a cross word or two and even added spice to the occasion. After all, matchplay, rare as it is, does inflame the passions more than a run-of-the-mill 72-holes strokeplay tournament. It's about *us* beating *them*, whichever team you happen to support, and if *they* get into deep rough or a bunker, spectators are likely to rejoice. In strokeplay, all of us think far more about how the players are faring. There will be applause after a good shot and a sympathetic groan when a player's ball plummets down into trouble.

When the last two matches were halved, the USA had pulled back 2 points that afternoon and the two sides were level, each having won six matches with three halved.

I remember our team was a little disappointed. We had lost our good lead from the first morning's play, and I felt the greater American strength in depth might tell over the final sixteen singles matches. It was a momentous day for me on a personal level. I had decided to give up international team golf, so this was my final match. I had a great opponent, Lee Trevino, US Open Champion the previous year but not yet quite the name he was to become over the next few years.

Playing at number one I had a great start, with birdies on the first two holes to go 2 up. The next four holes were halved in par figures, but Trevino birdied three of the next four holes to be up in the match for the first time at the 10th. The next five holes were all halved with pars, but I faltered at the 16th, 401 yards, dropping a shot to be 2 down with 2 to play. At this point I got my third birdie of the morning on this 510-yard hole but, alas for Alliss, so did Trevino, running out the winner 2 and 1. I had dropped just that one shot to par in my round and was 2 under at the finish, but Trevino produced the best scoring to be 5 under. I had missed eight putts of under ten feet and that, I thought, was enough of that.

My defeat was a jolt to our team hopes and matters became worse when our number two, Peter Townsend, went down 5 and 4 to Dave Hill.

Could Neil Coles deal with Tommy Aaron, one of the Americans not on good form? He was in the lead at the turn by one hole, and took the 10th as well. Neil then ran into trouble, losing three holes in a row to be down in the match for the first time with holes running out. The 14th and 15th were halved, but Coles levelled the match when he holed a good putt on the 16th. Even better was to follow. On the par-5 17th, Coles drove well and got his 4-wood shot to within inches of the hole. He was 1 up again and went on to take the match. The rot seemed to have stopped. Christy O'Connor defeated Frank Beard far from home 5 and 4, but Brian Barnes lost a close match to Billy Casper by one hole.

At this point the Great Britain tail wagged vigorously. Maurice Bembridge and Peter Butler each won 1 up. On to the last match, which featured our Open Champion, Tony Jacklin, and Jack Nicklaus. It drew the biggest crowds, and Jacklin put on a fine show, victoriously coasting in 4 and 3.

Once again Great Britain had had the better of a morning's play and regained a 2-point lead. Three wins and a half in the afternoon's eight singles would bring the Ryder Cup home.

The play that followed is best remembered for the tremendous climax. The strain by now was telling on all the players, and you could hardly say that more than three players produced good figures. At number one and three both Brian Barnes and Maurice Bembridge played downright badly and beat themselves, but Bernard Gallacher, replacing Peter Townsend or me, went some way towards redressing the balance. He was 4 under par when he beat Trevino 4 and 3. That was one of the $3\frac{1}{2}$ points.

Peter Butler seemed to be bringing in another with ease when he was 3 up on Dale Douglas after four holes. The American fought back, however, to level the match after the 10th. But Peter Butler was a steely competitor and continued undisturbed to a 3 and 2 victory. Only a win and a half were needed from the last four matches. The signs were good, for we had won them all in the morning.

It was a very different story this time. O'Connor was below his best against Gene Littler and lost 2 and 1. Neil Coles was not himself and was 5 over par when he lost 4 and 3 to Dan Sikes. Suddenly those $1\frac{1}{2}$ points had to come from just two matches, Brian Huggett against Billy Casper and Tony Jacklin against Jack Nicklaus.

The Huggett/Casper match was square at the turn, but the American took a one-hole lead when Huggett dropped a shot at the 10th. Five halves followed, but then Casper was twice bunkered at the 16th and had to concede the hole. Match all square.

The last two holes at Royal Birkdale measured 510 and 513 yards, but both were clear birdie opportunities. On the 17th Casper chipped dead for his and left Huggett facing a putt of four feet or so to get his half. This he bravely did.

On the last, both Casper and Huggett reached the green in 2. With a thirty-foot putt to win the match Huggett went boldly at it; rather too boldly in fact. He ran the ball a little more than four feet past, and shortly after heard a roar from the crowd at the 17th green. To Huggett this meant that Jacklin had won his match with Nicklaus, and that he had to hole the four-footer for a half to win the Ryder Cup. He did so and collapsed in a mixture of relief and triumph. But all was not over, as he had thought.

Behind, Jacklin and Nicklaus had been having a tremendous battle, the lead ever changing hands, first one player then the other being pulled back to all square and never more than one hole in it. At the 16th, however, Jacklin dropped a shot to go 1 down, and on the 17th Nicklaus had the best of things when he put his iron shot about eighteen feet from the flag with Jacklin as many yards away. Jacklin holed his huge putt, the reason for that great roar from the crowd. Nicklaus didn't. Match all square.

So the Ryder Cup hadn't been won after all; the outcome of the match now depended on how the two men played just one hole, ironic after the hundreds played over the three days. Either man could win or lose the Cup.

Both drove well and Nicklaus was first to play to the green, a good one, his ball ending about half a dozen yards from the flag. Jacklin's ball flew straight on target but ran past to the back of the green, a great deal further away. He had a putt probably to win the Ryder Cup while to 3-putt made the reverse inevitable. His ball ran on line, but pulled up about two-and-a-half feet short. It was Nicklaus's turn to try to take the trophy. He was determined not to be short, nor was he. He had to hole the one back from about four feet or the Cup would go to Great Britain.

Although Nicklaus is not perhaps known as one of the world's greatest putters, he's the man I'd always choose to hole a vital putt. As he says, 'You have to bear down on them. Any jerk can miss them gracefully.'

Nicklaus did hole and quickly conceded Jacklin's putt, saying, 'I don't think you would have missed but in these circumstances

I would never give you the opportunity.' The gesture set the seal on this great occasion and removed all trace of the ill feeling that had broken out in the fourball matches. Even so, Jacklin said afterwards, 'Half of his team were bitching about the fact he gave me that putt.'

At a far more vital moment, it somehow echoed my own gesture with Palmer at Lytham eight years before and was a fitting end to my own Ryder Cup career. I had watched for more than half the match from the commentary box. That was to be my viewpoint in the years that lay ahead.

My putting had become a tremendous strain, not helped I am sure by the strains in my married life. An important move to Moor Allerton was also on and I decided to announce that I no longer wanted to be considered for international match selection. The 1969 Ryder Cup was my swan song as a player but this great event has been able to bumble along quite nicely without me!

6

WORLD CUP GOLF

'I discovered that all the kamikaze pilots did not die in World War Two – they were driving taxis in Tokyo'

Before I leave my memories of my playing days I might mention two other events in which it was my great privilege to participate.

The Canada Cup was started in 1953, with the rationale 'International Goodwill through Golf'. The plan was to bring together two professional players from every golfing nation in the world at a different venue each year, and have them play four rounds of golf for team and individual prizes. The competition still survives, in spite of several hiccups along the way. It was sponsored initially by John Jay Hopkins, presiding tycoon of General Dynamics Corporation, a vast Canadian enterprise beavering away at the business of constructing nuclear submarines, space hardware, aircraft and various other items of military equipment for the US government. If Hopkins was a merchant of death, perhaps the goodwill part of the thing might have represented compensation, or sublimation, for John Jay. As I understand it, Hopkins had been persuaded to underwrite the whole thing by Fred Corcoran, a Boston Irishman and entrepreneur extraordinary.

Corcoran, who died in the late seventies at the age of seventy-two, had been, among other things, tournament director of the American PGA, four times their Ryder Cup team manager, personal manager to Sam Snead, and had started a tournament circuit for US women professionals. To organise the Canada Cup, he became head of the International Golf Association, an organisation that still exists. The first two events were held in Montreal, the first being won by Tony Cerda and Roberto de Vicenzo for Argentina. The Canada Cup, which in 1966 became more grandly known as the World Cup, has gone on ever since, through good times and bad.

I first played in 1954 with Harry Weetman at the Laval-sur-le-Lac Golf Club in Montreal. I was to play ten times in all and from that very first year I saw the event as a passport to the world. We were provided with air fares, hotel accommodation and a fee of $500. I didn't blow my money but brought it home intact after paying the necessary local taxes. Before this trip, I had been to Paris and Buenos Aires, but here I was in Montreal, all expenses paid, money in my pocket, in an annual event that could take me to a different world capital every year! Montreal I thought a delightful city, very cosmopolitan, with lovely squares, trees, statues and restaurants. Its spicy French flavour gives it a particularly different ambience. At that stage in my career, I thought this golf game was wholly marvellous. No one had mentioned that putting might after all be quite difficult.

Harry Weetman and I had a wonderful trip together in the great days when we were practically inseparable. We played fairly well in very intense summer heat and in a tournament in which it was taking more than three hours to play twelve holes. The 12th hole came back to the clubhouse, the 13th was short, and there were invariably three or four fourballs on the tee. We made the fatal error twice of having a drink on this tee. When it is very hot, drinking on the golf course does not help, even if it is orange squash. By the time we reached the 17th, another short hole, we were even more thirsty. There, they had run out of soft drinks and had only beer left. With so many people waiting to play, we decided to have a taste of this iced beer. We drank I suppose about half a tin each, but sitting in that hot sunshine, despite the very little amount of alcohol we had taken, knocked us out. We each wanted a 3, 4 finish for fairly low rounds, 71 or 72, but when at last our turn to drive came round, we could hardly see the ball. Harry finished 5, 5 and I finished 4, 6, and neither of us have been much inclined to take drinks on any golf course since, no matter how hot the weather. We scored in the low 70s most of the time, but other people were in the 60s, and we did not get near to winning.

Peter Thomson and Kel Nagle took the Canada Cup for Australia, playing wonderfully well, and Stan Leonard the Canadian, a neat, dapper but strong player with a fine putting touch, made the individual award a native-son win for Canada. We came straight home, with nothing but very pleasant memories of our trip to Montreal.

The Canada Cup took me to the Far East, to Tokyo with Ken Bousfield in 1957, and again with Tony Jacklin in 1966. It also took me to Australia for the first time, to Washington, Mexico City, Puerto Rico, Buenos Aires and Hawaii.

My chief impression of Japan was of its being like an ant's nest. I discovered that all the kamikaze pilots did not die in

World War Two – they were driving taxis in Tokyo, hurling cars all over the place. I've always thought that the Place de la Concorde was a shade hairy, but traffic in Tokyo had to be seen to be believed. Such a perplexing country, with so many faces. True Japanese-style homes I thought were charming – shoes off at the door, bamboo screens, matting floors. How sensible to take your shoes off at the door. Our way is nonsensical – you're entertaining, just had the new carpet fitted, it's deep snow or hissing with rain outside when the guests come in, shake their umbrellas all over the hall, leave them in the wrong place, someone rubs a shoe on the new settee and all the boot polish comes off and they say, 'Oh, I've marked your settee, most terribly sorry,' and you say, 'Oh, doesn't really matter, just an old thing,' while inwardly you are absolutely seething! How sensible to take off shoes, and put on little paper slippers.

But I never did get to grips with the Japanese breakfast. It seemed designed for a cross between a sea lion and a canary. For me, it would never replace the Great British Breakfast.

I first went to Melbourne in 1959 and found quite marvellous golf courses. The composite course for the Canada Cup at Royal Melbourne was simply majestic. This was the first time I had ever seen blue gum trees and koala bears, the first time I rubbed a leaf between my hands and smelled eucalyptus, the first time I had seen such a collection of all sorts of Victorian architecture, houses with verandas, iron and concrete roofs – strange recollections. It seemed a wonderfully tranquil, sedate, Anglo-Saxon city.

I played in the Piccadilly World Matchplay Championship, as it was then, at Wentworth in 1965 but by the middle of that year I was reduced to cross-handed putting, early symptoms of the 'twitch'. In fact, I had been handling it OK, I'd played well in the Dunlop Tournament and the Ryder Cup at Royal Birkdale and, in partnership with my great friend Christy O'Connor, had won 5 points out of 6. It was this result that got me into the World Matchplay event; one of the big boys didn't turn up so I was invited. The event, conceived by Mark McCormack, had begun in 1964, sponsored by Rothman's cigarettes and forty years on it's as healthy as ever, although it has gone through a number of commercial changes and a number of different sponsors. But everything looks fair now HSBC have signed up to do the event for another eight years, an extraordinarily generous commitment.

The concept was simple – eight of the best players in the world would meet over 36 holes of matchplay. Winners of all the majors each year would be invited, the others would be selected on the basis of lifetime achievement or significant current success. Each player had his travel expenses paid, and those of his wife or companion, and an elegant London hotel suite, first in the newly opened Carlton Tower in Knightsbridge, then later on there were river suites for all at the Savoy Hotel. Each player had a limousine and driver at his disposal for the entire week and, if beaten, was invited to stay for the rest of the event. At the club, the ladies' locker room was set aside for the players. There were special dinners, shopping trips and visits to the theatre for the wives. But the journey from the Savoy to Wentworth was just too tedious. The players had to get up far too early and didn't get back to the hotel till seven or eight o'clock at night. It was taking some of the gilt off the ginger-bread, so they took to renting private houses on, or near, the Wentworth Estate. Each one was fully staffed, including a Cordon Bleu chef, and had a well-stocked larder, refrigerator and wine cupboard. The owners received several thousand pounds a week and took off gaily, no doubt to the Bahamas. The fact that the family or the wives of the players were invited to stay for the entire period was a master stroke in public relations by Piccadilly. It was something the players just couldn't resist. Arnold Palmer, still at the height of his powers, won the first event and it was off and running, claiming a place in the golfing public's heart that it has never lost. Regardless of the player invitations, which occasionally have been controversial, it has produced huge crowds, astonishing scoring and marvellous matches, regardless of the weather.

I played Tony Lema in my first match and, as so often, did not have my head straight about the whole thing. I suppose I wasn't prepared mentally for the event. The players then were still based up in London but I decided to stay at the Berystede in Ascot, a place I'd been staying at for a number of years and only three miles away. I drove my own car, spurning the limo. With hindsight, I should have taken the car and the posh hotel suite, held my head up high saying in effect, 'I'm as good as any of you supermen, Palmer, Player, Lema.' The morning round was very close, it may have even been all square, but I was very foolish. I went into the lunch room and there was a feast laid out totally untouched. I ate well and perhaps even had one, maybe one and a half, glasses of wine. I should have had a sandwich or a bowl of soup. I teed off that afternoon feeling slightly bloated and, yes, you know what happened, Lema beat me quite easily 4 and 3, or it might even have been 5 and 4. So much for my World Matchplay career.

In 1966 I went, for the first time, to Augusta to play in the fabled Masters. I'd had a couple of invitations before but had turned them down – sounds totally ridiculous now, doesn't it? But it was a long way to go, and I didn't think winning was a possibility. How could it be with the likes of Jimmy Demaret, Sam Snead, Billy Casper, Ben Hogan, Cary Middlecoff and Uncle Tom Cobleigh and all waiting to beat the living daylights out of you? I was rather overwhelmed by the whole thing, the huge galleries, the noise, the colour, the entire gung-ho American dream. It was here I got the 'twitch'. It was on the 11th green, my partner Gene Littler. I think I 5 putted from about six feet, or was it 6 putts from five feet? So much for my Masters career, those fiery Augusta greens had consumed me. That's why I had the most tremendous admiration for Peter Butler, Maurice Bembridge and Ramon Soto who went and played the course so brilliantly.

It was in the sixties that the Shell Oil Company promoted *Shell's Wonderful World of Golf*, filmed solely for television – a very good vehicle for the company, taking their name around the world and entertaining 200 to 300 guests wherever the matches were played, and they were played in a variety of countries, some historic, some with exceptional beauty and some in faraway places with strange sounding names. The players were well rewarded with first-class expenses.

Gene Sarazen and Jimmy Demaret did the on-course commentaries. The several hours of film would be edited down for a fifty-minute television show. The matches were very successful and ran for many years. In fact, they have been reinstated over the past four or five years by Terry Jastrow who, for so many years, was producer of golf for ABC Television. I played in three matches and never won one. The first was at Penina, which had just opened, designed by Henry Cotton on an old rice plantation. It was awful; there wasn't a tree in sight. I wondered if it would ever amount to anything but it certainly has. The golf course is fine and the hotel one of my favourites.

Another memory from *Shell's Wonderful World of Golf* was my match with Dow Finsterwald at the Tryall Golf & Country Club in Jamaica. Due to problems with the light, it turned out to be the longest match ever filmed for TV, running into a third day. Yes, a game of golf running into a third day. After two days we were just short of the final green in 2. That night Dow introduced me to a drink called a daiquiri. To me it tasted superb, but I don't recommend you to have ten or twelve before a game of golf the next morning with temperatures of about 100 and humidity about the same. He won on the last green!

One of my favourite matches was in Bermuda where I played Tony Lema at the Mid Ocean Club. I played some of the best golf of my life. Shot after shot peppered the flag but my putting was in total disarray, so much so that Jimmy Demaret said that 'I had put cross-handed putting back twenty years.' Lema had a putt of perhaps four feet on the last green to win the match. The greens were very slow, he hit it too hard, the ball spun out and so we split $3,000. I was never sure if he did it on purpose. Lema was a lovely fellow; we had become solid friends in a very short time. Tragically, he and his wife Betty died just a year later when their light aircraft crashed on a golf course.

7

MOOR ALLERTON

*'So much went on during those years . . . it was
a happy club, we had a happy home'*

By the early sixties my marriage to Joan was beginning to
crumble. My lifestyle with weeks away from home did not make
for domestic tranquillity. Joan certainly did nothing wrong
except, she used to say, she loved me too much, which, to
me, became a form of possessiveness. The house and the
children were always immaculate, she didn't drink, she wasn't
promiscuous, although she could on occasion be a delicious flirt.
Much of the decline in our marriage was due to the fact that at
the Senior Service Tournament at the Dalmahoy Golf Club on
the west side of Edinburgh in 1965 I had met Jackie Grey. I had
been aware of her presence for some time before we spoke. She
was working as an interpreter for the sponsors, being fluent in
French and German. One day I was having a drink at the bar
with David Thomas and Guy Wolstenholme when she walked
in. They suddenly went off to play and I found myself sitting
alone and asked her if she'd care to come for dinner that night.

She said yes, we drove south of Edinburgh for a few miles and had a very pleasant evening.

That really was the start, and it has not ended yet. Our relationship grew. How it did was sometimes beyond my comprehension because we didn't see each other for at least a year. As it turned out she was very independent, a 'thoroughly modern Milly', sharing a flat in Wimbledon with a Dutch girl and with her own car. I was becoming torn between my feelings for Jackie and the family. This clandestine relationship brought the inevitable explosion and it happened just after the Ryder Cup matches played in 1967 in Houston, Texas. After the series David Thomas and his wife Robbie, Joan and I went to Las Vegas; we were playing in a special Pro-Am event. Dave and Robbie knew of my affair and I, quite wrongly perhaps, arranged for Jackie to communicate with me through Robbie. The whole drama ignited when the desk clerk innocently handed over a letter addressed to me care of Robbie while Joan was standing alongside her at reception. All hell broke loose! Joan was much comforted by Bernard Hunt and his wife Margaret but the atmosphere was horrendous and she was soon homeward bound.

There was much to-ing and fro-ing and soul-searching on my part. Everything took a long time to conclude. My son Gary was fourteen and had just started school at Milton Abbey; Carol was eight. It was a very difficult time for everyone, particularly the youngsters. The grand house was sold, although we kept fifteen acres of land that might, we thought, become available for development. It was what they called 'white' land. A local builder took a bit of a flyer and paid something in the region of £20,000 for the acreage in the hope that it would, one day, be free, which of course it was, and went on to be worth many hundreds of thousands of pounds. After everything was done and all payments made, I was seriously broke. Through this difficult period I was greatly sustained by my bank manager, Anthony Reid. He was a Barclays man and worked out of a little branch office in Ferndown. This was long before bullet-proof glass and gun-toting guards, just an open counter and a drawer full of money, a chair and a phone. I found the only things I actually owned were a Rover TC motor car with 12,000 miles on the clock and a large number of Sumrie suits, which had come courtesy of my dear friend Ronnie Sumrie from his family factory in Leeds.

The swinging sixties were drawing to a close, I had to take stock and the result was not very stimulating. My relations with Parkstone Golf Club were fine, although in those far-off days nobody was too keen to hear of anyone getting divorced; it just wasn't done. I was pushing forty, hugely in debt and my conscience troubled me – some might say rightly so. I was beginning to feel very alone. My brother had married into the Curry family, the vast cycle and television company, and had moved away from Parkstone and basically out of my life. I was not living at home any more and felt cut off from the children; mother had died, and father was ageing fast. When Percy eventually died I had a comforting letter from Henry Cotton who wrote:

Dear Peter and Alec, We are both so sorry to learn that your father only made six over par (78) but I'm sure he enjoyed his life particularly seeing you make the grade. I know you appreciate how good a golfer he was and understand that we long ago realised that he was some player, the best; in fact as an iron player there have been

few equal. He was great and if prizes had been given for clean hitting, he would have been the richest golfer of them all.
Sincere condolences,
Yours, Henry

My putting was crumbling, which realistically meant that my tournament career was in sharp decline. After eight Ryder Cup selections, the last in 1969, and ten Canada Cup appearances, I was coming to the end of that particular road. Suddenly a phone call, a voice said, 'Would you consider coming up to Moor Allerton to be our professional?' From out of nowhere my life was changed. The call was from Irwin Bellow. What an invitation, come to Moor Allerton. At that time Moor Allerton was predominantly a Jewish club on the north side of Leeds. They were in the process of selling their old course for redevelopment and were re-opening a couple of miles away with a marvellous new clubhouse, 27 holes, great practice facilities, plus tennis courts, bowling greens, etc etc. I thought this new opportunity, allied to my television and media work, could be the answer and it put new dimensions into my life.

And so it came to pass. Irwin and his brother Marshall were good and keen golfers with a huge involvement in the club. As the months went by Irwin went into politics and revolutionised the council-housing situation in Leeds and, I believe, made a blueprint that many other city councils followed. For that he was rewarded with a title and became Lord Bellwin of Leeds. His brother Marshall stayed on to run the family business. The firm was the main agent for Pfaff, the giant German engineering company who, through their wonderful inventions, had virtually put the Singer Sewing Machine company out of business, among other things. He and his wife Carol became staunch friends.

Leeds was an entirely new world with new people, although it also meant I was closer to Ronnie Sumrie, who remained a stalwart friend. His clothes firm once employed 1,200 people in its great factory on the east side of the city but cheaper labour costs abroad put an end to all that.

Depending on which bit of gossip you believed, the old golf club was sold for somewhere between £500,000 and £750,000, a huge sum in those times. The new club was to be first-class. They brought over Robert Trent Jones, the most famous, and certainly one of the most expensive, golf-course architects in the world, to design the course. The clubhouse would be functional but, at the same time, lavish. Alf Sanders, the club professional for many years, was retiring so if I decided to take the job it would be a clean entry. I had permission to play tournaments and continue my television work and anything else that might come along. The Bellow brothers were, in fact, saying that any exposure I could generate for the club would help them to get this rather large show on the road and they were very keen about the possibility of staging a big pro tournament there every year.

I knew the area quite well. I'd lived in Scott Hall Road as a boy when my father was the professional at Temple Newsam, and had played often enough in the *Yorkshire Evening News* tournament, which alternated between the Sand Moor and Moortown Golf Clubs. Leeds, at that time, had an outstanding football team, rugby league was in its pomp, Yorkshire cricket was tops, the town was alive. Now, thirty years on, it's probably one of the most vibrant cities in Europe. This all happened early in 1969. Joan and I were together but things were very strained. I drove her up to Leeds to have a look at Moor Allerton and its surrounds and we stayed with Marshall and his wife. I thought Joan's reaction to the place, its people, would be a last chance to save our marriage but on the drive home I finally realised it was all over. It was a tearful journey, overshadowed by the awareness of Jackie. I found her forcing herself more and more into my mind. She was confident and self-possessed, perhaps more than anyone I'd ever known. She was bright, kind, attractive. She absorbed all my stories, complaints and moods. She's one of the most talented people I've ever known and when we'd spoken she seemed very positive about Moor Allerton and the possible lifestyle there on its many levels.

The work of Robert Trent Jones was met with a mixture of opinion. His style was to construct huge tee-ing grounds, substantial water hazards, large, wickedly sloping greens and he also seemed determined to reshape the entire landscape! The course has changed dramatically over the years. Many hundreds of trees were planted and they're now twenty to thirty feet high, which has given it an entirely new look. At that time it was open and very bleak. You could see across the course to the Vale of York and the Great White Horse, which cut into the hills thirty to forty miles away. Boy, oh boy, did the wind whistle in from the northeast. Had they made a terrible mistake in moving away from the gentle acres of the old Moor Allerton?

I had now made the decision to ask Jackie to come with me to Moor Allerton. She had put up with all my to-ing and fro-ing as, indeed, had Joan. The old saying that it's always the woman who gets the divorce was never truer. Joan decided that was that. Shortly after the divorce came through in 1970 I married Jackie. We went to Leeds full of hope and the ten years spent there were among the best of my life.

When the club bought the land for the new course there was

an old farmhouse on the property. It was totally derelict. The only thing still in place was a wonderful stone roof. All the windows had been smashed, the floorboards pulled up, fire-places ripped out. It was, to say the least, a mess. We looked around at all sorts of properties but didn't have any money to put down a deposit, so buying, or even renting, a property was out of the question. The club said we could live there and, if we wished, restore the farmhouse. We'd work something out later regarding payment. In time the work was done – how we ever managed to get the wherewithal to do it was beyond my comprehension. A year or two later we even added a 1,000 square foot extension. The building costs in those far-off times, believe it or not, were £5 per square foot. Nowadays I doubt whether you'd get much change out of £100 per square foot.

We lived upside down. A small dining room and lounge with a big handmade fireplace were on the first floor, the main bedroom and adjoining bathroom, three small bedrooms and kitchen downstairs. Colin Geddes, the head greenkeeper, and his family lived in a bungalow next door. He, and all the ground staff, became our friends. I remember watching our son Simon sitting on the tractor driven by Stephen Young, one of the greenkeepers. It reminded me of the times I had done exactly the same thing at Ferndown with Jim Bracher. So much went on during those ten years. It was a happy club, we had a happy home, although there were moments of great sadness.

One of the other attractions of going up to Leeds was that David Thomas, my great friend, was only an hour or so away living in south Manchester. Through the seventies we became more and more involved in a golf-course architecture venture we'd embarked upon. I still played some tournament golf and wrote a column in Mark McCormack's golf magazine but television was taking an increasingly large part of my life, culminating in the BBC *Pro-Celebrity Golf* series, which began in August 1974. The BBC thought that a series of golf matches, which would be filmed in August and shown during the winter, might have a life of three or four years. In fact, it ran for fourteen before it went on to other networks and other stations and, who knows, one day it may be resuscitated – but more of that later.

It was clear, if I was going to continue my way of life, I would have to provide the club with a reliable shop manager, a partner, a lesson-giver, someone worthy of such a big club. I immediately thought of Bert Williamson, who was from a very prominent Nottinghamshire golfing family. He'd been a companion of mine for a long time and I thought he was wonderful. Bert had been the professional at the Kingswood Golf Club in Surrey for a number of years. He was an excellent player and a fine teacher but he was now based at the Olgiata Golf Club on the outskirts of Rome, a very smart club where the 1968 Canada Cup matches had been held. Italian golf clubs, like much of Italian life, are prone to in-fighting and political wrangling. Bert seemed to have been rather marginalised and his input progressively ignored. He was getting itchy feet. I thought he might be just the man to handle Moor Allerton's needs in my absence and I was delighted when he responded to my invitation with a letter which opened simply, 'That whirring noise is the sound of my helicopter landing on your roof.' We were in business.

Bert and his lovely Italian wife Carla moved into a house in the little village of East Keswick, a mile or two away from the course. Bert was a likeable man who lived frugally – in fact, he was mean, but likeable. Bert was very efficient at running the club but he got up the backs of a few members because he simply wasn't prepared to do any wheeling and dealing, which a number of the members quite enjoyed – they liked the opportunity of doing a little bartering.

After a few years, and when I was well into the *Pro-Celebrity Golf* series, the club decided that they wished me to spend more time at Moor Allerton. I got the impression that they wanted me to tell Bert it was over, he had to go. However, another section of the membership, where he had some staunch supporters, had come to the conclusion that it was *me* who had to go. I could represent the club and continue to live at Blackmoor Farm but the responsibilities of the shop, and all that meant, would be in Bert's hands. I would have a small retainer, Bert would have the rest, and life would go on. Bert would be the king of the Moor Allerton castle.

And so it was for a number of years until another opportunity came along for Bert. Is Molas Golf Club, situated on the southern tip of Sardinia, was looking for a professional. It was a fine new club and, of course, Carla being Italian helped his cause and, who knows, perhaps she was getting a little tired of life in Yorkshire. Anyway, Bert was up, off and running. But life went on. Peter Blaze took over as the professional and what a good job he made of it.

For Jackie and me, our time at Moor Allerton was fulfilling and educational and gave us fascinating insights into the Jewish way of life. We had been warmly welcomed and made some wonderful friends. In the early days I had long conversations with a dear old boy called Doddy Aber who insisted on calling me 'Mr Alliss'. He regaled me with tales of the Jewish culture. I liked Moor Allerton because it had a caring ethos. They looked after their old folk. Many of them observed the Friday night customs, the family circle. The club closed early on a Friday so as not to offend those who still maintained the standards of yesterday. They were not great drinkers but they had a beautiful bar at the club. Perhaps most of all I loved their sense of humour: General Moshe Dayan was asked how he had managed to win the Six-day War – it was over in a flash. 'Well,' he said, 'I lined up all the doctors on the left, all the lawyers on the right and all the accountants in the middle, then I stood on a hill and shouted "Charge" and, boy, do those guys know how to charge!' When I first arrived I took my car to be Simonized. When I returned I found they'd cut three inches off the exhaust pipe. And one must not forget the Jewish lament: if Moses had turned right instead of left when he crossed the Red Sea, we'd have had all the oil and the Arabs would have had the oranges.

Shortly after we had settled at Moor Allerton, along came Sara Elizabeth Jane Alliss, Jackie's first child, the first of my second family, and dearly beloved by both of us. Thirteen months later came Victoria and the greatest tragedy of our lives. Victoria was born with massive brain damage, so much so that she was never definitely diagnosed. Shortly after she was born we realised that she was not responding to her environment, to noise, movement, light or dark. We returned to the local hospital where a lady doctor, highly qualified we were assured, shone lights, tinkled bells in Victoria's face, and said, 'Oh, Victoria's just a little backward – take her home and give her plenty of love and affection.' Tender loving care Jackie had in abundance, but a few more weeks brought no change whatsoever so we were referred to the Hospital for Sick Children in London's Great Ormond Street, a world-renowned institution.

There, our child was subjected to the most extensive tests – blood, tissues, fluids were analysed; they drilled into her head and eventually, and remarkably, said they didn't know exactly what was wrong. They thought it might be some genetic thing, they had only three or four such cases in a year. They thought it could happen again and we would have to think seriously about having more children.

We brought Victoria back to Leeds where she had devoted care and kindness from the staff at St James's and Seacroft Hospitals. She later went to the Oaks School at Boston Spa for exercise and physiotherapy. She needed constant care every hour of the day and night. In all her life I don't suppose she was out of hospital for more than a few weeks. Her life expectancy was given as eight years. In the event, she lived to be eleven.

Jackie was shattered, almost destroyed. She could not comprehend the unfairness of all this and the fact that we could do so little for her. I say 'almost' because Jackie became a giant, she took command. She visited Victoria twice every day, cuddling her, loving her, talking to her, all this without knowing how much, if anything, Victoria was aware of the love that was being given her. It was all doomed to end in nothingness and, with a lively sixteen-month-old daughter at home to nurture and love, these were very testing times for us all.

We had moments of bitterness. Why us? What did we do wrong? Needless to say we found no answers to such questions. I behaved badly. I became an ostrich. I couldn't make myself visit Victoria. No doubt it was plainly and simply self-pity, the most indulgent of all the emotions, but my thinking was of crippled or deformed children – if the brain was intact always something could be done. They could learn to read and write, speak, communicate, have *some* kind of life. But with Victoria there was nothing. In this case, I found myself thinking, it would be better for all of us if Victoria just slipped away. Yet Victoria was our child, our creation, a creature who deserved all our love, all our strength, all our energy. From Jackie she had all that.

Jackie became pregnant again. Long conversations and discussions were held with her gynaecologist, 'Theo' Redman. He advised us that there was a chance that Victoria's condition might be repeated. It simply wasn't worth the risk and he wondered whether Jackie was strong enough to cope with another possible disaster. A medical termination was advised at St James's Hospital. The procedure was successful and she was home after a few days. I was slowly becoming aware of another of the great mysteries of life, one that men can never quite unravel, the mystery of childbirth and motherhood. And I was gradually coming to understand that almost everyone has a private grief, private because it's unspoken. I hoped I learned more respect for other people, their emotions and their behaviour.

Two years went by. We'd been back to Great Ormond Street with Victoria but there was still no positive diagnosis. She was being well cared for in Leeds but Jackie was fretting for another child. We talked long and hard and eventually decided to go ahead and risk having another baby. Sara was about three when Jackie became pregnant. The baby was born at St James's Hospital, which was almost becoming Jackie's second home, again under the watchful eye of Mr Redman. Simon Peter Grey Alliss joined this world, sound in wind and limb and with the light of life in his eyes. Our joy was unconfined.

We moved south in 1980 and brought Victoria with us where she became a resident at a small children's nursing home in Grayshott, a nearby village. This made things much easier for Jackie; also Sara and Simon were able to pop in and out most days.

I think the big lesson for my children out of all of this is that they have absolutely no fear of any form of handicap and are the first to bend down to help or pick up a disabled child or adult. But Jackie was still 'needing' another child, she felt cheated, and in 1982 we took a chance and she became pregnant. Yet again fate took a hand. Six months into her pregnancy, Victoria died. As anyone who has ever buried a child will know, it has to be one of life's most distressing experiences. Again, my wife coped with huge courage. Her strength was to be severely tested as a month to the day after having Henry Peter Charles David, her beloved father, Geoff Grey, died.

Henry, our fourth child, was a healthy, happy and contented baby. He was beloved by all and brought an air of peace into our world.

8

GREAT
ADVERSARIES

*'It was the day I first set eyes on Peter Thomson
of Melbourne, Australia, who was later to
become a true and valued friend'*

During my career as a tournament professional there were
certain special players, men who stamped their personalities and
their achievements on the game. I have mentioned Henry
Cotton and Arnold Palmer earlier. They surely were among
the greatest of my time and I must add four more names to that
roll of honour.

When Bobby Locke finished joint second to Sam Snead in the
first postwar Open at St Andrews, he invited Snead to join him
in a series of exhibition matches in South Africa. Locke won
twelve of the fourteen matches played. He asked Snead if he
could make a living in America. Snead replied, 'If you putt like
that, you'll get very rich very quickly.' Sam did – betting on
Locke!

In my judgment Bobby Locke was the finest putter golf has known. His procedure on the greens was unchanging. He would crouch behind the ball, establishing the line, then a walk to examine any grain close to the hole. The last three or four feet were, in his opinion, the most important, especially if there was any grain, then right foot drawn back into a closed stance; two practice swings then 'pop', away it would go, usually into the hole. Quite phenomenal. It was a routine that never varied.

He went to the States in 1947. His first appearance was at the Masters where he finished fourteenth. In his next four tournaments he finished first, first, third and second in an extraordinary sequence. In his first year in America he won an astonishing seven times and finished marginally second on the money list to Jimmy Demaret who had played the entire year. The next year he won three times in America. One of his wins, in Chicago, was by a record 16 strokes. But then the American PGA banned him because, contrary to the rules, he had not played in a couple of tournaments he had entered. In the words of Gene Sarazen, it was 'the most disgraceful action by any golf organisation'.

Now in his thirties, Locke turned his back on America and embarked on the most fruitful, the most memorable decade of his life. He won the first of four Open Championships at Royal St George's in 1949, after a 36-hole play-off with Harry Bradshaw. A stunning 68 over the first 18 holes of the play-off broke the Irishman. He defended his title successfully the next year at Troon. Indeed, apart from Max Faulkner in 1951 and Ben Hogan in 1953, Locke and Peter Thomson dominated the championship from 1949 until 1959 when another South African, Gary Player, stepped up for the claret jug and inherited the mantle of Bobby Locke.

Locke won the Open in 1949, 1950, 1952 and 1957. Thomson went one better. He won three in a row – 1954, 1955 and 1956 – and then in 1958, and seven years later made it five at Royal Birkdale. Early in his career, Bobby Locke had flighted his shots left to right, the classic fade. As he grew older he switched to right to left, the classic draw, more and more as his girth grew greater. He was now aiming off almost 45° – a very different action, which, nevertheless, caused the ball to return unerringly to the centre of the fairway or the green. He was a great judge of distance, always judged by eye. I never saw him misjudge a shot into a green by more than a few yards.

He dressed uniformly. In the UK and Europe, it was always navy plus-fours, white shoes and stockings, a Cambridge blue sweater and a white cap, and he always wore a white shirt and a tie that was invariably in the colours of the South African PGA or Air Force. In the States the plus-fours became knickerbockers, which made him as noticeable as his golf. In his time, Locke won the championships of France, Germany, Switzerland, Egypt, Australia, New Zealand and Canada, and more than eighty events worldwide.

Alas, his retirement back in Johannesburg brought disaster. While driving across an un-gated level crossing, his car was hit by a train. Locke was seriously injured, indeed lucky to survive. He lost the sight of one eye and his brain was affected but he'd still play games with his friends, or indeed anyone who asked. They were very slow affairs, often not covering the full 18, but he never lost his deep love of the game that he graced in such an elegant way. Bobby Locke died at the age of seventy. He was a golfer of the very highest class. I enjoyed his company enormously and played dozens of games with him. He spent a lot of his time at the Farnham Golf Club in Surrey, which he always said had the most magnificent greens. He was great fun to be with, which belied his looks!

Samuel Jackson Snead was the youngest, by a few months, of the Big Three – Nelson, Hogan and Snead – who dominated US golf in the forties and fifties of the twentieth century, succeeding the original Triumvirate of J.H. Taylor, James Braid and Harry Vardon of fifty years earlier and preceding the Big Three of Palmer, Player and Nicklaus of the sixties and seventies.

All three were born in 1912, a vintage year by any standard. Snead was a hillbilly from the mountains of Virginia and many people reckoned he remained a hillbilly for the rest of his life. He was not a polished person but he was a magnificent athlete. No one ever had a golf swing that was as pretty or more thrilling to the eye in its rhythms and flowing power. Snead was one of the great long hitters in golf – seventy years ago, with equipment much less sophisticated than today's, he regularly hit drives well beyond the 300-yard marker. The nickname he acquired was 'Slammin' Sammy Snead', later simply 'the Slammer'. I suppose it was well deserved but some say it held him back because he spent much of his early golfing career just trying to hit the cover off the ball but, once he'd learned how to play, which didn't take him too long, he was quite wondrous.

Snead had magnetism. The press loved him with his southern accent and quaint expressions. Sam went on to win almost all the game's great prizes – the Masters in 1949, 1952, 1954, the PGA in 1942, 1949, 1951, the Open Championship in 1946. (He played competitive golf into his sixties and won the PGA Seniors Championship in 1964, 1965, 1967, 1970, 1972 and 1973!) But the US Open was to be his *bête noire*.

At his first attempt in his very first year at Oakland Hills, he won the US Open *for half an hour*. His 283 made him 'leader in the clubhouse'. The genial young hillbilly was swamped by the writers and promoters, all anxious to get a piece of this colourful young champion. But on the course something stirred. Ralph Guldahl, about as solemn as Snead was sparky, came to the last hole needing a par to tie Snead's total. Instead, he holed a monster putt for an eagle at the par-5 18th to win by 2. A year later Guldahl was to prevail again to retain the title. To this day it's still thought of as one of the, perhaps it would be too cruel to say, major flukes in the world of golf, but not far off. To win the US Open two years in a row and not, in all fairness, much else was remarkable.

In 1947 came Snead's last chance. He holed a birdie putt on the 72nd to tie Lew Worsham. On the final hole of the 18 holes play-off, both had putts of under three feet to keep them level but as Snead, thinking it was him to play, settled over his putt, Worsham asked for the putts to be measured. It turned out to be Snead's putt after all. He putted – missed. Worsham putted, holed and won the Open by a stroke.

Snead's Open Championship experience was quite different. He always claimed that 'when you left the States, you were camping out'. If the money was right of course, Sam would travel to the ends of the earth. He was never thought of as one of life's big spenders but he picked the perfect place and time to confirm his philosophy – St Andrews in 1946 and the first postwar Open and all the austerity you could imagine. He was virtually forced to enter the Open by the Wilson Sporting Goods Company, to which Sam was contracted. He said he would only go if his great friend and fellow professional Johnny Bulla would accompany him. Johnny Bulla was contacted. 'Look,' they said, 'you're a great friend of Snead, you both work for Wilson, you can talk him into going,' which he did. All was agreed.

At that time the Open finished with two rounds on a Friday. Going into the final round, three were tied for the lead on 215 – Snead, Bulla and Dai Rees, with Henry Cotton one stroke behind and Bobby Locke on 218. The weather worsened that afternoon, the wind increased and so did the scoring. When Snead took 6 on the par-4 6th hole, he threw his club on the ground in disgust and his body language suggested he'd given up all hope. His thoughts turned to going home and a chance to get out of this dreadful place. He reached the turn in 40, then suddenly he was in the lead. Why? Because he birdied the 10th, 12th and the 14th. Life was suddenly worth living again. He eventually coasted home to win by 4. Guess who was second? You've got it, Johnny Bulla. So, if Bulla had come alone and hadn't talked Sam into making the journey, he could well have won the Open Championship 1946.

Sam Snead had some delightful little eccentric touches. His trademark was a straw hat with colourful bands; he used to travel with at least half a dozen of them in a long polythene bag. He used to tuck a $100 bill underneath each of the bands. Once, when we were competing in the Canada Cup matches in Puerto Rico, he left his beloved hats on the bus. There was panic because Sam knew there was $600 going a-begging. Anyway, they turned up and all was well.

He had another lovely habit of folding a dollar bill up into the smallest square, smaller than I've ever seen. If anyone gave him any service which he quite liked, or he felt obliged to leave a tip, he used to place it in the hand of the waiter or the bell boy, or whoever it was, with the words, 'Here boy, put that in your hollow tooth.' He'd then walk away. The bill was so small it would take some time before it was all smoothed out. Then of course the recipient saw it wasn't a five or a ten, just a humble one, but it's the thought that counts!

Here's another Snead story that amuses me. After he'd won the Rancho Santa Fe Open in 1937 a friend brought him a cutting from a newspaper, showing Snead holding the trophy on high. The paper? The *New York Times*. When Sam saw it he remarked, 'Hey, how'd they get the picture of me? I ain't never been to New York.' Such was the then simplicity of Sam Snead but his lack of education didn't stop him becoming an enormously wealthy man owning huge tracts of land in Florida. It was said that much of the land he did own was where the Disney organisation have their vast playground today. If so, goodness knows how much money Sam left, and I often wonder to whom?

I met him at the Masters just after his seventieth birthday. I asked him how he was and what it was like to be seventy. He replied, 'Never trust a fart, always take a pee when you can and if you get an erection, use it even if you're alone.' Not quite Homer or Shakespeare but he was making a point, in fact three.

There are those who would say that Ben Hogan was the finest golfer who ever lived – just the thing to get some action started in the club bar on a dreary winter afternoon. What is certain is that those who did see him play have no doubt that he would be one of, say, half a dozen of the titans, peerless in the entire long history of the game. Perhaps his keenest accolade came from the golf journalist who wrote that he was 'the golfer least likely to make a mistake'.

Hogan practised relentlessly. In 1940 the breakthrough came. He won the North and South Open at Pinehurst in April. He was leading money-winner that year and again in 1941. What should have been three prime years were spent in the US Army

Air Corps but he was back in action in 1945. In 1946 he won the PGA, the first of his major championships. From then on he dominated the rest of that decade and deep into the fifties. In 1948 he won the US Open and the PGA. In the thirteen months to February 1949, Hogan won thirteen tournaments but on 2 February the Hogans were involved in a dreadful car crash when a Greyhound bus, overtaking in fog on a two-lane highway, hit the Hogan car head on. Ben suffered a double fracture of the pelvis, broken ankle, broken rib, broken collarbone. He was in hospital for two months. When he arrived home he weighed 95lbs.

By the summer he was well enough to be a non-playing captain of the US Ryder Cup team at Ganton. By the autumn he could putt and chip, then play a few holes and finally 18. Then he entered the Los Angeles Open, due in January 1950, and stunned all of America by scoring 73, 69, 69, 69, for a 280. He lost the play-off to Sam Snead. They said Hogan's legs were just not strong enough to carry his heart around but this event proved to Hogan that he could still be a contender – a champion.

When he came to his only Open Championship at Carnoustie in 1953, he had already won the Masters and the US Open that year. This was my third Open and I well remember the tremendous excitement from the huge crowds who flocked to see him play, and win, improving his score in every round.

As though after 1953 there were no more fields left to conquer and no great point in doing it all over again, Hogan never returned to our Open, never won another major. He caught the beginning of the television age, so personified by Arnold Palmer in the sixties, but made no attempt to embrace it. He was a hugely contained man who never tolerated fools gladly, as I saw at the Ryder Cup match at the Champions Club in Houston in 1967 when he captained the US team. Some called him introverted, and why not, after his father's death. There were no children of his marriage to Valerie. Save for one or two confidants, he kept the media at arm's length. He was conservative and dressed conservatively in grey or pale blue with, always, a white cap. When he retired he absolutely ceased to be a public figure, with no interest in travel, public appearances, media interviews. He wrote a perceptive book entitled *The Modern Fundamentals of Golf.* There is a Ben Hogan Trophy Room at the Colonial Club in Fort Worth and that is about the legacy of an astonishing career and remarkable life. Typically, unlike his contemporary Snead, he showed not the slightest interest in senior golf. He was almost a hermit and drank rather heavily. It's a pity he didn't leave a bigger legacy to the world of golf. Asked on his eightieth birthday how he would like to be remembered, he said, 'First as a gentleman – then as a golfer.'

The date 15 June 1951 will go down in my personal history not only because it was the day I completed my two years' National Service with the RAF Regiment, but also because it was the day I first set eyes on Peter Thomson of Melbourne, Australia who was later to become a true and valued friend.

I had been demobbed and travelled back from Watchet on the North Somerset coast to my father's home near Ferndown Golf Club, then in to Bournemouth to watch the final hours of the Penfold Festival of Britain Golf Tournament, which was being played at the Queens Park Golf Club. It's still there but has been slightly spoiled by the new bypass allowing visitors free flow into Bournemouth. They lost a couple of cracking holes but never mind, never mind. Still to this day it's a very good test.

I looked over the fence and down on to the 18th green and there was Thomson holing out. I can remember exactly what he was wearing – white shoes, dark green trousers, a white shirt and a white tennis visor.

Thomson, by any standard, was a very great player, particularly with the small ball that was in use during his halcyon years, essentially the fifties of the last century, during which time he won four of his five Open Championships, including three in successive years – 1954, 1955 and 1956. He won his first Open Championship at Royal Birkdale when he was just twenty-five years of age, one of the youngest winners in modern times. So rational was Thomson as a golfer and as a man, I often thought he didn't need any luck at all. He always saw his way clearly and appeared to have his golf and life under control.

His record in the Open Championship is intriguing. In his first appearance at Royal Portrush in 1951 he finished joint sixth behind the winner, Max Faulkner. In his second outing at Royal Lytham & St Anne's he was but one stroke behind the winner, Bobby Locke, and then at Carnoustie in 1953, Hogan's Open, he was joint second. No doubt, by this time, he had found the knack of links golf and felt that his time was coming and it was to come with a vengeance. He won the next three Opens at Birkdale, St Andrews and Hoylake. He was master of the old adage that links are best played backwards from green to tee. This is simply a way of expressing positional play, making a study of the green and the best entrance up to it, the place on the fairway that gave you the best line into that particular entrance and then where to put the tee shot on the fairway to set the whole thing up – and if the green was sloping one way or t'other he tried to leave himself an uphill putt! Ahem!

Thomson had a detached air about him, rather like Ben

Hogan, although he never had Hogan's forbidding manner. He had an open sunny face and walked down the fairway at a brisk clip but you somehow knew that he would not suffer fools gladly. He was never one to hang around the clubhouse with the boys after play. He was likely to have a bit of a chat and perhaps one beer and then say lightly, 'Well, I've had enough of you fellows, I'm off.' And off he went back into the town or to his hotel where you always felt he had things to do.

Invariably, he started each year with a couple of months in the USA tuning up for his assault on the European Tour. A lot of Americans over the years patronised him and his play. They thought that he should have won more but I can assure you that he always came away with a handsome profit. He did, in 1956, win the Texas Open and finished fourth in the US Open, which was won by Dr Cary Middlecoff, and ended the year in the top ten money-winners. He then concentrated on playing in Europe, Australia and the Far East, but when he turned fifty he thought he'd give the US Senior Tour a crack, although he might have been fifty-one, moving on to fifty-two, before he finally jumped on to their band wagon. It took him a year or two to get back into his stride but he had started taking the game seriously again. He won the World Seniors Invitation by a stroke from Arnold Palmer and, generally speaking, he was doing OK as a fledgling senior. But in 1985 something amazing happened – he won nine titles, a record that had only just been equalled by Hale Irwin. After that, what do you think he did? He simply retired. It was almost as if he said, 'Well, there you are boys, some of you thought I couldn't play. I've won nine times this year and with a bit of luck, if a few more putts had gone in, I might have won a dozen – I'm off. But remember the name P. Thomson, Australia.'

During his career Thomson won three Australian Opens and the championships of Italy, Spain, Germany, Hong Kong, India and the Philippines – twenty-six victories in all throughout Europe and thirty around the world.

9

FIRST YEARS
IN TELEVISION

*'I was introduced to the black art of
commentary by Ray Lakeland, then a major
BBC producer, based in Manchester'*

My first television broadcast was from Birkdale, now the
Royal Birkdale Golf Club, at the Championship of 1961, won
by Arnold Palmer in a storm. I was introduced to the black art of
commentary by Ray Lakeland, then a major BBC producer,
based in Manchester covering all sport – football, golf, horse
racing, rugby. Evidently, he had sat behind me on a flight back
to Dublin after the 1960 Irish Hospitals Tournament. I'd
regaled the boys with how well I had played and how I'd been
robbed of victory by Kel Nagle who had putted quite magnificently. He'd won by 4 strokes but the third placed man, Bobby
Locke, was 11 strokes behind me!

Some weeks later a letter arrived from Ray saying he'd been
interested in my summing-up of the situation and would I like

to be part of the BBC commentary team at the Open Championship the following year. I wrote back saying that I hoped to be playing! He said, 'That's OK, if you play in the morning, come up in the afternoon, just sit with the boys and tell us how the greens were, how it played, the wind conditions and so on.' I did and from the moment I climbed up their rickety tower I was hooked, regardless of the rather primitive conditions. A good trivia question: 'Who was our Steve Rider of the day and our anchorman and who were the commentators?' Got it? Well, the 'Steve Rider' on that occasion was Cliff Michelmore, Henry Longhurst was lead commentator, abetted by Bill Cox and Ben Wright. John Jacobs, too, was on hand. In time, he left to run the European Tour, then introduced golf to commercial television with Yorkshire TV. Climbing up that tower was a long road for me, taking me to all the major events of the game worldwide and to work for both the BBC and ABC, the American Broadcasting Corporation, one of the three huge networks in the United States, plus work in Canada and Australia.

Finding capable commentators is not easy. Over the past twenty or thirty years many people have written in complaining to the BBC about the incompetence of broadcasters and how they could do it better. There was a time when they would be invited to try their skills at the PGA Championship at Wentworth in May or the World Matchplay on the West course in October. I never thought the BBC gave any of these 'contestants' a real chance. Their attitude was 'show us what you can do'. They'd put the innocents in a commentary box in front of a blank television screen, give them a set of earphones and a microphone and say, 'Now watch the screen.' Presently, they'd hear a voice in their ears from the director saying, 'Are you all right, are you ready to go?' 'Yes, I'm ready.' 'OK, this is the 14th tee, West course Wentworth.' Nothing more, no other information, no scores, nothing . . . just players on the tee.

What they were looking for was no sign of fluster or bluster, just 'Here's Bobby Locke and Ben Hogan on the 14th tee. It's Hogan's honour. He's 5 under par and he's playing a 2-iron.' In other words, make it up, say things with confidence and show them here's someone who can think on his feet. No one ever did and, when being spoken to by the director or producer, many committed the cardinal sin of answering him back on air. You know the sort of thing. Director says, 'we're going to the second shots at the 16th.' Would-be commentator says, 'OK, I'm ready for that.' Too late, too late, that has already gone out to the listening, watching world and those folks at home who sit around with a notepad looking for traces of failure, rubbing their hands with glee, are jotting down mistake number 34 in the space of a mere twenty minutes.

Of course, there are many pitfalls for the commentator on golf. Let me give just one example. If you go to a course early in the year and it's in poor condition and everyone can see that the fairways are bare and the tees are awful, and you happen to remark on that, someone's bound to take you on one side and say, 'Don't you know we've had the worst winter in living memory? You wouldn't appreciate how many people have been working here seven days a week. Joe Smith and his team of greenkeepers, and lots of volunteers from the club and other greenkeepers from round and about, have actually been working their socks off to get this course into a playable condition and you come along to destroy and denigrate their efforts in a few words. You ought to be ashamed of yourself.' Ashamed isn't quite right but you're sorry if your words have wounded those who have put so much into it. That's why you can't speak the truth all the time.

This came home to me years ago when I was working for the network ABC in Hawaii. In those days they had their commentators up twenty-foot high towers behind various greens dotted around the course. (CBS still work that system.) Well I was some twenty-five yards from the ocean, it was a beautiful day but, in the space of forty-five minutes, the temperature must have dropped 30 degrees. A cold breeze coming off the sea almost cut me in half. I managed to find one of the big blue canvas covers they put on cameras to keep them dry during the night, and wrapped myself up in that, remarking that the temperature had dropped very quickly. 'And here's Asao Aoki putting on his fourth sweater,' etc, etc. That night at a cocktail party I was approached by the Junior Minister of Tourism, who I think had been over-imbibing. He was slightly stumbly and wagged his finger aggressively in my face and said I had single-handedly destroyed the island's tourist industry by remarking that the temperature had dropped some 30 degrees in the space of forty-five minutes. In all honesty, I didn't know how to answer that. What do you do when the camera is pointing at people pulling on waterproof trousers and jackets in Hawaii, the Sunshine State where everything in the garden is supposed to be rosy, certainly for 340 days in the year? I made a strategic withdrawal, but it was a lesson learned.

The other day I came across a letter from the BBC in the person of E.K. Wilson, Senior Booking Manager, to Archie Preston, then handling my business affairs, in 1969. The offer was for a two-year contract with an option for a further two years to be exercised six months before the end of the first two-year period. This contract was to give the BBC complete exclusivity for television and radio broadcasting rights world-wide. To paraphrase a lengthy letter, the BBC was offering me a minimum annual guarantee of £800 plus a fee of £200 per annum as golf advisor. Their requirement was coverage of the Open, the Dunlop Masters, the Piccadilly Tournament and another tournament yet to be named; Target Golf and linking work on American tournaments. The suggested fee scale was:

For tournaments	£35 per commentary day
	£25 for rehearsal day
	£10 for extra standby day (this would be made up to £35 if it turned into a normal day's commentating)
For Target Golf	£30 per engagement

Linking work on American tournaments 4 days per year

Things have moved on! But you could buy a four-bedroomed house in a good part of town for £2,850. Happy days.

My mentor as a golf commentator was Henry Longhurst, who died just over twenty-five years ago. For a generation, therefore, he is no more than a misty name but for those of us who lived in his time, Longhurst's place in the annals of the game is secure. He was a distinguished journalist and a communicator, who established a particular philosophy towards the business of commentating on the game as it was presented by the television screen. Longhurst, in the televising of golf from its earliest days, quickly realised the fact that millions of people, literally millions, who might be watching the action and hearing his words, were not, in a sense, his audience. His audience was essentially two people, perhaps of mature years, in their own living room, perhaps drinking a cup of tea and watching the golf. He spoke to them with an ease and familiarity. If television commentary was but one facet, however important, in a many-faceted game, Longhurst persuaded himself – and all his perceptive successors, as it happens – that the key to doing it was to be, quite simply, conversational, to talk to those two people in their own living room as though he was there with them. A further justification for this philosophy was, and is, the fact that golf is a slow game. Major championships involve continuous play for twelve hours or more each day and last four days, for all the world like a Test Match in cricket.

The Longhursts were a prosperous family who owned a department store, Longhurst & Skinner in Bedford. Longhurst, born in 1909, had a rather privileged upbringing, including Charterhouse School and Clare College, Cambridge. He took a team of undergraduates on a golfing tour of the US and ever after delighted in his many visits to America. He was good enough as a player to win the German Amateur Championship of 1936 and to finish second in the French Amateur one year later. After university he quickly found work as a journalist and in the thirties produced a weekly article for *The Tatler* magazine for 365 weeks, a staggering seven years! That must be the equivalent of two majors! Then he started a record run that still makes print journalists catch their breath. Longhurst wrote an 800-word column in *The Sunday Times* each week without interruption for twenty-five years. Shall we call that the equivalent of four majors? In addition to this, there were sundry magazine articles, the odd book and radio broadcasts, plus a place at the birth of the BBC's televising of golf in the fifties. That amounted to Henry standing by a green at Moor Park talking into a hand-held microphone to one camera. The pictures were in black and white and, to say the least, grainy.

Henry remained on the throne until illness attacked him in the early seventies. He died, after a fearful fight against cancer, in the summer of 1978, aged sixty-eight. In my early days, as the new boy, I became something of a Longhurst 'minder', a travel companion who checked the tickets, the baggage and generally got things done as increasingly we travelled to American events. At one point Henry had been employed simultaneously by the American networks ABC and CBS as well as the BBC – an unholy trinity. Exclusive contracts put an end to that. He encouraged my writing for Mark McCormack's *Golf International* – the fewer words the better, the simpler words the better, he would say. Despite our age differences, he became one of my best friends as television work progressively began to take over much of my life.

In addition to commentating on professional golf tournaments, Henry and I became associated with a new form of television programme involving golf, which became very popular. In 1974 we began *Pro-Celebrity Golf.* We made 140 programmes, a vast number. Our initial sponsor was Marley, the giant building supply company based in Kent, whose chairman, Jack Aisher, was a mad keen golfer who loved to play the game and watch it on television. He became the President at the Royal Cinque Ports Golf Club near Deal and was, and still is, a tremendous benefactor to the club. For the first two or three years it was almost Jack's private party. He brought up to eighteen or twenty friends for five or six days' fun. Also they all helped to make up the gallery. Believe it or not, it was quite hard to find people who would act in the galleries in those far-off times. On many occasions our stalwart stage manager, Harry Coventry, recruited locals who were paid somewhere between £5 and £10 per day just for the pleasure of being out on the course and watching the filming.

The first ten programmes were recorded at the Turnberry Hotel and what an array of talent there was on view. Telly Savalas was at the height of his fame as the fictional New York detective Kojak, Sean Connery was riding high as 007, Bobby Charlton was on the verge of retiring after a glittering career for Manchester United and England, actor and light comedian Fred McMurray came along with his glamorous wife Gloria de Haven, Robert Stack of *The Untouchables* was also on hand. The first professionals were Johnny Miller and Peter Oosterhuis. Miller was at the very top of his form in the early seventies and was regularly winning six or seven tournaments a year. He appeared unstoppable. Various sponsors were very generous, particularly Slazenger, who provided all the clothing worn by the players. The weather on the whole was fair, so a wonderful garden party atmosphere was created.

We recorded two shows each day, starting at approximately 8.30 a.m. Nine holes were taped and about seven shown, depending on the prowess of the players and the situation of the game. Only once in the 140 programmes was a shot replayed and, due to the expertise in the editing room, hardly anyone noticed anything awry.

It wasn't long before the matches switched to the Gleneagles Hotel. There was quite a bit of rivalry between the two over where the series would be filmed. Both venues were magnificent with perhaps Gleneagles having the edge because there was more to do for those attending but not participating in the golf. Henry Longhurst's health was deteriorating rapidly. He now disliked being on camera and I found myself thrust more and more into the action, introducing the programmes etc, but Henry still put some words in to the commentary. He did so enjoy being at Gleneagles in August. Why? Because we were usually there on the 'Glorious Twelfth' and it gave him the opportunity to enjoy an early grouse. As he used to say, 'So much for hanging them by the neck for three weeks in the garage, then declaring them absolutely ripe for eating.' Some of the ones we had there were probably shot only an hour or two before they reached the table. He was a canny one though; he certainly knew the difference between a tough old bird and a sweet youngster!

I shall have much to say about our celebrity guests later on but I should mention here the professionals who made the greatest impact on me, for different reasons.

Johnny Miller was a professional with a difference; he somehow made everything rather hard work, but this may have been due to his shyness. Fuzzy Zoeller and Lee Trevino were a hot combination and the one-liners flew thick and fast between them. But, on balance, I guess Trevino could give Zoeller a 2-up start over 18. He was, without doubt, the most entertaining, interesting and interested professional we ever had playing in the series. During fourteen years I came to know him well. Trevino was born in poverty but there was something in him that made him fight his way out from that bleak background to become one of the world's greatest sportsmen. He won the US, Canadian and British Opens in successive weeks in 1971. He had a social conscience and an enquiring mind and he wanted to know about everything; how our parliament worked, the difference between England, Scotland, Wales, Northern Ireland and Southern Ireland and what on earth and where was Eire? He wanted to know how we all came together, he was interested in our history, he wanted to know how to play cricket, how you made Yorkshire puddings and porridge, and why we drove on the left-hand side of the road. I gave him the explanation that many years earlier it was easier for right-handed people to draw their swords while passing another horseman on what passed for roads in Great Britain and Ireland hundreds of years ago.

He was a complex person but his attitude to the filming was entirely rational. He knew he was in the entertainment business, so at 8.15 in the morning he would be on hand and surrender himself entirely to the demands of the director. But forty-five minutes after the day's final wrap, he became his own man. You only had to tell him the plans for the following day, he'd nod, take it all in and, after a couple of beers with me and the crew, he'd tiptoe off to his room, shower, order room service and settle down for an evening's television. He avoided the hotel restaurant, no chance of a quiet dinner there, all those people wanting to shake your hand, talk or sign autographs. Of course, he attended all official functions and dinners that were part of the Marley/TV scene, but for most of the time he kept out of the way. He enjoyed our newspapers and read them from cover to cover. An impressive personality, Mr Trevino.

As you might imagine, we got a lot of letters from viewers when we ran our *Pro-Celebrity* series. We had quite a bit of support but there were one or two dissatisfied clients who used to send letters reading 'Love you but', e.g. 'First may I say how much I enjoy your golf commentaries. I think you're shaping up very nicely as a worthy successor to Henry Longhurst but on another tack, I don't think *Pro-Celebrity Golf* is a worthy programme for the money spent on it and I see no need to waste valuable television time by attempting to "popularise" golf in search of a mass audience.'

By 1978 the world of television was rapidly changing. The BBC's dominance in the broadcasting of so many of our leading sporting events was beginning to show signs of creaking.

Satellite TV was rather patronised in its early days but it soon began to make serious inroads into our homes, particularly when Rupert Murdoch became involved and the fattest and fastest cheque book in the world was brandished on every possible occasion, not only in the UK but also in the United States. The world of professional sport would never be the same again. The BBC was forced to fight its corner as never before. A lot of people don't realise the BBC is a billion pounds a year industry, although the money is perhaps less important than finding time slots in which to present programmes.

Professional and celebrity golf were on hand again in the form of *Around with Alliss*. The format was simple although we had to employ a little skulduggery at times. The programme ran for twenty-eight minutes and we played three holes. It was obvious, if one of us won the first two holes, the programme would be ten minutes short! So we had to make certain that the first two holes were halved, or we won one each, making the match all square, or one of us was 1 up with 1 to play.

The idea of *Around with Alliss* came from BBC producer Bob Abrahams. Between us, we produced thirty-six programmes, which are still remembered, I like to think, fondly to this day. The idea was to show me on a golf course with some captains of industry, public figures or sporting personalities and allow the viewer to be privy to our private conversation as we went round the course. It was very well done. We both had personal microphones and there were five cameras, always one viewing from long range. That way the viewer could plainly see no one else was nearby listening in.

Many interesting things happened during this six-year run. Perhaps the funniest concerned Dan Maskell at the Morton Hampstead Golf Club, now known as Bovey Castle and recently

taken over and refurbished totally by Peter De Savary. It used to
be part of the British Transport Hotel chain. For those who
don't know the course, I will explain. The first tee is right
outside the hotel/clubhouse. You play down a steep hill; it's a
driveable par-4. The river Bovey cascades about twenty-five feet
wide in front of the green, fast flowing, perhaps two or three feet
deep most of the time; it looks an absolute picture. My honour,
I cracked a good drive over the water left of the green some
fifteen yards in rough but lying well.

Dan had arrived with a finger-stall on the first finger of his
right hand. I asked what happened and he said he'd been rather
foolish. He'd been cutting the lawn and the blades on the
mower had jammed up with grass. He'd put his hand in to free
same, the blades spun and, oh dear, perhaps he was lucky not to
lose a finger. He didn't think it would hurt his play too much, he
could stick his right finger out and all would be well. He got his
first drive away, a little high but in play on the right-hand side of
the fairway. It ran down the bank some thirty or forty yards,
leaving him perhaps 110 yards from the green. The ball was
lying on quite a severe down slope, not the easiest of shots. I
suggested an 8-iron. Dan had many, many goes. Every ball he
hit, all new I hasten to add, went into the water . . . gone
forever.

Now one of the problems was it was early in the morning and
there was a little dew on the ground. The establishing shot had
been set up directly opposite Dan. Behind him there was a fine
rhododendron in full bloom so it was obvious we couldn't
suddenly change the position, too much work would be involved setting up a new shot. With all the tramping about, the
dew began to get more and more worn, divots began to show
but, using a good deal of imagination, it didn't look too bad.

Eventually, Dan got one over the stream but by this time everyone had lost count of how many he'd played. In fact, we'd had to send one of the caddies back to the pro shop to get more golf balls.

I played a good chip up to about six feet. Dan came on to the green, did a bit of to-ing and fro-ing and, at the end of it all, managed a 5 net 4! I had a quick stab at mine – well, we'd already been out over an hour and hadn't finished the first hole! I missed, so it was a half in 4. Dan was distraught. 'Sorry, sorry, I'm so sorry.' Dan's problems continued at the 2nd; he had eight or nine shots before holing out. Perhaps his finger was troubling him more than we realised. I managed to get a 4, so it ended up as another half. The 3rd is a pretty, short hole, water on the right, big trees on the left. Dan got one away just short of the green, I was on the back. Now my memory seems to cloud over here. I have a feeling that he chipped up, hit the pin and got a net 2. So be it, I certainly didn't begrudge Dan his moment of glory and, as it was in a continuous shot, you could see there were no cutaways, his shot was genuine. I gave mine a whack and, miracle of all miracles, it went in the hole, a half in 2 and a halved match.

But Dan was distraught. 'Oh, I'm so sorry.' I lost count of his sorries, he was almost in tears. 'How can you ever make anything of that, please, please, I'm so sorry, I'm so sorry.' They assured him that the programme wouldn't look too bad when it was eventually broadcast. I'm not sure Dan believed us. Anyway, he went away and was informed when the programme was to go out. As promised, it didn't look half bad. In fact, the ending was very dramatic. Dan was very happy and many friends congratulated him on his fine play despite having a bad finger. He was in seventh heaven and took all the many plaudits that came his way with great aplomb.

Then came the time for Dan to say farewell to the world of television. A party was organised to say goodbye. The BBC's Bill Cotton was the host and, with seventy or eighty people gathered at the TV Centre for the great but, in a way, sad occasion, Bill suddenly announced, 'Dan, we've got a surprise for you, we're going to show the game you had with Peter Alliss in *Around with Alliss* down at Morton Hampstead. I'm sure not all your friends have seen it.' It took a little time to set it all up and Dan was asked by a number of people how it had gone. He remembered how well the programme had looked when it was broadcast and said he'd played pretty well and perhaps he'd been rather unlucky. 'You see, Peter holed this monster putt on the last hole, otherwise I would have won.'

Everyone settled down and the show began. Well, you may have guessed, they showed the uncut version, much to Dan's horror. He took it all in very good part. Watching all those shots, the to-ing and fro-ing, chasing back to the clubhouse for more ammunition, the language got a touch heated at times, even Dan managing a couple of 'bothers'. It was yet another bit of television magic, which only a few people have ever seen. Who knows, perhaps it might one day be seen on *Auntie's Bloomers* – on the other hand, perhaps not.

10

'DEAR MR ALLISS'

*'There seems to be a wide range of opinion
concerning the talents or shortcomings of "Alliss,
the commentator"'*

Funny game, golf. It is a ball game in which, for most of the
time, the ball is stationary, non-existent in a sense. Then, the
golfers simply walk across the countryside. It is a countryside
reasonably manicured for the purpose, but it is essentially the
great outdoors – grass, hillocks, trees, bushes, heather, whins,
streams and ponds. The least of it is pretty, the best of it is
stunningly beautiful. It's a flora and fauna game and I have
received dozens of letters from people, often women, who say
that they are avid watchers of televised golf tournaments, without knowing (or overmuch caring) about the game, because it is
'so pretty'.

Journalist friends in the old days (I'm sure it still applies) used
to tell me that only 'crackpots', O.A.P.s or bee-in-the-bonneters
ever wrote to newspapers. They simply never had letters of
praise. When I was a tournament player, I'd get the odd letter

from someone I may have met up and down the country, saying this or that, seldom of any great consequence. Since I became a television person, my mail has been intriguing, a constant fascination. People do feel strongly about things and about me. There seems to be a wide range of opinion concerning the talents or shortcomings of 'Alliss the commentator'. Alas, much as I want to be loved, not everyone loves me! One letter I had from a gentleman in Oxford read:

> As an old member of Muirfield, I enjoy watching golf but I resent it when my pleasure is marred – is ruined – by the inane drivel that comes non-stop from you and your colleagues. Nine-tenths of it is unwanted and unnecessary.

In a follow-up letter, the same man said:

> You really must be careful. Your verbal diarrhoea is getting worse. Babbling of black and yellow Labradors. It will be little green men next. You really are a dreadful young man.
> Yours neither faithfully nor sincerely

Looking back, many of the choicest I must say came in the seventies and eighties of the last century when I was doing *Pro-Celebrity Golf* and *Around with Alliss*. Perhaps I was learning the trade at the time.

A 'terribly disappointed' from near Chippenham in Wiltshire tears me apart then says he writes with the best intentions:

> May I plead, if you are to continue as the BBC's commentator on golfing matters, you try to emulate Henry Longhurst's admirably restrained instructive and

non-grating manner. With respect, I and many of my
golfing friends find your comments far too facetious,
repetitive and not always in good taste. I give, as
examples, use of such words as 'beauty', 'all depends on
the bounce', 'dig in' etc. As for your latest effort 'take
that you swine', I can only say that such remarks are
unworthy of you.

Then he twists the knife by saying:

Please accept this letter in the spirit intended, i.e. helpful
advice.
Yours sincerely

A 'fan' from Dagenham sent me a letter in which he said:

My reason for writing is to tell you something that, no
doubt, you already know . . .

From Fife came:

I enjoy your golf commentaries. There are none better.
But please will you stop prefacing the golfer's name with
the word 'young' – it sounds so patronising.

In 1986, referring to an event in 1977, an impassioned Scot
from Falkirk told me that he was:

. . . writing to tell you that I am sick and tired of
hearing from you and other golf commentators the praise
you give Tom Watson for his unforgettable last two
rounds with Jack Nicklaus at the British Open at
Turnberry. Praise for Jack Nicklaus indeed – the man is
a legend in golf – but praise for Watson? You must be
joking. What you don't know or have forgotten is that

> *Tom Watson was using illegal clubs when he won the*
> *'Duel in the Sun' as they now call it, by one stroke . . . a*
> *few months earlier Watson had also won the US Masters*
> *using the same clubs, beating Nicklaus into second place*
> *by two shots . . . As far as I am concerned, Nicklaus has*
> *now won twenty-two majors. There is no way Jack*
> *Nicklaus would have accepted these two majors in*
> *winning in such an underhand way.*
> *P.S. When Tom Watson won his only US Open title at*
> *Pebble Beach using illegal golf balls guess who was second*
> *– yes, you are right – Jack Nicklaus. From a Nicklaus*
> *fan, one of many.*

From Sanderstead, Surrey – the reference to the author Leslie Thomas relates, no doubt, to one of the *Around with Alliss* programmes:

> *I was looking forward to seeing some golf in your*
> *programme of June 15 but instead we got an overdose of*
> *conversation from Leslie Thomas with innumerable and*
> *meaningless 'you knows'. You got a touch of that*
> *complaint too so I switched off after about ten minutes.*
> *Do try and give us more golf and less gobbledegook next*
> *time please.*

Look out – this is from the Sheriff Court House in Lanark, September 1985:

> *Like St John in Revelation 2.4 'I have somewhat against*
> *you'. During the recent Ryder Cup I have suffered the*
> *careless and incorrect use of the sacred term 'dormie' by*
> *some of your commentators (I hasten to add I exonerate*
> *you and Clive Clark from any blame).*

It is very annoying to hear people who should know better telling us that someone is 'dormie 4 up' or worse 'dormie 3 down'. The Rules of Golf are quite clear on the point and I refer to Rule 2/3 where it says a 'side is dormie when it is as many holes up as there are remaining to be played'. It is obvious that only a player in the lead can even be 'dormie' and the proper expression is to say that a player is 'dormie', or perhaps 'dormie' followed by a number.

These errors made publicly are unfortunate since they are repeated by youngsters learning the game and rules, the mistake becoming harder than ever to correct. Can you please have a word with your men before the next matchplay event at Wentworth?

From Queens Park in Bournemouth, in 1985, near my old stomping grounds at Ferndown and Parkstone:

For many years my husband and I have thoroughly enjoyed your golf broadcasts and sincerely hope that there will be many more to come. However, we beg of you and your fellow commentators, please do not fall into the American trap of thinking that the winning of lots of money matters. It is rather irritating to be reminded of the amount at stake so regularly. We know that a missed putt can be expensive without being told. Surely golf is one of the few remaining sports where the 'game's the thing' – certainly from the spectators' viewpoint.

The following was addressed to 'The BBC Commentators, The Open Golf' in July 1979:

Dear Sirs,
Please refrain from referring to threesomes, which do not
occur in the Open (see Rules of Golf, Section 11,
Definition 28).
  'Sides and Matches' reads 'Threesome. A match in
which one plays against two and each side plays one ball.
I thank you.

This was to prepare and pre-warn us before the Open Championship won by Severiano Ballesteros at Royal Lytham with 283.

Now a change of mood from Devizes in Wiltshire:

As a professional student and 14-handicap player of this
wonderful game, do we have to put up with the banal
utterances of Mark McCormack. He described Greg
Norman today as 'the world's number one golfer'. The
Sony rankings have little or no credence. Based on
current performance and results, Nick Faldo deserves
that attribution. Why does the BBC keep adding to its
number of commentators? Why can't there be a cut in
the commentary team after two rounds also?

Today, he/she may have a point!

From Milngavie in Glasgow (and the department of no comment):

Feel I must report to you the following snatch of dialogue
during your Open Championship coverage. Voice of Alliss
on TV – 'and it will be Sandy Lyle to play his second shot
first'.
  My wife, with puzzled frown, 'Is he allowed to do
that?'

'Do what?'

'Play his second shot before he's played his first shot.'

Collapse of stout party. She's not very bright but she's got great tits.

Natural history intruded after the Loch Lomond event in the summer of 2003. As a pair of mute swans went sliding by on the loch, I mentioned that it was possible to tell male or female by a 'knob on the beak'. Quick as a flash from the heartland of England, in Stafford, came a correction:

It is not possible to tell by simple observation. All adult swans have a knob on the beak – as any bird will tell you! Fortunately, cobs and pens know! Best wishes – don't even think of replying to this.

Our broadcasts, again with reference to the Loch Lomond event, produce all kinds of passions. Here's a letter from Devon:

12 July 2003

Dear Peter Alliss

I write, as I have written before, with a PLEA regarding golf TV presentation!

Since Thursday we have had an excellent presentation as usual on Lomond side, under exacting conditions for the whole team, indoor or outdoor – thanks and congratulations to all!

But why why why, when the excellent graphics of holes etc are being shown, or when current scores are shown and run through, often in both cases with commentary simultaneously, are we compelled to hear additional trivial, irrelevant and intrusive MUSIC? I can conceive of no useful purpose for this and regard it as an important demerit *in the overall technique of golf presentation in which the BBC team excels. What is it for?*

I know from discussion with others, golfers and non-golfer viewers alike, that this criticism is widely held. I beg you to see it seriously raised for discussion internally and would urge most sincerely that this distracting *and* pointless *aspect of presentation should be dropped for good.*

Across the years it has to be said there are pedants. To be grammatically impeccable when watching screens, listening to instructions, observing the action and talking all at the same time is not easy. Was it George Bernard Shaw, accused of the odd blip, who said 'I'm not writing for professors of English grammar'. From Eton College no less, in October 1986, came the following, after the now-statutory thanks for many hours of enjoyment 'this season':

A minor quibble or two; should you continue to identify with those who absurdly persist in talking of Nicklaus's twenty Major titles? There are four Majors, no more no less, and there are certainly many other pro titles far more competitive than a US Amateur title. What is the point of calling it a major title?

Shame on you sir! Shame on you for falling into the FOOT trap. I refer to your remarks about Bernhard Langer's ball being lodged in the tree TWELVE FOOT from the ground – how many yards is that?

You may say, quite correctly, that someone has a ten-

*foot putt but that putt measures ten FEET . . . join me
in a campaign against this inaccuracy.*

That fellow is clearly a professor of pedantic semantics.

This from someone in Islington who certainly does not care
for Alliss:

*I am writing to you concerning your personal coverage of
the Ryder Cup [1989]. I just couldn't believe my ears at
some of your remarks about how hard done by the Yanks
had been over Press remarks . . . There was our team
playing there [sic] guts out and you were saying how
good the Yanks had behaved . . . not being a winner
yourself of anything important in your career, I could
understand you but at least our golfers showed guts.*

*As I said Mr Alliss, not being a winner yourself it's
probably all you're used to saying, you have a very good
job, try to make comments worth listening to and don't
bum the Yanks for your comments. My guests on Sunday
at home were appalled.*

From a winner to a loser

No name or telephone number were supplied. An Islington
soul-mate from Sundridge Herts:

*May I protest in the strongest terms to you for your
scandalous comments at The Open at Muirfield when
Paul Azinger struck his second shot into the bunker on
the 18th and you sought to rationalise the disgraceful
cheering of the crowd at his misfortune . . . you should
have roundly condemned the crowd for its unsporting
cheering and jeering . . . Your conduct was shameful*

> *and a disgrace to golf, the BBC and your own father*
> *who, like me, would have been appalled at your mighty*
> *indiscretion . . . Dare we hope for your resignation . . .*
> *you should consider whether or not your useful days in*
> *golf have come to an end.*

These people are certainly not foundation members of the Peter Alliss Fan Club!

The reference here, says my correspondent from Glasgow, is the 1985 Ryder Cup matches:

> *I have addressed this letter of criticism to you as you are*
> *widely regarded as the ringleader of those who present golf*
> *for the BBC TV. I don't see how you can be overburdened*
> *with work covering a mere handful of golfers travelling at*
> *a pace which, compared with some other sports, could be*
> *reasonably described as 'leisurely'. Couldn't one of you*
> *therefore have devoted a few of your 'off the air' minutes*
> *conducting a little research into how Señores Ballesteros,*
> *Canizares, Pinero and Rivero pronounce their names?*
> *Collectively these names were heard several hundred times*
> *with at least ten variations,* sadly not one of them even
> once correct. *As an example you may wish to ask Pinero*
> *(Peen-yayro) if he prefers Pinero.*
> *P.S. when you were knocking the ball about were you ever*
> *called AH-YEECE?*

Yes – in Japan, Hong Kong and many other points east!

Department of 'Worth a Try':

> *I am writing to inquire if there is a possibility of*
> Around with Alliss *to celebrate my sister's fiftieth*
> *birthday.*

*I realise that this is a very busy time of your year but if
we could arrange even a few holes I would be very
pleased. My sister is a member of Worcester Golf and
Country Club with a handicap of 16. If this is at all
possible, please let me know your fee. I have enclosed an
s.a.e. for your convenience.*

That from a gentleman in Selsdon Surrey. This from a gentleman from Solihull in the West Midlands:

*Four members of our golf club are paying their annual
pilgrimage to The Open at Sandwich. One of our
number, Doug Fedeski, a past Captain of our Club, is
65 on July 18th and although we are planning a
surprise party for him, something extra such as a TV
interview with a golf nut who once said he'd 'love it if
one of Jack Nicklaus's shots felled him' would be a
pleasant occasion. Perhaps alternatively you could ask Mr
Nicklaus to send him a birthday card to the address of
friends with whom we are staying . . . ASH, Canterbury.
If you do not think this letter an absolute load of rubbish
and would be kind enough to help on this birthday, a
message left on seat H1/3 on the Composite seat stand
will find us.*

An unknown fan from West Bengal writes:

Respected Sir
*How I wish this fine breeze blowing outside could carry
to you my hearty wishes on your birthday on 28th
February. This letter will take a long time to reach you
and I am very annoyed with the slowness of our 'quick'
means of communication.*

But now it seems to me that you have vowed not to reply my letters of deep admiration. Please tell me, is it good to break the heart, you are ruling? In fact, I can't resist the charm of your superb style of golf upon my words, you are absolutely unique and you are my ideal of a perfect personality.

Therefore, I shall be highly obliged, if you please send me your autographed photograph for momento. Please take a very good care of yourself. Once again, 'Many Happy Returns of the Day!'

Yours, in adoration [with a picture of two hearts and a happy birthday]
With high regards

No. 10 Downing Street:

Dear Peter
Thank you for your charming letter of 23 Nov. For 20 years I have tried to maintain the lowest possible profile with reasonable success by NOT making speeches (except on sports occasions) by NEVER giving Press interviews nor going on the box.

You personally are very popular as is Around with Alliss *and too many people would see and hear me, to say nothing of watching my ghastly golf, were I to accept your kind invitation. All the requests for interviews, 'chat' shows, speeches and what you will which I have been politely turning down for years would come flooding in and refusals would be difficult, in some cases impossible. THEN heaven knows what trouble I could or would get into. So I fear the answer must be 'no', flattered as I must be by your invitation.*

I hope I shall see you again soon.
Best regards,
Sincerely
Denis Thatcher

From Ben Hogan, Fort Worth, Texas:

Dear Peter
Many thanks for your letter and invitations to
participate in your forthcoming project. Please
understand when I tell you that I simply do not want to
do this. I have never considered myself any good at this
sort of thing. I did appreciate very much your thinking
of me in this connection and I do hope you will be in
sympathy with my feelings.
Ben

One thing about Alliss – his refusals are always high-class refusals.

The Jocks, of course, are always with us – and why not? They started the whole thing. From Macduff in Banff, a slap on the wrist:

May I take this opportunity to congratulate you on the
wonderful commentary given by you . . . during [BBC2
Irish Open] . . . rather annoyed by your favouring one of
the finalists. You kept on referring to 'Sebbe' and
'Langer'. Perhaps next time you will give both finalists
their Christian names.
P.S. Mr Langer's Christian name is Bernhard.

From an exiled Scot in Hitchin Herts:

My family of boys, 20, 21 and 15, and I always enjoy
Pro-Celebrity Golf with your conversational
interviewing – BUT why at beautiful Gleneagles does the
presentation crystal have to be Waterford? Surely it
should be Scottish Edinburgh Crystal ! ! ! Thank you for
the pleasure you give us BUT . . .

Now letters of delight, first from a lady in Bristol:

I very much enjoy the BBC coverage of all the golf,
particularly on dreary afternoons when there is a pile of
washing to be done. Do you know there is an added
bonus for those of us watching at home, especially when
the event is from one of the inland courses. It is the
birdsong picked up by the outside microphones. The
chaffinches at Woburn last week were a delight.

A second from a lady in Baldock:

Everyone enjoys yours and your colleagues golf
commentaries but to me the added bonus, free of charge,
are the lovely songs of the birds especially in the vicinity of
the tees and greens. No other sport gives this bonus.

Finally, from Bournemouth University:

Dear Mr Alliss
As clerk to the University Board, I am writing to inform
you that the University would like to confer on you the
honorary degree of Doctor of Letters . . .

11

COURSE DESIGN

'The greens were shaped, the seed sown, soon we had the most wonderful crop of turnips, potatoes, parsnips and carrots'

By the end of the seventies our time in the north at Moor Allerton was coming to an end. The ultimate reason for ending that period in our lives was my partnership with David Thomas in the golf-course construction business. I had less and less time to spare for the club, although our personal relationships with the members never wavered. Everything changed when Ken Wood of electrical appliance fame contacted Alliss Thomas Golf Construction saying he'd got a property called Old Thorns Farm near Liphook in Hampshire and he wanted to create a golf course. His own house, an eight-bedroomed mansion, would be the core of the clubhouse. He'd also got permission for twenty-eight suites with planning for thirty more. He envisaged a swimming pool and sauna, beauty and massage parlours, facilities for business seminars – he wanted a really pukka private club, which would certainly be a huge asset in a very busy area of the south of England. There would be room at Old Thorns for the Alliss Thomas Golf Construction Company to have offices. Everything was set in motion.

David Thomas decided to stay in south Manchester near Hale but our other partner, Pat Dawson, decided that he had to live on the site and bought a property called Weavers Down House, which sits alongside the 3rd tee on the present golf course. So it was house-hunting time again for the Allisses. My father's estate, after all the bills had been paid, left £20,000, which Alec and I split between us. The committee at Moor Allerton had offered to sell me Blackmoor Farm on a leasehold arrangement and I paid £35,000 for the property in 1975, with a peppercorn rent per year for a period of 100 years. In 1978, when it was time to move on, I found a buyer for £78,000 and that was enough to put a down payment on a property in Hindhead on the Surrey/Hampshire borders, where we live to this day.

Ken Wood's dream of an exclusive golf club where the service would be impeccable in this delightful, mature Hampshire landscape, was beginning to take shape. We staffed our office and started to build the golf course, which was fairly tight as the whole area was just about 100 acres and Ken, as befitted a good businessman, kept back certain corners of the property for possible future development. My oldest son Gary, who had been the professional at the Harpenden Golf Club for a few years, came to join us, the plan being that the Alliss family would be part of golf there for evermore, giving us a comfortable living, a sort of pension for life. Alas, it didn't work out that way. Ken Wood and Pat Dawson met some Japanese investors and suddenly the course was sold, much to the dismay of David Thomas and me. There was much to-ing and fro-ing and a great deal of disappointment. However, that deal was not completed and it was to go through several other near sales before it finally went to the Koseido Group, who now own Les Bordes in France and the Old Course Hotel at St Andrews, to name but two.

It is interesting to think that I was recently made Honorary President of Old Thorns – and proud I am of that!

We had a second development next door to Heathrow. This was another great idea that would be our meal ticket for years to come but again the golden fleece was snatched from our fingers. It was eventually bought by David Lloyd of tennis fame. By this time I was beginning to think that big business was not for me. As my original accountant, David Gow, used to say, 'Stick to what you know and you know about golf.' But I was sticking to the world of golf, dammit, and I should know what's going on. I was, in some ways, like a lamb to the slaughter. After that, Dawson went on his merry way and by the mid nineties I'd lost all track of him. Working with him was something of a roller-coaster ride but I enjoyed his enthusiasm.

In the end, David Thomas and I parted. I still miss his company very much. Sadly, his marriage to Robbie ended in 2003. I still think of them with much affection. It was one of the saddest days of my life when David and I split up, although it didn't hit me immediately. He thought that, while I had plenty of other things to do and could make a living in several directions, his main source of income was coming from the golf-course design business. I was getting money I didn't really need! I didn't agree with that. It's like saying that Morecambe and Wise shouldn't have split everything 50:50 because Wise was not as funny as Morecambe. It takes at least two to make a partnership and I felt my contribution to our business had been immense. I was the 'meeter and greeter', the front man. I thought I played my part very well and was able to add much to the business.

David set up his own office near Manchester and brought his son Paul into the business and over the years has become one of the most successful golf-course architects in Europe, if not *the* most successful.

I sat down and took stock of things and remembered how it all began. A letter from a highly qualified civil engineer in Belfast called Tom McAuley said he could be very helpful to David and me and asked had we thought of getting into the golf-course design and construction business. His letter intrigued us. We met and so it came to pass, we threw in our lot with the new-found friend in Ulster. Within a short time small bits of work began to appear, particularly in the Manchester area. A couple of new holes here, re-bunkering there, then came our first major job, Haggs Castle Golf Club on the south side of Glasgow. It was near the Rangers football ground and a very busy, hugely successful club.

Then there was Clandeboye, a few miles outside Belfast. The idea was to re-vamp nine of its 27 holes, adding some new ones to give the club a 36-hole circuit. There were one or two teething problems but, with the help and understanding of interested members and some input from the German architect Bernard von Limberger, we got the job done.

Next came the chance to participate in an exotic scheme in Iran on a piece of property bordering the Caspian Sea, in fact the home of the Shah of Persia. The Peacock Throne was wobbling and, in all truth, it was a very fanciful development. A few trips were made, some plans were drawn up but, at the end of the day, money was the root of all evil. The family members all fell out. Then came the revolution – the Shah fled and the scheme died the death of a thousand lies. Sadly, no money for us.

By 1973 Tom McAuley had gone. A long story, suffice to say he thought he was doing most of the work and should get most of the spoils. We soldiered on, broadening our experiences with a course at Hessle near Hull. The old course had to be moved due to the construction of the wonderful Humber Bridge, which still takes my breath away every time I see it. But surely it's a wonderful white elephant, although not as bad as the Millennium Dome. The Hessle course was a difficult site, open, heavy soil, some clay, windswept, all in all, I thought we did a good job.

Designing and constructing a golf course invariably throw up unexpected problems. At King's Lynn in Norfolk we laid out a golf course on a lovely piece of golfing ground – birch trees, bushes, wild boggy areas, a very interesting site. We soon discovered during construction that we were going to be short of topsoil for the greens. A member of the committee who was a farmer said our problems were over. He had all sorts of root vegetables that were harvested in the autumn. They had to be cleaned off so he had tons of good soil that he would let the club have at a very advantageous price. The deed was done, the greens shaped, the seed sown and soon we had the most wonderful crop of turnips, potatoes, parsnips, carrots, everything in fact you could wave Charlie Dimmock at, coming up all over the nineteen greens we had so lovingly prepared. And who do you think got the major bollocking? Certainly not the committee man who sold us the dirt, no, it was David and yours truly. But time is a great healer, the clubhouse is very attractive, the golf course a delight and over the years we've heard nothing but good reports from people who have played and had a most enjoyable time there.

We received an enquiry from Blairgowrie, asking us if we'd have a look at the possibility of creating a second course. This was to be cut out through a mass of spindly pine trees. There was quite a bit of opposition to the new course. A meeting was called in the village hall, things looked bad. Then I made, if I might say, an impassioned speech that won the day. I certainly earned my wages on that occasion. We purposely left the fairways narrow. Why? Because it's easier to take a few trees out giving it width rather than trying to create something that mother nature's been doing for thirty or forty years.

Then came our first overseas venture – the place, Alicante. This was followed by courses in Nigeria, France, the Ivory Coast, Iran and Borneo, all fascinating challenges. Unfortunately, the developers in Alicante ran out of money before the course works were completed, so we packed our bags and left. Fortunately, we had been paid in advance.

The two courses in Nigeria were finished but the country at the time was so corrupt we were never fully paid for all the work done. Still, to this day there's a considerable amount of money lying in one of the numerous banks that don't seem to abide by the rules of normal banking. We even paid a medicine man a small fee so we could begin work, his bill is enclosed in this unusual letter:

From   *Nwankwo Okike*
                 Akam's Compound
                 Ngegwu Village
                 Oguta
12 January 1975

Dear Sir,
With reference to the Juju shrine prepared by my father
and kept at Ogbeno, Kalabari Beach, Oguta, I hereby

Jackie with Simon, father and godfathers lined up in the background (*from left*) me, Bruce Forsyth, Henry Longhurst and Cliff Michelmore.

Blackmoor Farm at Moor Allerton, Leeds, was our first real home. We lived there for ten years.

Proud father with baby Simon.

Australian Peter Thomson won the Open five times – a great competitor who remains a great friend.

Dave Marr, top-class tournament player, Ryder Cup captain, and fellow commentator with a wonderful, quirky turn of phrase – now sadly missed.

Tony Jacklin and Jack Nicklaus shake hands during the 1969 Ryder Cup at Birkdale. Theirs was a memorable match.

Our home, Bucklands, in 1963.

Gary Player set up a marvellous school at his home in South Africa. He called it Blair Atholl after the ancestral home of the Duke of Atholl.

The crew of Apollo 15 autographed this picture of their moon buggy for me.

TO PETER ALLISS WITH THE BEST WISHES OF THE APOLLO 15 CREW.

One of my favourite photos of Henry Longhurst, my colleague and mentor as a golf commentator. This shot was taken behind the clubhouse at Wentworth in the sixties.

Filming *Play Better Golf* in 1977 at Downfield Golf Club, Dundee, where I first met Greg Norman.

We had enormous fun filming *Pro-Celebrity Golf*. Here I am with two of the funniest men in the business, Eric Sykes (*left*) and Jimmy Tarbuck.

At Turnberry, we spent a memorable few days with the remarkable war hero Douglas Bader, here on the 10th.

For one programme, we filmed the Bing Crosby Cup. *From left*: Johnny Miller, Bing Crosby, me, Tony Jacklin and Sean Connery.

The 9th tee at Turnberry – one of the most dramatic tee shots in the world of golf.

*write to inform you that the following things must be
presented to me for sacrifice to the Juju before it can be
moved to my town.*

1 one goat
2 one he sheep
3 one dog
4 three fowls
5 one schnapps
6 one piece of white cloth and
7 one head of tobacco.

*All these items must be ready at the spot before I can
perform anything. Furthermore, when this is removed to
my home, a house will be built to place it. Transportation
of the Juju and feeding allowances must be included.
This Juju was prepared for members of my family.*

*After the above the total will be 2,000 nira [about
£2,000 at the time]. It is out of this estimated amount
that after building this house at my home, part of it will
be used to buy a cow for the first sacrifice to it.*

*With the above explanations you should realise that my
charge to it is not very much. On the day I will come for
the removal you will give me labourers to assist me
destroy the place.*

Thanks in anticipation
Yours faithfully
N Okike

The Ivory Coast was another flirtation that worked reasonably
well but trying to get things done legally and properly at that
time was hopeless.

Then it was back to France and La Baule in Brittany, which was great fun. There were no witch doctors but the usual problems with contractors. However, with the passing of time, it has all worked out very well and they now have a second course. La Baule, aaah, that wonderful beach. If you get the chance to have a holiday there, stay at the Hermitage Hotel, but don't go in August, the whole of France turns up!

In 1976 we were asked if we could suggest some alterations to the Ailsa course at Turnberry in readiness for the Open Championship which was to be played there the next year. We came up with a total scheme that would have cost about £30,000. We were so excited at being given the chance of doing something for the R&A that we were barely covering our costs for the job. But again disappointment was on the horizon. Nobody was prepared to pay that amount of money for the alterations. The hotel owners at the time didn't have the wherewithal and this was long before the R&A had spare money in the coffers to do exotic things. We made our suggestions, some of which were implemented and added something to the course, which I still think could be one of the greatest tests in the world if one was given a reasonable budget and a free hand. One of our main suggestions, still used to this day when big competitions are played and to aid congestion, is the walk from the 17th green to the 18th tee of the Arran Course, creating a dogleg right to left to the finishing hole. Work still needs to be done for when there's no wind. There's not a par 5 on the course. That could easily be changed with some judicious bunkering and one or two changes of tee and green locations. The Championship will always be remembered for the wonderful confrontation between Tom Watson and Jack Nicklaus. As Hubert Green said when he finished third, 'Well, I won the tournament I was playing in.' We thought a golden opportunity had been missed but Turnberry has come a long, long way from those far-off days and is now a stunning holiday venue. But I'd still like to be let loose with a few bob to make some changes. Ah well, you can't win 'em all, but again, as Ben Hogan always wondered, 'Why not?'

Bigger and better things were to come. Alan Hunter, at the time the estates manager for the Greenall Whitley Brewers and owners of the Belfry Hotel near Sutton Coldfield, eight miles or so north of Birmingham, asked if we could build an 18-hole golf course on land round the hotel. We viewed and suggested they might get the PGA involved. Who knows, they might, in time, bring major events to the course. After many hours of burning the midnight oil, eighteen holes were designed. Alan Hunter was a busy man and good supporter but, before we could draw breath, Ellermans, the shipping and travel group, were in as partners and suddenly there was a new concept. It was to be a 36-hole complex. The PGA were to move their national offices from London to the Belfry, which would be the site of the Ryder Cup matches as soon as the course was ready, perhaps as soon as 1981.

The land was poor; it had been used for rough grazing and potato fields. More land was eventually bought to give a total of 325 acres. One of the problems was a row of electric pylons that ran through the property, but we were able, certainly in the first two courses, the Derby and the Brabazon, to hide them so they weren't too intrusive. The land was undramatic, a flat, open plain that needed much earth moving. The greens had to be raised, mounding introduced to give some sort of character and provide viewing platforms, and we also needed trees. The year was 1975. There was a small lake in front of the old hotel, which we enlarged, and the present putting green was the car park for the modest hotel. The lakes would go a long way to provide the watering system and so on and so on. I lost count of the times David Thomas used to say, 'My God, what will Jack, Lee and Tom think when they come and see this?' A perfectionist was David.

Work continued at a rare pace. Huge dumper trucks were everywhere – ten at one point, paddling round the site, creating lakes, tees, mounds and dust. Oh, that bloody dust! I did pity the few neighbours but all was ready for seeding in the summer of 1976, or so we thought. Thirty to forty thousand trees were put in but they were little whips, tiny little trees, and, of course, sod's law, we had that wonderful summer, starting on 12 March and ending on 22 October. Hardly a drop of rain fell and, yes, you've guessed it, the watering system, designed and installed by specialist contractors, costing £100,000 out of a total budget of about £370,000, didn't work properly. Everything died, or perhaps I lie; maybe fifteen or twenty of the thousands of trees survived. Looking across this barren plain, it resembled a cross between the Sahara Desert and a derelict field of asparagus. Then at the end of the year rain, rain and more rain just to make absolutely sure that whatever topsoil was left was washed away, creating other problems. Contractually, we managed to end the job in 1978 but kept going back time and time again. Unfortunately, the greenkeeping staff had not appreciated that, with all the compaction during construction, the course had not been allowed to breath. It had to be aerated, hollow tined, anything to break up the surface, with feeding and top dressing, re-seeding where necessary. Progress was slow.

The Ryder Cup matches had been scheduled for September 1981. As there were several growing seasons between 1978 and

1981, I felt, with a fair run, everything could be ready. But at the English Classic event, played there in the summer of 1979, Brian Barnes, Mark James and several other professionals were reported in the media as saying that the course would not be ready for the Ryder Cup matches in 1981. In fact, in their opinion, it would never be ready for anything, it was absolute rubbish, the worst course they'd ever seen. The PGA took fright and switched the matches to the Walton Heath Golf Club near Epsom. As a result of those reported comments, reservations at the Belfry Hotel fell by 50 per cent. The owners were not pleased and suggested that the critics should watch their words. But all's well that ends well. Some twenty-five years later the Belfry, its golf courses and 450-bedroom hotel is one of the, if not *the*, premier conference resort golf venues in Europe. It's certainly the most profitable.

In the late seventies when the Belfry was about to open, I visited the club along with Jackie and her mother and father. It was to be a special occasion. As we were making our way through the crowded bar, I felt a tug on the sleeve of my coat and, looking down, saw a ruddy-faced, plump man gazing up at me. In a very broad Midlands accent he said, 'Hello Peter, I'm from Kings Norton Golf Club.'

'Oh, yes,' I replied. 'My club, Moor Allerton, have a regular match against you which they find very enjoyable.'

Stout party replied, 'Why do you never come?'

Being polite I said, 'Well, it usually takes place when I'm engaged in other business – a televised event early in the season or some other venture that doesn't allow me to participate, but I've seen them loading up the coach with a goodly supply of smoked salmon sandwiches, a couple of bottles of champagne and plenty of coffee.'

'But you've never come,' replied ruddy face.

By this time I was becoming aware that my in-laws were standing by looking rather agitated and Jackie, too, had a rather strange look on her face.

'We thought you were far too stook up.'

'Oh, no, no, no, it's just that the dates always clash,' to which he fatally replied, 'Well, you should come. I'll send me Rolls-Royce for you.'

Suddenly I lost all sense of rhyme or reason and found a cruel tongue. Staring him straight in the eye, I replied, 'I've got my own effing Rolls-Royce.' I turned to move away and gazed into the eyes of my mother- and father-in-law who, not to put too fine a point on it, looked aghast. I felt elated and yet, at the same time, ashamed that I'd been quite so rude. It had come out so quickly, so easily, so viciously. That, fortunately, or unfortunately, became more and more a trait of mine as the years went by; some would say I lost the ability to suffer fools gladly. I'd certainly done that but, somehow or other, I felt I had gone too far. But the deed was done.

12

LET ME SWING AMONG THE STARS

*'"Good morning, boys, good morning." It was
Bing Crosby himself, dressed for golf'*

'**O**h, Mr Alliss, sir, Mr Alliss, can I have a word, please?'
'Of course you can.'
'Please, sir, could you come over?'
These were the words spoken by the young under-manager at
the Gleneagles Hotel as I wandered down the grand staircase on
my way to breakfast. For those of you who know the hotel,
you'll remember that as you go from the main staircase towards
the dining room, there's a small anteroom on the right-hand
side. Our pro-celebrity TV sponsor, Marley, was using this to
entertain guests with cocktails and canapés after a hard day's
play.

I followed the young man inside and discovered, lying behind
a chaise-longue, curled up cuddling an empty Jack Daniels
bottle, the great actor George C. Scott. Surely this couldn't

be General Patton? But it was, with an almost angelic smile on his face and another empty bottle by his side, plus several McEwans Strong Ale tins strewn willy nilly about the place. What to do with him, whatever to do with him? A sound came from outside the door, accompanied, perhaps, by a slight sound of someone humming 'When the Blue of the Night meets the Gold of the Day'. The voice was unmistakable.

'Good morning, boys, good morning.' It was Bing Crosby himself, dressed for golf, his hat set at a jaunty angle, just on his way for a dish of tea and a bit of toast and perhaps a bowl of porridge before teeing off.

'Mr Crosby, Bing, sir, could I have a word,' says I.

'What is it, dear boy?'

'Come and look here, please.'

He came and looked down at George who, by now, had a rather silly smile on his face.

'Oh dear, oh dear,' Bing said, 'Uncle George appears to have been on the sauce again.' With that he touched Scott on the shoulder gently with a highly polished shoe and said, 'Dear George, good morning. You seem to be in some slight distress. Is there anything I can do for you?'

The great man stirred and said, 'Yes, I'd like to take a piss and go home.'

Without a pause, 'Der Bingle' replied, 'Well, my dear boy, you can do both. They are well within your compass.' George once more slumped into semi-consciousness. We had now been joined by the hotel manager, Jimmy Bannatyne, a fine chap, very cool under fire and a great charmer, but it was Bing who took charge, as if he'd seen this sort of happening many times before. Suddenly, one of the many limousines at the party's disposal was backed up over the lawn so Mr Scott could be placed onto the back seat with the fewest number of witnesses viewing his departure.

As the back door was about to close the timorous under-manager said, 'Oh, Mr Scott, Mr Scott, what shall we do with your clothes?' The great man raised himself up and with an imperious wave uttered the immortal words, 'Burn them – and my clubs.' The car pulled away and that was the end of that.

I never did hear where the limousine took him or how he returned to the United States, but he survived. On that occasion, George C. Scott never made it to the first tee but four years later he returned, accompanied by his wife who somehow had managed to steer George away from the drink. He behaved well and created much mirth and merriment but you could see behind those extraordinary eyes a flame still burned, a danger-ous flame. He had a very positive personality. Don't forget he refused an Oscar – not many do that.

But I digress. Jimmy Bannatyne and I watched the limousine pull away and then he revealed to me the hotel's secret ploys in dealing with unfortunate happenings among its clientele, which happened to include death. If a guest died in a public place, the first thing to do was to get him or her out of sight. If the guest died in bed, this caused less of a problem. The first thing was to search his room for money. Doesn't that sound awful, but he assured me that's the way it happens. The manager and the head porter look for cash, traveller's cheques, bonds, anything ne-gotiable, put them in an envelope, with witnesses of course, and place them in the hotel safe. Finally, in moving the deceased out of the hotel, and assuming there are no laundry baskets suitable, the deceased would be moved recumbent on a trolley fully covered with a sheet except for his face. Then, if on the way to the back door they should stumble upon some other guest, the trick was to pretend he was still alive by talking to him. 'Don't worry, sir, the ambulance is on its way. We'll soon have you in hospital.' Aah, the tricks of the trade.

Jack Lemmon was a delight when he visited Gleneagles although he was in the deep throes of alcoholism. His daily intake went something like this – breakfast time: vodka and tomato juice, mid morning: vodka and orange juice, lunchtime and early afternoon: vodka and tonic, early evening: vodka on the rocks. All this before getting into the serious business of drinking fine wines at dinner. I remember one night we were dining together, he was looking through the extensive wine list and discovered a Château Rothschild 1961 that was cheaper than at the Bel Air Golf Club in Los Angeles where he was a member. 'Oh, dear friends,' he exclaimed, 'we must have a bottle or two of this fine wine.' It slipped down like Diet Coke. I wonder what today's modern wine buffs would have made of it? But the label was sufficient, we weren't worried about the bouquet, taste, the weight, the balance, that special moment on the tongue or, perhaps, the thought that this wine will be the one that brings your nose to a point! It all went down the same way. Despite it all, Jack never gave a moment's impression of not being totally in charge of the situation. It was amazing. It wasn't long after this visit that he gave up alcohol and went on to star in many more superb films. He died a couple of years ago and is sadly missed by his many friends and admirers.

Peter Falk, alias 'Columbo', was another great character who behaved exactly as he did in all those detective programmes and movies he made over the years. He was wonderful value and a good golfer, playing off 12 handicap. What a list of 'runners' and 'riders' we had.

It was sometimes difficult to get new celebrities to join us for these matches. Take the case of actor Leslie Nielsen, an American actor who has probably been in more than 200 films, perhaps most famous for his portrayal of the bumbling detective Frank Dribben in the films *Naked Gun*, *Naked Gun 2½* and *Naked Gun 33⅓* . He was approached at the Bel Air Golf Club in Los Angeles and asked if he enjoyed golf.

'Oh yes,' he said.

'Would you like to take part in the BBC Pro-Celebrity series which is filmed in Scotland each August.'

'Indeed I would, what do I have to do?'

'Well you, your wife, friend, anyone you wish, will be given first-class tickets from Los Angeles to New York, transferred to Concorde into London then on BEA [as it was then] to Glasgow, be picked up by a chauffeured car and taken to whichever venue is being used.'

'Excellent,' said Neilsson. 'I'll bring a companion.' The companion turned out to be a stunning young woman of about twenty-four summers who was into the cult of naturism.

The first inkling we had of any trouble was when a rather agitated Harry Coventry, our long-suffering stage manager, came to me.

'Peter, can I have a word?'

'Yes, Harry, what's afoot?'

'Well, I don't think Mr Neilsson's up to it. I've just watched him on the practice ground and he doesn't have any idea.'

This turned out to be the understatement of the year. I doubt if Leslie had ever had a lesson at that time. Oh he'd been to golf courses, he'd been taken there for lunch and various other outings. You know the sort of thing – 'Come and join us at the club, Leslie, sit on the terrace, have a drink, enjoy life' – but I don't think he'd actually ever played. A difficult situation.

However, we thought we were up to it. For this particular series at Gleneagles we were starting at the par-3 8th on the King's Course. Leslie arrived on the tee, the two professionals struck off and hit the green. Then on some 20 or 30 yards to the celebrities tee. Celebrity A was Charlie Drake, who struck a reasonable shot into the front right-hand bunker. Now it was Leslie's turn. Six air shots followed in quick succession then he caught the top of the ball and it ran some twelve feet into impenetrable ferns and heather never to be seen again. The director's voice was very clear in my ear, 'Never mind, Peter. We'll pick it up at the second hole.' On we went. From the 8th we crossed over to the 11th, another par-3, but this time longer and quite formidable. The professionals played from the back tee, both needing long irons, and found the green; Charlie Drake was just short. Leslie, after several weird-looking practice swings, hit a 5-wood thin but it got over the mounds and ended up in the front bunker. 'Oh good,' I thought, 'at least he made contact, he's off and running.' Into the bunker he went, one, two, three, four, five, six, seven . . . nine, ten . . . the green was gradually being covered in sand. Then suddenly he caught the ball as clean as a whistle, up it flew, over the flag, over the crowd. I can still see the spectators' heads turning as the ball flew thirty feet above their heads into the trees behind the 12th tee. 'Never mind, Peter,' said the voice in my ear. 'We'll fill this in when we dub the commentary later. I'm sure we can make it work.' Famous last words.

The match ended after the tee shots on the next hole, the 12th. Our professional friends hit their usual beautiful drives over the saddle and safely away. Charlie D scuttled his short of the ridge, and now it was Leslie's turn. A few practice waggles, still very ungainly, and then the dreaded happened. As the club was being drawn back, I happened to glance up the fairway and noticed a spectator leaning forward to get a better view. He was resting his hands on the top of his umbrella and, at that very moment, Leslie struck the drive a full-blooded blow. Now he's a big man and he swings at it pretty hard. He caught the ball on the toe end and it flew low and hard some twenty yards and cracked this poor spectator bang on his right thumb, which ballooned to about ten times its normal size within seconds. Voice in ear, 'That's it, that's it, bring 'em in, bring 'em in.' 'What shall I do?' says I. 'You'll think of something, I'm sure,' the voice said. So, while our wounded warrior was being attended to, I called the players together. 'Look, chaps, we've got a problem. The main generator has packed up so we'll have to go back to the hotel I'm afraid. It's all off for the day. They can't get a replacement.' They were all very philosophical. 'These things happen in the world of television and film, we understand,' they said, and off they went.

I hadn't realised the complications of my words. Someone suggested it didn't seem right to suggest human error had caused this breakdown, dammit, someone might get the blame. We made our way back to the hotel but, unfortunately, all my communications to the director went through each and every courtesy television set dotted through the hotel, the pro shop, the dormie house, the restaurant, everywhere. To say that I had used every four-letter Anglo-Saxon swear word I could lay my hands on would not be an exaggeration. In fact, I probably made up a few new ones that nobody had heard before. I entered the hotel foyer and noticed I was getting some disapproving looks from a number of elegant ladies and gentlemen who were just standing about. I couldn't understand it. It wasn't long before they told me that all my effing and blinding had been booming through the hotel for at least forty-five minutes. Ah well, when the full story was explained, they almost understood. But what of Leslie Neilsson? When told by the powers that be that they thought the course was a little too difficult for him, he never batted an eyelid, and neither did his gorgeous companion. They stayed the full week.

Sean Connery, Bruce Forsyth and Jimmy Tarbuck all disliked losing, particularly if they hadn't played very well, and their displeasure manifested itself in many forms. Sean just became rather quiet and uncommunicative.

'Come on, let's walk down the fairway and chat about something,' I suggested to him once.

'What's to talk about?' he responded. 'Give me a script and I'll do it.'

I thought, surely he can tell us something. In fact, I had an inspirational moment and suggested he could tell us about the Connery Scottish Trust, which had just been set up. It was reported that he had started the ball rolling with £1 million. Well, he was away and in full flow. We could have spent half an hour on the subject instead of the allotted one and a half minutes.

Tarbuck just got cross if he felt he was being out-stroked by the opposition. This happened a couple of times, the most serious one being with Kenny Dalglish, the great Scottish soccer player. Kenny arrived to play and told everyone that he was very much out of practice and he really could do with a stroke a hole. We weren't quite as generous as that but Jimmy thought that Kenny was receiving far too many shots. Jimmy had been proud to announce that he was playing off 3 and was hoping to play in the English Amateur Championship. Dalglish said he was somewhere between 12 and 14. Jim hit a nice conservative drive of about 230 yards bang up the middle; Dalglish bombed one about 285 with a good-looking swing. It wasn't the happiest of three-hour golfing jaunts.

Bruce Forsyth, a dear friend, usually found something to complain about if his golf was a little shaky, the butterflies mating in the lower meadow or the birdsong wafting over on the westerly wind from the Mull of Kintyre.

Christopher Lee, a member of the Royal Company of Edinburgh Golfers, better known perhaps as Muirfield, was a great stalwart in those early matches and what a very imposing figure he cut. His handicap fluctuated between scratch and 5. Sadly, he was plagued with a bad back but somehow or other he managed to keep it under control and played some excellent golf. For a big man he had a fine figure but I wondered how disciplined he would be when it came to sampling the hotel's culinary delights. I found out one day. My wife and I went in for a nice lunch. Christopher joined us and had a bowl of peas, yes peas. Can you imagine it, sitting in that magnificent room eating a bowl of peas?

Actor Robert Stack regaled us with stories of how his family had conquered California 250 years ago virtually single-handed and were part of American aristocracy, if there was such a thing. A handsome man with a very attractive but rather grand wife, he was somewhat disappointed that most people only knew him for his role in the TV series *The Untouchables*; he was the detective Eliot Ness.

Another participant in the programme was England cricketer and golfer extraordinaire Ted Dexter, who would certainly have been a Walker Cup player if he had diverted a little more time away from Test matches. I always had the feeling with Ted that he could be striking the ball quite beautifully with whatever clubs he found lying around and then become slightly bored with the proceedings and see if he could finish the round using left-handed clubs or perhaps playing one-handed. I was told he was a bit like that with his cricket. On occasions, things were just a little bit too simple and he experimented. Sometimes it worked, sometimes it didn't, and I guess Ted just saw things in a different way from most. He and actor/writer/comedian Peter Cook had been at the same public school, Radley. In fact, Cook was Dexter's fag. According to Cook, he was often beaten for insubordination.

Peter Cook was a comic genius. Some of his early work, particularly in harness with Dudley Moore, was quite brilliant in its originality. After his early death many people were quick to criticise a wasted talent. Well, he may have been wayward but he left behind many golden treasures. He arrived for his *Pro-Celebrity* debut at the Gleneagles Hotel with the most stunning looking black girl I've ever seen. He introduced her to one and all as his niece, which he assured me was a custom heavily lent upon by Catholic priests when seen in the company of young ladies at race meetings. It turned out she'd had a couple of acting parts in one of the soaps but it was obvious to us all that she'd also been affected by the cult of naturism. I don't think she ever appeared anywhere during her five-day stay wearing more than four pieces of clothing, three of those being a pair of shoes and a handbag.

Sitting in the ballroom after dinner consuming the odd liqueur, there was an interesting mixture of mellow folk, elegantly dressed, listening to the hotel's ensemble. Slowly and very sensually she would move on to the empty dance floor and gyrate. Now the Gleneagles musicians were, to say the least, men of mature years, playing piano, drums, bass and saxophone doubling with accordion. The temperature in the room soared as her gyrations grew more sensuous. The leader of the band was a small, rotund man who wore a white tuxedo that had obviously been made for a man well over six foot tall and had seen better days. The lapels were so wide they could easily have accommodated a small rhododendron bush let alone a carnation. When the lady returned to the table there was much relief and mopping of brows. She was magnificent.

Peter produced a small, battered silver box. He opened it and took out an assortment of hand-rolled cigarettes of various thicknesses and lengths. After due consideration, one was chosen, lit up and passed between the two. There was much deep breathing, closing of eyes and sighs of what I assume was euphoria. Someone suggested they were special cigarettes made for asthmatics. I hasten to add that Peter was between marriages at this stage in his life. He gave one of his wives the wonderful nickname of 'Sexburger', a cute description.

We were slightly worried about Peter's golfing ability but, after watching him hit a few shots on the practice ground, I was satisfied that he could do it. He had a good swing and, if he didn't do anything particularly stupid, he could well put up a good performance. It certainly looked that way when he struck his opening tee shot bang up the middle of the first fairway on the King's Course, then a 7-iron to the heart of the green. An enthusiastic crowd of about 1,500 gave him a rapturous reception. Alas, he took 7 putts, or was it 10, we lost count. But, after a hole or two, he settled down and went on to play a pretty good game.

After his match had been completed, Peter and his companion decided to stay on and he suggested that he would like to referee the match I was to play in partnership with Ted Dexter

against Ben Crenshaw and James Hunt, who came complete
with Oscar, a magnificent Alsatian and quite the largest dog I've
ever seen in my life, and the most beautifully behaved. He was
never on a lead; only a thin collar with his boss's telephone
number on it was needed to keep Oscar on the straight and
narrow. He used to pad quietly behind his master, even into the
great dining room. James would point, Oscar would sit like a
statue, his eyes following his master as he made his way to his
table, never taking his eyes off him until dinner was over. Oscar
also loved the golf course but he had a strange habit of sitting
with his nose about eighteen inches from the ball as it was about
to be driven. As soon as the shot was on its way, Oscar would
charge down the fairway in a great effort to see where it had
gone. He never got more than seventy or eighty yards before
returning but, for some, it was disconcerting, particularly when
Oscar started to move before the club head had reached the ball.

Well, the great day dawned and Cook arrived at the first tee a
good thirty minutes before the allotted time and sat on the
bench outside Ian Marchbank's pro shop. There he struck up a
conversation with a charming, middle-aged lady who was very
excited about the prospect of watching television golf being
made. After a moment or two he asked her if she carried any
make-up. Her reply was yes. He asked her if he could borrow
whatever she had, lipstick, powder, mascara. She looked a little
puzzled but agreed and he proceeded to put on full make-up,
full, that is, bearing in mind the goods at his disposal. He then
slipped away into the back of the pro shop where the excellent
Derek Brown, Ian Marchbank's number one assistant, who,
incidentally, now runs Valderrama for Señor Jaime Ortiz-
Patino, was waiting. Five minutes later he emerged in character,
wearing the full Erich von Stroheim kit. I'm sure some of you

will remember the bullet-headed German actor and film director, perhaps best known as the long-suffering servant to Gloria Swanson in the classic film *Sunset Boulevard*. There was Cook in highly polished jackboots, riding jodhpurs, long-sleeved shirt with a yellow cravat tied rather racily at the throat, a dark brown blouson jacket, a monocle and a Tyrolean hat. In one hand he carried a riding crop and in the other a small goldfish bowl with a solitary fish going round and round. This caused quite a stir and distracted somewhat from the opening ceremony. When asked about the goldfish Cook introduced him as Abe Finkelstein, his agent, who had arrived at the hotel the night before. Cook thought it would be a nice idea if Abe came out to watch the golf and take a stroll round the golf course while he refereed the match.

Introductions over, opening drives were set up, Oscar the huge Alsatian positioning himself no more than two feet from the ball. At that moment Peter Cook solemnly placed the goldfish bowl, complete with Abe, alongside Oscar. Now this may not appear to be funny but I can assure you it was hilarious. Where would it all lead? How could we get through the next two and a half to three hours? Well, balls were struck, putts were holed, Oscar galloped up and down the fairways, Abe Finkelstein had a personal caddy for the full length of the nine holes played and Peter Cook continued to give a magnificent display of Teutonic firmness when called upon for any rules or decisions. He certainly kept yours truly, Crenshaw, Ted Dexter and James Hunt in stitches.

We had some wonderful nights during the filming of our golf series. One I remember very clearly took place at the Gleneagles Hotel. There had been a celebratory dinner in the ballroom. People had gradually drifted away and tables been cleared, but a hard core remained, myself included, as were Jimmy Tarbuck, Sean Connery, Bruce Forsyth, singer/songwriter/comedian Kenny Lynch and a couple of their friends. There was a piano on stage and Bruce was soon up there thumping away in fine style. A sing-song began. Suddenly, Tarbuck noticed a slight movement in the drapes at the side of the stage, tiptoed over and whipped them back, revealing a small man looking rather forlorn in a brown storeman's overall, which was certainly two sizes too big.

'Ah,' said Tarby. 'Come on, come on, we've been looking for you.' He dragged the poor unfortunate soul into the centre of the stage where, to say the least, he looked slightly out of place. It wasn't long before the poor fellow was being goaded into giving us a song.

'Come on,' said Tarby, 'you've got Bruce Forsyth on piano, there's 007 down there and Kenny Lynch "Up on the Roof" – what an audience.' He went on and on.

Our man spoke with a delightfully soft Irish brogue and said he would give us a rendition of 'Danny Boy'. Bruce struck up a few opening bars, gave him the nod and off he went. He had a beautiful voice and the smirking faces, my own included, suddenly felt rather ashamed that we inflicted this ordeal upon such a gentle soul. No matter, he sang it through to the bitter end, never missed a note, never missed a word and, at the end, got a very enthusiastic round of applause from the small but élite audience. He bowed and left the stage. There was absolute silence for a few moments and then we all burst again into spontaneous applause. It was a memorable night and another lesson learned that you never know what's in people. Hidden depths, hidden talents. We all went to bed very quietly, all with our own thoughts.

13

THE NAKED TRUTH

'There they stood, naked as the day they were born, in the freezing cold'

Many years ago David Thomas and Hugh Lewis, neither of whom could be called a stripling, found themselves at a very smart hotel by a lake in Sweden. David at that time was very much into saunas and massage. He convinced Hugh, who had not the slightest interest in these things, that it would be a good idea to go down to the hotel's cabin by the lake and sweat! Sure enough, off they went into the cabin where the sauna was going full blast, stripped off, poured scented pine water on the stones and suddenly it was hotter than a summer nightshift at the Llanwern Steelworks in South Wales.

'It's too hot for me in here,' says Lewis.

'I've just the answer,' says Thomas. 'Follow me.' Out they went into the freezing cold.

'What do we do now?' asks Lewis.

'Into the lake – if you survive a heart attack, back into the sauna to warm up. It's stimulating and will do you the world of good,' says Thomas.

Picture the scene. Each of these fellows is over six feet tall and they were, to say the least, a tad overweight. I would say they were certainly carrying a surplus of two and a half sets of golf clubs each. So let's say they were running at about seventeen stone apiece. They rushed into the icy water, survived their heart attacks, then raced back to the sauna. But the Yale lock had snicked behind them. There they stood, naked as the day they were born, in the freezing cold, not a friend in sight. What to do, what to do?

There was no way of breaking the door down. They scouted round the sauna and discovered a small oblong window at the rear. Could they prise it open, could they get in? They found a piece of iron on the beach and managed to prise the window loose without doing too much damage. Next Hugh, being slightly the smaller, stood on David's naked shoulders and attempted to get in through a hole that would have been a triumph for an eleven year old. He got his head and half a shoulder through and then abandoned ship. By this time they were turning blue. The lights of the hotel, some 150 yards away, beckoned tantalisingly.

'There's nothing for it, we'll have to go into the hotel and get the key. All our clothes, everything, are in this sauna.'

'Don't be a fool, how are we going to do that?'

As luck would have it, there was a rubbish bin nearby, which wasn't too full of objectionable things. So, after tipping the contents out and kicking the bottom out of the bag, David managed to wriggle into it, rather like those ladies of a certain age used to do years ago when attempting to step into a girdle. Hugh, in the meantime, was doing all the exercises known to man, flapping his arms about in an attempt to get his blood circulating. Dave made his way up to the hotel and, with as much dignity and confidence as he could muster, walked through the foyer to reception, trying desperately to stop his teeth from chattering, and asked for the spare key to the sauna. The foyer was silent. Dozens of pairs of eyes followed him as he made his stately way back out through the swing doors and down to the water's edge.

After about thirty minutes back inside in a temperature that would have killed most, they had thawed out and the world was back to normal. Ah, the joys of travel. I often wonder if anything like that has happened to any of the modern players.

On another occasion some of us had arrived a day or two early at Geneagles in readiness for the filming of *Pro-Celebrity Golf*. We had a rather good dinner together and decided that the very next day the eight of us would each put a tenner in the pot and play a Stableford competition off handicap. Suffice to say, we stayed up rather late. This was the occasion I was introduced to a drink called a Rusty Nail, which slipped down very nicely indeed, but *wow* – you don't want too many of those to get the job done. We decided we'd go to bed but we did have a master plan just in case the weather was poor the next day. Whoever woke up first would ring round and let the others know the weather forecast and, if we decided that golf was out of the question, we'd rendezvous in the sauna. I woke at about 6.30 with what sounded like airgun pellets hitting the window of my room. Now there are degrees of rain at the Gleneagles Hotel in Perthshire. Occasionally, there's a light mist that drifts down the glen and gets you a bit wet if you stay out in it too long. Then you have, what I was observing at the time, airgun pellets, which became shotgun pellets of the 12-bore variety, working up to 303 heavy calibre machine-gun fire. This one grew rapidly and by the time I got my head together and found out the room numbers of my companions, it was still belting down. I called round and we decided those who could would rendezvous in the sauna at about 8.30 a.m.

The sauna was quite large; it would seat eight or ten people comfortably. When I arrived Sean Connery was perched in the corner stark naked, sitting on a small towel next to a tub of pine-scented water with a big wooden ladle in his hand, which he dipped into the beautiful liquid and then emptied over the hot coals. The immense cloud of steam that arose took one's breath away. It was red hot, but the smell was delicious. I arranged my small towel on the wooden slats and sat down. Suddenly I noticed, lying on the floor, the great jockey, Geoff Lewis.

'What are you doing down there?' I asked, which is a pretty silly question when you think of it. His reply was intriguing.

'Do you know,' he said, 'I must have had ten thousand saunas in my life. Heat rises, so if you want to stay in a long time, you lie on the floor. You still get very hot, you sweat, so you should drink something. I'm on my holidays, remember, so I bought a bottle of champagne, which contains no calories. So I'm just going to lie on the floor, and occasionally have a sip of champagne. I can tell you it does you the world of good.' I thought, I must try that.

Through the door came Jimmy Tarbuck, closely followed by Bruce Forsyth. They arranged their towels and Sean poured more water on the coals, creating even more steam and heat. Next to arrive was Kenny Lynch, an amusing cove and great side-kick of Mr Tarbuck. The heat was almost unbearable. Sweat was dripping off our bodies on to the poor, unfortunate Mr Lewis, who didn't seem to care a jot. There were one or two moans, the odd belch, then suddenly, through the glass door we saw Eric Sykes approaching.

Quick as a flash Tarbuck said, 'Here's Eric coming. Don't say anything when he arrives, everybody shush, not a word. Odds on he won't have his hearing aid in.'

Eric came through the door. Slipping out of his robe he arranged his towel and sat down. Now to say Eric was thin would be an understatement. His ribs looked like the deck of a stacked xylophone. He sat down, looked around and said, 'What a pity this rain. I was so looking forward to playing today.' Silence, everyone looking straight ahead. Eric continued, 'You know what I've found playing here at Gleneagles, you really need a local caddy. You can go hopelessly wrong if you don't have someone who knows the line on the greens.' Nothing, just drip, drip, drip. The sweat continued to drop on to poor old Geoff.

Connery poured another spoonful of scented water on the coals, the heat rose, there were one or two more groans, again the odd belch, heads were held in hands and someone broke wind silently, there was a distinct aroma in the air. The scene was one of self-inflicted agony. Sean, as 007, was at the height of his fame. He stood up to rearrange his towel and his physique was quite magnificent. There was a good deal of observation of what the Americans call 'noble parts'. My wife had always had a crush on Sean and I was sorry she wasn't there because his noble parts were perhaps not much more noble than mine. But I digress.

Eric looked around at this strange scene, bodies of various shapes and skins of different hues dripping sweat, slight moaning and groaning, and uttered the immortal words, 'Can anyone tell me what time this train gets into Calcutta?' We all broke up and decided that that line in that particular situation should be recorded for all time. It was absolutely brilliant.

14

ALLISS & CLARK

'Everyone at the time seemed to be building golf courses wherever they could get a piece of land'

After the parting of the ways with David Thomas I went through a fallow period but during a conversation early in the eighties a propos nothing, Clive Clark suggested we could join forces in the golf-course architectural line and operate out of a room in his mother's house in Sunningdale. A good idea, so off we went. We had immediate success. Clive had had an interesting and varied career. He'd twice been a finalist in the English Amateur Championship and had got to the final of the Amateur Championship only to be beaten 2 and 1 by Michael Bonallack at Royal Lytham & St Anne's in 1965. That was the year Bonallack and Clark shared all the spoils of amateur golf between them but Michael took the two big prizes. Clive played in a Walker Cup team and, at the age of twenty, holed a thirty-five-foot putt to halve his match with Mark Hopkins at the Five Farms course near Baltimore in the USA. It was a great occasion because it was the first time the Great Britain and Ireland team had ever returned from the United States unbeaten.

He turned professional that same year and during the course of his career won four tournaments on the European circuit and played in the 1973 Ryder Cup matches. He then became the professional at the Sunningdale Golf Club. Several eyebrows were raised at this appointment of such a relatively young man for he was taking over from one of the game's greatest characters, Arthur Lees, who had first gone to the club in the late forties. Although he wasn't to everyone's taste, I thought he did a splendid job; some thought Arthur's shop was lacking in golf equipment and other goodies to tempt the golfers but Clive stocked his out magnificently and surrounded himself with superb assistants.

It was during his time at Sunningdale that he joined the BBC golf commentary team and found success as 'our man on the fairways'. How often was he asked, 'What's it look like down there, Clive?' And he always gave us a sensible answer. Clive and I went through a boom period. The R&A had announced that some 200 new golf courses were needed to satisfy the anticipated demand before the turn of the century. Sadly, it never materialised. We stayed at Clive's mother's for quite some time but eventually things were getting a little cramped. We were now employing half a dozen people, including the identical twins, Bruce and David Weller, both beautiful draughtsmen and delightful young men. We found an office in Farnham, which suited them very well as they lived within walking distance of St George's Yard, where our office was based.

Clive and I had already worked on some thirty or forty golf courses before John Steven entered our lives in the late 1980s but first Roy Cooper, my partner, had to check things out. Roy is a chartered accountant whom David Thomas and I first met in the mid-sixties. We both became clients of his accountancy practice and over the years he has acted for me in an advisory capacity. Then in 1992 he retired from the group, in which he was a financial director, and pretty well joined us on a full-time basis. Roy can be quite feisty, fiery in fact, but dependable, friendly, an aggressive businessman and someone who's been a wonderful help and support to me from the very beginning, a member of the Potters Bar Golf Club. I wouldn't be surprised if he doesn't end up being captain before the ink on this book is dry.

Everyone at that time seemed to be building golf courses wherever they could get a piece of land. Planning permission seemed relatively easy to get and the public rushed in like lemmings to deposit money to ensure memberships. In the late eighties Clive and I, trading as Peter Alliss Clive Clark Golf Designs, were approached by John Steven of Compton Holdings to design and supervise the construction of golf courses on behalf of his company. Steven's method of working was to acquire the land with completion delayed until a date when he anticipated opening the golf club and would therefore have the funds to pay for it from the proceeds of sales of memberships. He made similar deals with the contractors for their work. I was asked to go on the board but held off until I was assured that an accountant, a partner in one of the major accountancy practices, had accepted a directorship. The policy was that the funds from the sale of memberships of any one course would be ring-fenced to cover the cost of construction of that course alone and were not to subsidise any other project. Things took off at a great rate of knots. We were able to design interesting golf courses, attractive clubhouses were built and members rolled up aplenty to sign on the dotted line.

One of the most fascinating jobs Clive Clark and I ever worked on was the creation of the first golf course at Brocket Hall, a fine estate a handful of miles north of the M25 at twelve o'clock. The estate was being run by a youthful looking Lord Brocket who was married to a beautiful American ex-model. He and his advisors had worked miracles restoring the estate and were in the process of trying to build up more conference business, and the idea of creating a golf course appealed to him. We paid many visits to the house and, although Lord Brocket was later to go to jail for attempting to defraud his insurance company, as far as we were concerned, he was a delightful companion who paid his bills promptly. More recently, his fame has been in Australia in the jungle – *I'm a Celebrity – Get Me Out of Here* with Jordan and others.

There were many restrictions on the site. From what was originally the main gate into the property the planners had no wish to see any sand, so the idea of placing bunkers hither and thither was a non-runner. But somehow, by creating hollows and small banks, we managed to hide the sand, so that, from where the planners stood, there was not a grain in view. Many things have changed since our original work on the course. The house where the Brocket family lived is now converted into the clubhouse and the second 18 holes have been built, running through the woods of the northeastern end of the property. I felt we did a pretty good job, considering we had the 'open' ground to work with, but we did have the use of the lake and river and, at Lord Brocket's suggestion, we made the third shot to the 18th hole a pitch across a wide expanse of water – even more exciting because he thought it would be a good idea to have a flat-bottomed boat to accommodate not only the players and caddies but golf carts as well.

Clive and I never got close enough to see the huge problems, as far as finance was concerned, and when we read that an amazing robbery had taken place and a couple of vintage cars and priceless engines had been stolen from Lord Brocket's magnificent collection of Ferraris, we didn't think much of it. But then the plot gradually unfolded. How was it the burglar alarm had been switched off? Why did nobody see or hear anything? The powers that be immediately smelt a rat and must have known of his lordship's financial problems. They dragged the lake looking for the millions of pounds worth of equipment that was reported missing. Months went by and eventually, in some (rather sordid) garages in north London, much of it was found. Lord Brocket was tried, found guilty and went to jail. What I found interesting was that so many of the people who had paid homage to him while he was running free immediately changed their tune the moment he was locked up.

The course was pleasant and we had the bonus of creating the fairways out of grassland that had been there for many years. It was just a question of finding a route, cutting, feeding, fertilising and, within a short time, we had the most magnificent fairways. Things began to prosper but the estate had to be sold because of the huge financial problems that were faced by Lord Brocket. A lease was taken out whereby, in thirty or forty years' time, it will revert back to Lord Brocket's heirs.

A second course was built and it was rather disappointing, having been associated with the first, not to have a telephone call asking if we would like to participate in the new course. But that's life, particularly in the design and construction business.

In 1992 Clive and I were in the process of planning the construction of a golf course at Pyrford near Woking. In fact, only the River Wey separated our property from the giant Wisley course just off the A3. We intended to keep this as an investment for ourselves but, when John Steven saw it, he rushed down in his helicopter to look at our project and insisted on buying the course. I was away at the time covering the US Open Championship at the Pebble Beach Club on the Monterey Peninsula on the west coast of the United States. He met Clive and Roy Cooper, our financial consultant, at a hotel nearby and, after lengthy negotiations, offered £4 million for what we had done so far, to be paid in instalments, the first coming two weeks before Christmas.

It must have been difficult for them to ignore that kind of money but when Roy telephoned me at Pebble Beach, I initially resisted the deal, saying, 'No, this is a chance we've wanted. It will be there for us and our families for ever, an income, an interest. No.' But eventually they talked me into it. Why? Well, they pointed out we had to do all the marketing, the selling, pulling it all together, there was still masses of work to do, including getting finance to build the clubhouse, etc. etc. By the middle of August 1992 the deal was done.

Everything appeared to be going along very nicely but about the second week in December, I had a phone call from John Steven saying that he could not meet the first payment. I immediately called Roy and asked him to get down to Reading to meet with Steven's holding company, Compton Holdings Limited. Up to this time we had done ten or eleven courses for Steven and felt that everything was going well. He was an excellent promoter, did everything at a first-class level, but unfortunately a recession was upon all of us. Sadly, Roy found administrative chaos with records that were not up to date and many that had been badly maintained. Nobody seemed to have much idea of the financial position of the various companies.

Men v. Women was another hugely enjoyable TV series – here with Beth Daniel, Bernhard Langer, Jan Stephenson and Greg Norman at Woburn.

The Alliss Thomas Golf Construction Company designed and built the course in lovely La Baule, France, among many others. A private plane took David and me, together with Hugh Lewis and Terence Frisbey, who wrote 'There's a Girl in My Soup', to view the site.

Outside the Turnberry Hotel with Guy Wolstenholme and Granny T. This was the last time I saw my dear friend Guy. He died of cancer shortly afterwards.

Ambushed by Eamonn Andrews with the big red book. I had no idea.

Annie Turner, better known as Granny T, a wonderful Yorkshire lady and our locum granny since 1973.

Marley were an early sponsor of *Pro-Celebrity Golf*. Chairman Jack Aisher (*third from left*) was a keen golfer. Also in this group are Lee Trevino (*far left*), Howard Keel (*fourth from left*), Sean Connery (*second from right*) and Seve Ballesteros (*far right*).

Peter Cook, comic genius, brought along Abe Finklestein, his pet goldfish, which doubled as his manager, for his round of pro-celebrity golf, and left James Hunt's enormous dog, Oscar, to guard it while he played his shots.

Gary Player, winner of 158 tournaments worldwide, including nine majors. Somehow I'm not totally convinced he received the accolades he truly deserved.

Mark McCormack taught me a great deal about work and life.

James Hunt's Oscar was impeccably mannered except when you came to drive off the tee when he would lie close up and then chase after the ball as soon as it flew up the fairway – diverting, not to say distracting, for Jerry Pate (*second from left*), Lee Trevino (*second from right*) and the volcanic George C. Scott (*far right*). James (*far left*) was used to it!

Two of our best friends, Terry and Helen Wogan. Their daughter Katherine's wedding was magical.

The Tobago team on the 1st tee – we had thirteen wonderful holidays in a row with Peter Gammon, Ronnie Sumrie and Martin Curtis.

A risky business, interviewing one's wife.

Jackie with Michelle Dotrice and Edward Woodward at Stratford upon Avon during the filming of her cookery programme for television.

Above: The Grand Match is well named – a brilliant two-day get-together between former Ryder and Walker Cup players, held at the Royal Cinque Ports Golf Club in Kent. Here I am with Bruce Critchley whose original concept it was.

Left: I was delighted to receive an honorary degree from the University of Humberside. Mother would have been proud.

Below: A mixed bag of Ryders and Walkers at the Grand Match.

Each golf course had been formulated as a corporate limited entity in which Compton Holdings was the main company. Roy brought in staff to investigate the financial situation and very soon realised that, contrary to policy, the funds were not, in fact, being ring-fenced and the clubs where sales were good were being used to subsidise others.

Shortly after this, Nick Pitt of *The Sunday Times* elected to write a critical article about the affair. He picked on me for some reason, probably because the name of Alliss was the best known. By this time most of the other directors had fled, with the exception of a local solicitor who stayed and tried to help sort out the mess. The thrust of Pitt's article was that the John Steven's courses were collapsing and there was a potential loss to the public of millions of pounds, which they had paid in because they liked and trusted Peter Alliss and 'he wouldn't be involved in anything that wasn't a hundred per cent'.

Pitt's campaign seemed to go on and on; it certainly did us no good. Roy tried to get Pitt to hold off on the grounds that the publicity would encourage people to demand their money back instantly, which would simply create a run and bring the whole business down like a pack of cards. Pitt was not inclined to listen to reason. It was a very difficult and nasty time.

To help us in this matter Roy employed the services of Lowe Bell Communication and we were advised by Tim Bell (later Sir Tim Bell) and Piers Pottinger. They were able to get some of the more inflammatory remarks about me removed. Compton Holdings collapsed and John Steven went into bankruptcy, but at the end of it all very few of the eight or nine thousand people who had bought into the various projects lost money.

At that time, the giant American Golf Corporation was interested in acquiring golf courses in the UK and had been having talks with John Steven along those lines. Roy took over these negotiations and was able to progress them successfully in respect of four courses – Mill Green in Hertfordshire, Milford south of Guildford, Cams Hall at Fareham near Portsmouth, and Dummer near Basingstoke – but American Golf would not conclude the business unless they could also have Pyrford. So it was agreed to sell Pyrford at a price that paid for the land and all the expenses that had, so far, been incurred. No profit whatsoever was made by anyone. Roy Cooper was able to dispose of all the courses under construction with all the memberships honoured and, at the end of the day, perhaps only a handful of the public suffered in any way. There were some participants who simply went away leaving their money where it was, seemingly treating it like an investment that didn't come off – bad luck, let's move on to the next. In the liquidation of Compton Holdings, I understand substantial sums were lost by trade creditors but most of the clubs concerned have gone forward and are very successful.

There was an unhappy postscript to all this. Clive Clark washed his hands of me and the entire situation. It did look pretty grim. He came out with the great line, 'Well, you were the chairman, I had nothing to do with the company, you're the one.' That was virtually that. He didn't want anything to do with it. He decamped to America and set up a golf-design business in Palm Springs. We had done much good work together, the last course of any importance being the Marquess, the third at Woburn. We had a very pleasant relationship with Lord and Lady Tavistock. Lady Tavistock, who is now the Dowager Duchess, is an amazing woman, bright as a button and someone who could be an outstanding broadcaster. She has great style and quality and is totally at ease in front of the camera, a gift given to very few.

I continued to run the business from Farnham but work was drying up and when the landlord wished to increase the rent by some 30 per cent, I decided, along with Roy, that it was no longer viable to have the office right in the middle of town. Help was at hand. My secretary, Helen Cameron, had a house with spare rooms.

'Why not move your office in with me?' she said. 'I could do with the rent money. I'm sure we can work out a package whereby everyone's happy.' And so we did. Although the golf-course design business has been very slow, there's a strong possibility of creating a new course on Lord Cardigan's estate, just south of Hungerford in Wiltshire, the site known as Tottenham House. Fingers and toes crossed, it might turn out to be a real gem.

I take the course-designing job very seriously, probably a damned sight more seriously than many people purporting these days to be golf-course designers. Those who are part of big organisations are able to get away with it, but I doubt whether some of them even know how to pull on a pair of Wellington boots. The fact is I enjoy the work and find it incredibly satisfying.

15

TELLY OVER HERE –
TV OVER THERE

*'I suppose the easiest way of summing it up
would be to say that almost everything in
America is overkill'*

I'm often asked to compare the differences between working
for the BBC and American television, in my case the American
Broadcasting Company. There is one interesting difference
between golf coverage in the US and UK. American commentators are called 'announcers'. This implies someone who makes
revelations or announces news or facts without much in the way
of opinion. In British television golf commentators are just that,
people who 'comment' on happenings, implying opinion or
chatter. The reason is clear. The pressure of time, the fifty-
minute hour, compels American broadcasters to be sharp, crisp,
fast and factual. A typical sequence might be: 'Tiger Woods on
sixteen, fifteen-feet putt for birdie – he's missed – let's go
to seventeen.' The man covering the 17th green will say

immediately, 'Mickelson over a twenty-footer for a birdie to tie Woods – he's made it – now back to the seventeenth tee.' And so it goes on – bang, bang, bang . . . If I exaggerate, it's not by much. The BBC's commentators, by comparison, often with two or more uninterrupted hours on their hands, can afford to be relaxed and take time out to smell the flowers.

People ask what I change in commentary when I go to the US. Well, I try not to change anything because if I do, they may understand what I'm talking about and I would no longer be a 'funny ornament' that they don't quite understand but quite enjoy! I fiercely resist the temptation to call a bunker 'a trap', the inward or homeward nine 'the back side' or to say that someone has struck his 'tee ball'. I don't much care for a lot of today's television jargon. Why, for example, does it have to be 'the putting surface'? You might as well say 'the green sward'. Dammit, it's the green. Why is it always a breeze, never a wind, and why does it always appear to be 'hurting'? Do you know what that means? Well, of course you do. You've heard it often enough: 'the breeze is from the right and hurting', which means it's just a little bit into the player's face so making the shot a shade more difficult. 'He's half a club short.' I often get viewers writing to me and asking where they can purchase these half clubs! 'It's come up short' – golf balls don't come *up*, they come *down*! It's all mumbo jumbo – cliché after cliché with that wonderful arrogance in that 'I-know-everything' tone of voice. Every shot's analysed and a reason found and given for everything, whether it be one that just misses the green by a few feet or one that careers eighty yards to the right out of bounds.

While in America a week or so before the 2004 Open championship, I came across the word 'nomenclature' – a person's or community's system of names for things – and wondered more about the differences. For example, we have chips, they have fries; we have bumpers, they have fenders; we have pavements, they have sidewalks. I could go on. Then I got to thinking about pronounciation – a bit like Cole Porter in the well-known song about tomatoes/tomaytoes. Why is it Moss-kow in America and Mossco in Britain, we say Colin, they say Co-lin,. They leave out the 'h' in herbs and why do they always say Loss Vegas when it's spelt Las Vegas? Fanny over there means something entirely different from over here, as does bum – a rear end here, a tramp there. Churchill was right – two great countries divided by a common language.

During that visit, I went to Washington and had the opportunity of visiting the Pentagon. What an extraordinary building – seven miles of corridors, 25,000 people going to work there every day. It was a cross between a museum for all the armed forces and a shopping centre – or mall, as they call it.

Over the years, the three American networks, CBS, NBC and ABC, have changed their methods of broadcasting. CBS still insists on having towers out on the course. You'll have noticed them during the coverage of the Masters from Augusta early in April 2004. They believe their commentators need to be right in the action. I don't know why. Henry Longhurst used to say that with a monitor, a microphone and information, he could do a commentary from his sitting room at home! From exposed camera towers there is the risk of the commentator's voice carrying to the players on the green, or bits of paper blowing off the tower could flutter down across the green. CBS hold their towers close to their hearts but I think they look antiquated.

They also insist on having headphones with a microphone built in so when you see people being interviewed, it looks as though they're speaking to you from another planet! Heavy headsets, clumsy microphones, when in all truth it's so easy to have an earpiece, like a hearing aid, and a miniature microphone pinned to the jacket or shirt. This picks up sound perfectly but they insist their systems produce a better quality of sound. The interesting thing is, since I've been going there, they have introduced (for my delight only!) one of the so-called old-fashioned lip mikes, where you actually hold the bar under your nose. This keeps you a constant inch or so away from the microphone so the level of speech is always the same. That, in *our* engineers' opinion, gives without doubt the clearest quality of all.

When working in the States I'm totally spoilt. I'm provided with first-class travel and collected at my destinations by a gentleman called Jeff Shapter. Slightly physically handicapped, he does the most wonderful job as a 'goffer' and part-time personal assistant; he's a jack of all trades and very much master of some. I find him an absolute delight. He whisks me to my hotel and I go to my room and unpack my small case (I always carry my luggage on board so I never have to wait for bags at the carousel). Then perhaps I'll meet a couple of the gang down-stairs for a drink before dinner, try to stay up reasonably late but, in all truth, no matter what time I get to bed I'm always awake at 3.00 a.m. UK time. I've stopped fighting it now – some of the best programmes are on TV at that time and I've discovered the History and Discovery channels, which provide me with great entertainment, also the occasional old movie, which I love. The faithful Jeff is there in the morning to pick me up and take me out to the course.

There are often occasions in the United States when the preparation of golf courses for television, for 'the picture', has become almost farcical. The greens are cut down so short that you are almost into bare earth and the ball runs at such a pace as to make putting ludicrous. There are certain courses, Augusta National comes to mind, where the only protection the course has is the speed of the greens and the flag positions. At Augusta, they have cut bunkers further into the fairways, developed fairway mounds, actually bought land from the adjoining Augusta Golf Club to lengthen one hole (the 13th) and this has not made the slightest difference to the playing of the hole for the big, even medium, hitters of the ball.

My understanding is that this bit of land cost the club the best part of one million dollars. Quite an outlay, but the modern player is so big, strong and talented and his equipment so sophisticated, the only thing that will make him think is rough – positive and challenging rough. Augusta National had an inch of rough in place a few years ago but it had no effect – a waste of time and money. The US Open and US PGA courses are always severe with fairways narrowed down to twenty yards and collars of deep rough around the entire green but still modern players contrive impressive scores. It's easy to pontificate from the side lines, but in our world today, common sense isn't as common as it used to be!

I suppose the easiest way of summing it up would be to say that almost everything in America is overkill, whereas the BBC operate under a much more frugal umbrella. For example, let's just take the situation of golf carts. On the American side there would be at least forty to sixty. Every commentator would have his own personal buggy so that he can flit hither and thither round the course, whereas the BBC would have a limited number of golf carts designed to carry cameramen, sound technicians etc. and on the production side you'd be lucky to have two or three at your disposal at any one time.

All this, of course, costs money – hundreds of dollars a week for the hire of each buggy. Then there are the Portaloos. In America, wherever our commentary position is established, there is always one alongside for the sole use of commentators and technical staff employed in that location – again, hundreds of dollars a week for such a luxury. Add to that refrigerators full of soft drinks of all types and bottled water, trays of sandwiches, donuts, biscuits, fruit, coffee percolating machines, miniature bars of chocolate and M&Ms, all there to make the lives of the workers more comfortable.

For every event at least twenty or thirty extra staff are hired to do small duties, usually college students or retired folk who have an interest in the game of golf. Their daily rate would be anything from $50 to $75, plus free meals produced to a very high standard. Similarly, the hired help when the BBC is doing a golf tournament is perhaps twenty-five. Many of them come to every tournament. It's almost a way of life. They love the game and it does give them a front-row seat. Richard and Sandra Kendrick handle pretty well all the BBC outdoor catering, not only at the golf but many other sporting occasions, and what a super job they do. Perhaps it's not quite on such a lavish or large scale as it is in America but they're catering for a third of the number.

I won't go as far as to say the BBC system is make-do-and-mend but all the technicians involved seem to have a marvellous ability to fix things, to make them work. I sometimes get the impression that I've seen their fathers, and perhaps their grand-fathers, in some wartime movie where the inmates of a particular prisoner of war camp manage to create a radio out of six empty cigarette packets, a pair of boot laces, some mustard powder and fingernail clippings.

The sports department has gone from a totally male-dominated arena to one where males have virtually disappeared at the top end of the ladder, so you're bound to get different thoughts, philosophies and working environments. Paul Davies is our excellent director but he is the lone male in the midst of half a dozen charming ladies who know television from A to Z but on rare occasions don't quite understand the philosophy of golf. At times they go where angels fear to tread, which isn't necessarily a bad thing – they sometimes end up getting the most remarkable interviews with people who normally are untouchable.

In the United States, television is ruled by ratings. Shows that do not succeed immediately are cut off mercilessly and thrown on the rubbish heap of television history. Attitudes in the UK, happily, are different. For example *The Last of the Summer Wine* would not have survived for a second series if that attitude had been adopted. The show has run for twenty years. The fact is that when it comes to hiring and firing, the Americans are just as gung-ho as they are at everything else. The philosophy is clear your desk, hand in your keys, leave the building *now* – not many tribunals to defend you over there, not many wrongful dismissal actions reach the courts in the US. In the States there are always a dozen people who reckon they can do it better than the incumbent and all they want is a chance.

In the world of television strange things are done. I was reminded of Dave Marr's sudden departure from ABC. Happily, Dave Marr joined us at the BBC. This was a good break for the BBC. Although we could not match the ABC fees, it was an opportunity for him to enjoy club-class air fares, decent hotels and several thousands of pounds for each visit to our shores, which eventually became about half a dozen each year. It took him some time to get into our system. He wasn't used to the luxury of having time to elaborate on various aspects of the game, but he gradually understood that he would have time to finish a sentence and trot out his homespun philosophy, which I loved.

Dave Marr had been a top-class American tournament player who won the US PGA Championship in 1965. He found himself captaining one of the most formidable of all US Ryder Cup teams, the one that beat Europe $18\frac{1}{2}$ –$9\frac{1}{2}$ in 1981 at Walton Heath. Asked about his team's prospects against what was an improving Europe team, he said, 'Don't worry – we have an escape submarine on standby.' And when his team fell a point behind after the first day, he said, 'Guess we'll just have to circle the wagons tomorrow.'

Marr, a Texan, had all the broad humour of that state. He was very quickwitted. When viewing a canny old campaigner on the course who was getting away with murder using all his guile to scrape a par here and the odd birdie there, he would say, 'Yes, he's a hard old dog to keep under the porch.' When there was a David and Goliath situation he'd say, 'Well lookee here, the lamb jumped up and bit the butcher.' On watching the American golfer Jim Thorpe, who plays on the Seniors Tour over there, now renamed the Champions Tour, someone mentioned Thorpe's great power. 'Yes,' said Marr, 'he has graphite arms and an outboard motor for an arse.' In conversation with Bing at the Crosby Tournament, Dave noted that Calvin Peete had had a diamond sunk into one of his front teeth. Crosby replied, 'Oh, how absolutely charming.'

Dave thought golf had become a 'lift and drop' game as the years went by. If someone was tearing up the course, out in 31 and putting for a birdie on the 10th (could he be thinking of one

Tiger Woods?) he'd say, 'He's hotter than a bucket of red ants.' For someone playing conservatively, sitting back watching his opponent make mistakes, Dave would say, 'Why dig for bait when you've got a boat full of fish.' Craig Stadler was battling his way up the 18th hole at the PGA Championship a few years ago. The humidity was very high and it looked as though someone had thrown a couple of buckets of water over him. Marr said, 'Here comes Stadler, dressed by the dreaded sisters, Polly and Esther.' At a tee shot on a par-3 hole, the player hits, the television commentator says, 'Ah, that's a little heavy.' The camera follows the flight of the ball, which ends a few feet from the hole. Marr's comment is, 'Yes, a little heavy, but perfect – just like Liz Taylor.'

Of Steve Pate, he of the volcanic temper, Dave judged he was 'meaner than a junk-yard dog'. After a particular conversation with a relatively well-known golf aficionado, Dave turned to me and said, 'How is it that old bores never die?' Mrs Bobbitt, you will remember, was the lady who became so displeased with her husband that she cut off the most private of his private parts and threw it out of the car window. From then on, if someone hit a wild slice, Marr would say that 'he's hit a Bobbitt.' When someone looked particularly agitated, having just dropped four strokes in a row, Dave would say, 'Stick a fork in him – he's done.' In more recent times, if a precocious young player overshot a green by a considerable distance, the gag would be, 'I guess he just pumped too much air into his Reeboks.'

When the great Fanny Sunesson first started to get vocal when caddying for Nick Faldo – 'no cameras please', 'stand still' – Dave said, tongue in cheek, 'You know, Fanny's beginning to sound just like a first wife.' He said of Bernhard Langer on a particularly sombre day, 'His sense of humour is no laughing matter.' Once a friend told Dave his daughter was pregnant. 'Hold on,' said Dave, 'I'll go and get my gun and we'll go and shoot the sonofabitch who did it.' When he was more serious he would say, 'Winners are only dreamers who didn't quit.'

Contrary to belief, he could be very feisty and even threatening when he had one too many sherbets but he was a good companion and added much to our broadcasts. He died of cancer, in middle age. I miss him very much.

16

THE AMERICAN WAY

'Baseball hat back-to-front, wearing clothes that didn't fit and all, seemingly, having size 14 feet'

No two men could be more different than Tommy Bolt and Mark McCormack but both have something of that unique American flavour. Due to the homogenised state we now live in, everybody in the world of sport, due to the various trials by television, has to be whiter than white, purer than pure. Not so that great American professional Tommy Bolt, as good a ball striker as the world has ever seen. Yes, he was *that* good, winner of the US Open 1958. And to say the least, he was one of *the* characters of the day. Why? Well, he used to throw the odd club, use an expletive or two and had a walk that wouldn't have disgraced a sheriff walking down the main street of some Texas town 125 years ago. Tommy disliked the college kids. It was all too new. Youngsters with modest talent were offered golf scholarships at universities. Some probably played more golf than the pros and perhaps still do to this day. They would finish their studies and then attack the world of professional golf with relish. He always said they had an awful lot to learn, they didn't even know how to throw clubs properly. Some of them were stupid enough to throw them *backwards* so someone had to go back and retrieve them.

Fining players for various misdemeanours had just been introduced. The penalties were for a variety of things. On one occasion Tommy walked on to the first tee at a course in Palm Springs looking absolutely immaculate. Pristine black and white shoes, the purest of white trousers, black shirt and red alpaca sweater. He took a step or two then, shaking a leg vigorously, let off a couple of raspers. Some people had the audacity to laugh; he was fined $50. Tommy remarked 'Sheet, these guys are taking all the colour out of the game.'

It was about this time the PGA introduced a rule whereby you could only hit a maximum of two shots into a green during a practice round. The reason? Well, for years players, particularly those who took the game seriously, would pepper the greens with five or six shots until they got the feel of the shot. On this occasion Tommy hit three, or maybe four, on to a green. An official rushed out, 'Tommy, Tommy, I'm sorry, we've got to fine you, you know the rule, you can only hit two, so far you've hit seven extra shots during the round and this is only the twelfth.' Tommy, who always carried a wad of cash, pulled out a roll of hundred dollar bills and gave him a couple saying airily, 'Keep the change, I may hit a couple more.'

Now that was not Mark McCormack's style at all. Mark Hume McCormack was born in Chicago in December 1930 and died in New York in May 2003. He was the founder of IMG, International Management Group, the world's largest sport and management company for artists and events and, starting from scratch, he created an empire that operated in thirty-three countries and generated $900 million a year. 'Starting from scratch' is only partially true. The whole colossus started in 1960 with McCormack shaking hands with Arnold Palmer, a promising golfer, and agreeing to look after his commercial affairs. Within two years, Palmer's endorsement income had risen from $5,000 to $300,000. Mark set standards and prices. He was the one who asked for, and got, $1,000 for Arnold Palmer to appear on the *Ed Sullivan Show*. Sullivan was the Michael Parkinson, Jonathan Ross and Terry Wogan of the day all rolled into one. His programme was enormously successful and they thought the people would just enjoy being on the show, regardless of the fee. McCormack changed all that when he asked for $1,000 and got it. No one, it was said, had ever been paid more than $100. He realised that nobody knew what to charge, there was no precedent for sports people in show business. So he simply set his own fee structure at a time when competition in television sport was becoming rife. Now there are a number of competent organisations in the field who can be considered rivals but none of them begin to match the huge scope and diversity of IMG. Presently dozens of show business personalities were beating a path to his door. In 1967 he set up a television production company, Trans World International (TWI), which became the biggest producer of television sport in the world. He handled television and marketing negotiations for the Royal & Ancient Golf Club and Wimbledon tennis, and created the World Matchplay Golf Championship at Wentworth. IMG diversified into music, modelling, publishing. It represented the profile of the Nobel Peace Prize and, on one occasion, the Pope!

McCormack had fingers in so many pies that it always amazed me that nobody said, 'Hey, are you sure this is all right. You are batting, bowling and fielding for both sides at the same time.' This was certainly true as far as the BBC was concerned. On at least two occasions Mark (who for a period did golf commentary for the BBC) produced a master plan showing how he and his organisation could do a better job for the BBC than the BBC. Work that out! He said he was capable of getting any commentators the R&A nominated and that he could demonstrate financial savings and also bring new blood and new ideas into how championships were shown on television. The BBC blasted all of this out of the water with a wonderful presentation to the R&A and their various committees.

With the BBC through the sixties and seventies increasing their coverage of American events, such as the Masters, their Open and Women's Open, my name became known to the USGA, whom McCormack represented. Over the years we talked rather casually about my contracts and eventually he represented me properly for my television work. We'd be sitting in an office that was more like a drawing room. He would review where our business affairs were, tell me what was pending and how this deal and that was going, then say, 'It's good to see you again, we'll keep in touch.'

There came a time when my contract with ABC was running out and I thought it would not be renewed. Under these circumstances I told him I would end our association – he was taking 25 per cent of my fees. He was not pleased, he wanted me to stay. It wasn't long after this I discovered that he had tried to set up a replacement for me with ABC Television. What they did not know was that Frank Hannigan, then the USGA Executive Director, and Terry Jastrow, then Producer of Golf at ABC, were battling hard on my behalf and they won the day.

Leaving McCormack and IMG meant a huge increase in my

income, for I subsequently agreed an improved contract with ABC, in fact a 25 per cent increase and no 25 per cent commission to IMG; it was a huge unexpected bonus.

An interesting aspect of McCormack's personality was that he never seemed to hold a grudge against any clients who left him or were uncomplimentary. Perhaps that was because his operation was so large, and their contributions so proportionally small. Tony Jacklin and Nick Faldo both went back as clients. A lesser person than McCormack might have thought, 'No, you left me, you get on with it, paddle your own canoe,' but not him. Perhaps it flattered his ego to think that they could not do without him.

In one of my many conversations with McCormack, he told me he'd only let one client go and that was Ilie Nastase. He found him very difficult and unreliable. I wonder what he did, apart from swearing and using vulgar gestures.

Mark McComack had the single greatest American quality – energy. His second definitive quality was vision – he saw very early on the immense effect television would have on sport, indeed, on all outdoor events. He created golf tournaments, tennis tournaments, outdoor music festivals. He maximised the association of sports champions and public names with the marketing strategies of major international corporations. All told, a remarkable man and when death came it seemed a pitiful end to Mark McCormack, an astonishing force of nature. I enjoyed his company very much. He taught me a great deal about work and life.

Early in 2004 a book entitled *The Wicked Game* was published by Sidgwick & Jackson. The author was Howard Sounes. Sounes turns over some very interesting stones, not least of which is the growth of black golfers in the United States.

On page 39 he tells a story of the Phoenix Open, yes, the great Phoenix Open, the year 1952. Joe Louis, the world boxing champion, through his celebrity status had managed to obtain exemptions for himself and a few other friends including Charlie Sifford, the first really good black pro of the day, to try to qualify for the Phoenix Open. When they got to Phoenix no hotel would put them up, they were not allowed into the locker room where the tournament was being held and were obliged to play the qualifying round early before the white players went out. When Charlie Sifford reached the first green, someone had taken a shit in the cup – no wonder he failed to qualify.

It's a fascinating book and it's happened in my life time. As I read, it was hard to equate the fact that nobody from the PGA of America at that time seemed to be fighting any battles for the black man or for his chances of making a living out of professional golf. One mustn't forget that in the late 1950s all America was up in arms regarding civil rights. I once more lived through that autumn of 1957 in Little Rock Arkansas when nine black children risked their lives to attend the Little Rock Central High School. The National Guard failed to maintain calm; President Eisenhower sent in the 104 First Airborne division to keep order so the children could go to class.

With the advent of Tiger Woods, his huge success and fame, things have come a long way in fifty years. Isn't it fascinating to think that if Arnold Palmer had been born black, we may never have heard of him.

Eisenhower and the Augusta National Golf Club play a big part in Sounes' book. The way he presents it, the club in the fifties was a bastion of white supremacy in the world of golf, aided and abetted by their chairman, Cliff Roberts, who is portrayed as a racist, although some would argue 'perhaps a kindly one', this exemplified by his reaction to Claude Tillman, who worked originally for one of the members of the club. That member died, so his widow sent Tillman to Roberts with a Christmas wreath around his neck and a card attached offering, no doubt, Christmas felicitations and also offering Tillman as a gift. Roberts placed his 'gift' in the club kitchen where Tillman worked from then on. Roberts relates the story in a book he published about the club in 1976 and presents it as an amusing anecdote. Hard to believe now, isn't it, the notion of a black servant, passed from the employ of one wealthy white man to another as recently as the 1950s. Roberts was an interesting man who got himself into a position where he was a dominant and domineering figure. He struck fear into everyone's heart. At the end of it all, he was a bully; it's said that he left his many millions to medical science specialising in birth control!

Whether Sounes' book will be bought, read, criticised or enjoyed by members of the Augusta National Golf Club or, indeed, anyone in the hierarchy of golf, remains to be seen but it's a very interesting read and brought home to me how things were so very different only fifty years ago. But flawed though it may have been, the Masters at Augusta is one of the world's truly great sporting events.

Sounes' book mentions the Phoenix Open and coincidentally I attended the tournament immediately before travelling to Augusta for the 2004 Masters. In many ways no two tournaments could be more different. The FBR Tournament, formerly the Phoenix Open which began in 1932, is without question the most attended golf tournament in the world. In 2004 it was played at the TPC at Scottsdale. They have two courses, the TP and the Desert; the Princess Hotel stands alongside; it is a magnificent building that can accommodate huge conferences, bar mitzvahs, weddings etc.

On 31 January 2004, the official attendance for day one was 141,320. That means that more than half-a-million spectators will have attended during the week. There's nothing like it in the world. The 16th hole is the key, a par-3 surrounded by hospitality boxes. Tens of thousands of fans, fuelled by drink, cheer the players to the rooftops if they hit the green. There's been a couple of holes-in-one here over the years. Tiger Woods had one – oh, the joy! You could hear the cheers 150 miles away. If the players don't like it, they can stay at home – some big names don't bother. The same could be said of the AT&T, which used to be called the Bing Crosby and played in the Monterey area of northern California, at Pebble Beach. There it just gets noisy and can be difficult for players to concentrate because of their Pro-Am partners. A few comedians who aren't all that funny can be, and are, a distraction. But it's a change from the other forty odd tournaments played throughout the year in the United States with the solemnity of a state funeral in Westminster Abbey. It's perhaps not golf in the accepted sense but millions of dollars are raised for charity and, at the end of it all, it's another page in the extraordinary book of golf – modern golf that is.

I noticed this year when the crowds had moved away, tons of paper cups and cans were left lying around – not for long, I hasten to add, but they were much tidier years ago. I guess that's all part of the modern scene – hundreds of beautiful young people, particularly the women who are now into the hipster pants, many with delicious belly buttons. A wonderful sea of flowers, but with an odd weed here and there. As for the men, well most of them looked like they were auditioning for a rap party, baseball hats back-to-front, wearing clothes that didn't fit and all, seemingly, having size 14 feet! Raucous yes, but very few, if any, ejections from the course. No fighting, which was refreshing, but noisy.

I travelled club class to Phoenix on a new Boeing 777 and, would you believe it, they've copied the old love-seats of the eighteenth and nineteenth centuries. You're embarrassingly close to your neighbour but you can get a little privacy by pulling up what looks like a replica of Lady Windermere's Fan. You can stow a few things like newspapers and magazines behind your seat, not in front, so if you're strapped in you've got to get up and go round. There's no elbow room so it's probably best to sit with your dining table up most of the time. Whoever invented it should be made to travel in it non-stop on a journey forever, rather like Dr Who! Everything else is fine. The BA staff were great, as usual.

There was a party of eight golfers, mature men, travelling to Phoenix with me. They were jolly enough but as the journey progressed they became noisier and noisier. Good humoured, good natured but loud. They were like sixth form boys on holiday flirting with the stewardesses who perhaps were a little too generous with the wine trolley. Don't get me wrong; they were pleasant, just noisy. Perhaps they were using their headsets and had no idea how loud they were speaking. That can happen. Oh, by the way, I don't think the word 'whisper' appears in any American dictionary!

It suddenly brought back to me an experience on one of my first visits to the United States over forty years before. I said America is a land of contrasts. Well Burning Tree Golf Club, near Washington left a mark on my memory that will prove indelible. I went there with the 1959 Ryder Cup team and we were hoping that President Eisenhower, who was a member, would find the time to come over and perhaps play with us. The clubhouse was not over-large, but carefully designed, neatly laid out and very comfortable. The hospitality was outstanding, but I noted for the first time the American preoccupation with 'How much money do you earn?' and 'How much weight are you putting on?' Cents and calories seemed the main conversational gambit. We had to go to a dinner given in our honour by the club; it was their annual Fall Dinner and we all dressed up in Ryder Cup blazers, white shirts, Ryder Cup ties, official slacks, black shoes, fingernails clean, hair brushed carefully, all very neat and tidy.

When we arrived outside the locker-room, David Thomas and I were greeted by the most tremendous thundering yells of 'Whooppee, whooppee! Arraboy!' coming from inside, and strains of music. We wondered what could possibly be happening. It sounded like some weird indoctrination rite. When we opened the door, there were four coloured musicians playing between rows of lockers and a gentleman standing in a corner wearing grey slacks with a tartan stripe down each side, a long, light-brown corduroy jacket and a string tie. He was stamping his foot to the tune of 'Dixie', leaping high in the air and blasting out these screams and whistles and yells of 'Whooppee!'

I looked at this in astonishment and turned to the chap standing by me and asked who this animated gentleman could be. I was told blithely that he was one of the best and most famous lawyers in the eastern states. Well, this was a good start to an evening which was to be wholly memorable. Here we stood in the locker-room under all the flags of different presidents of the club and famous members, admirals and generals and so on. All had their personal flags hanging from the beams, and there were drawings and caricatures all round the locker-room. We had a couple of drinks there and moved on to the dining room, where I was somewhat shattered to see the members of this fashionable club gathered for their Fall Dinner in shirt sleeves, open-necked shirts, leather or corduroy jackets – one of the most exclusive clubs in America all of a sudden looked like a NAAFI.

Suddenly I looked up to see two men dancing. They were identified as the president of a very large airline and the president of a very famous railroad. At last dinner was finished. Came the time for the awards to various members, first for the 'American Drinking Team'. It seemed that a bunch of the boys had gone on holiday to Florida and each day they had had a drinking competition. They all stood round and sang the Burning Tree song.

Finally came a parson, bishop of one of the counties around Washington, who was to speak for all the members who had died over the preceding twelve months, and this was the strangest experience of the evening. The first one he mentioned was John Smith 'who we all remembered; he had been with us for many years and a good pal to us all. And then one day, on the 14th July, nineteen hundred fifty-nine, as he was approaching the 11th green only 2 over par, the hand of Almighty God reached out and took him before he could play his chip shot. And there John Smith died but will always be remembered with fondness in our hearts.'

And while this was going on, the open-necked shirt brigade, the sweater wearers, the Davy Crockett jacket brigade were all weeping, some were cursing, some were saying, 'Ah, Jeez, Johnnie' – and all of them seemed to be trying to get another drink.

The reverend continued, 'I think we should put a plaque on the tree by the 11th saying "Here died John Smith: God rest his soul." ' This went on for eight or nine members of the club who had passed away.

Of course, although we made some fun of it all, we had seen America at perhaps its worst. If Khrushchev had seen the shenanigans at that club on that night, I wonder what he would have thought. Maybe it was a release from work, for all of them were responsible people. I have no doubt they worked very hard but this was not really America, just a slice of it, and for us it was rather an anti-climax; we had so looked forward to seeing this wonderful club.

The Burning Tree in 1959 was a once-in-a-lifetime experience, I doubt whether any American golf clubs are like that today.

In Arizona, I promise you, I saw fairways painted green. The terribly hot, dry sun just overpowers the grass, so the Americans, true to themselves, thought nothing of dyeing them, presumably on the theory that at least they could have them look like fairways.

And, a final question. America is the most powerful nation in the world yet it has the flimsiest lavatory paper! Why?

17

RYDER CUP COMMENTATOR

'It was not pleasant watching the over-partisan crowd enjoying their triumphalism'

I have described earlier my memories of the eight Ryder Cup matches when I was privileged to be a player. In those far-off days, of course, I represented 'Great Britain & Ireland' against the United States. My last match as a player was in 1969 and ten years later golfers from the British Isles had been supplemented by fellow professionals from the continent of Europe. We have had a Spanish captain and now one from Germany. I wonder what Henry Cotton – or Percy Alliss – would have made of that. But whatever the make-up of the teams, the Ryder Cup matches have always represented one of the ultimate tests of skill, and most certainly of the character and nerve of a professional golfer.

Two years after my retirement in 1969 Eric Brown was again the captain when the matches were played in St Louis, Missouri. Jay Hebert was the US captain and, in all truth, the result of a 5 point victory to the USA was by no means a crushing defeat, with many of the matches going to the final hole.

In 1973 I offered my services as referee, the matches were being played at Muirfield, and the result was a resounding victory to the US by 19 to 13.

Bernard Hunt captained the home team and Jack Burke the United States. Bernard Hunt, a dear friend and one of the most solid of citizens, played an extraordinary hand when it came to kitting out his players. Lined up for the team photograph, it looked for all the world as if they were competing with Joe Loss or the Ted Heath Band to play at the Palladium. As usual the first two days went fairly well but the singles went the United States' way although, once more, there were some close matches. Hunt's captaincy was very low key compared to the flamboyant Scot, Eric Brown. During this period, being captain was a four-year job and, once again, Hunt captained Great Britain & Ireland against an American side led by Arnold Palmer. This time the Americans won by a clear 10 points. Yet, again, there were some very close matches. For example, in the last of the singles, Norman Wood defeated Lee Trevino 2 and 1, a great victory and it was on this occasion Brian Barnes defeated Jack Nicklaus twice in one day.

The 1977 Ryder Cup at Royal Lytham & St Anne's was an interesting occasion and this time GB&I were led by Brian Huggett, the American captain being Dow Finsterwald. That year's matches were subject to a change in format – all four-somes on the first day, fourballs on the second and only singles played on the last day. Peter Oosterhuis continued his good play in Ryder Cup competition and Nick Faldo won his first single, defeating Tom Watson on the home hole.

Captain Huggett was very disappointed in the attitude of

some of his players. He was very verbal on this matter and perhaps that was why he was not asked to captain the side again, the honour going in 1979 to John Jacobs.

From 1979, GB&I had now become a European team but the result was much the same, a USA victory by 17 points to 11. The format was also changed, fourballs in the morning and foursomes in the afternoon. I think this was the beginning of five-hour rounds for foursomes, which has plagued us ever since. Greenbrier in West Virginia was the venue and Billy Casper captained the Americans. Seve Ballesteros and Antonio Garrido were the two Europeans who had made the team but in all truth they did not acquit themselves very well, winning 1 point between them. So perhaps, after all, bringing in European players had not produced the magic formula that some had thought. Incidentally, Jack Nicklaus was very instrumental in this idea. He felt the matches were dying on their feet. America was winning too often. What could be done to liven up the proceedings? Let's have more games for spectators to watch and introduce European players into the arena – and so it came to pass. But it didn't come off, not in 1979 anyway.

Suddenly, in 1981, when the matches were played at Walton Heath, things might have been very different. John Jacobs was brought in to captain the Europeans and Dave Marr the USA. Marr was quoted as saying he thought this was the most powerful team America had ever put together and, when you looked at their names and the way they performed, he wasn't far off the target. The end result was a win for the USA by 9 clear points. After the first day, things were very even. But day two was a golfing disaster for the home team, Langer and Pinero being the only winners of the second day morning fourballs, all four foursomes matches going to the US in the afternoon. The

European team was without Tony Jacklin and Seve Ballesteros, two of the finest players in the world at that time. To this day, I'm not absolutely certain what happened. Everyone seems to have a different version of events but, suffice to say, the introduction of Europeans into the side was not working.

Two years later, the matches were at the PGA National Club in Florida and suddenly there was light on the horizon. Tony Jacklin captained the Europeans, Jack Nicklaus the USA and if it hadn't been for a couple of master strokes by Calvin Peete and Lanny Wadkins for the United States, plus a couple of elementary mistakes by the European side, Europe would have notched up their first victory in years. I shall never forget the scenes of jubilation from the Americans as they grabbed victory from the jaws of defeat. On that occasion a super critic could have placed the blame firmly on the shoulders of the two Spaniards, Seve Ballesteros and José Maria Canizares, who, although they both secured half points, should have won.

But things were looking better. The matches were at the previously much criticised Belfry in 1985. Captain Jacklin retained his place; the Americans brought in Lee Trevino whose captaincy was criticised by his team for not communicating enough. He didn't see it that way; I think Trevino thought he'd got a very fine team and they didn't need much geeing up because it was virtually a foregone conclusion that his side would win. The European team that year contained Ballesteros, Pinero, Canizares from Spain and Langer from Germany. On this occasion the Europeans came through in fine style, Ballesteros and Pinero winning three of their four opening fourball and foursome matches and between them contributing $1\frac{1}{2}$ points on the final day. We also had José Rivero, so there were four Spaniards in the team; Rivero was brought in for the singles. He lost to Calvin Peete by one hole so he didn't disgrace himself.

In 1987 I had the honour of being the Captain of the Professional Golfers' Association. Tony Jacklin retained his captaincy of the Ryder Cup team and the Americans brought back Jack Nicklaus. One could almost see him riding a white charger into battle leading his troops into action to erase the memory of that horrible defeat at the Belfry, which surely was just a hiccup – it shouldn't have happened. Well, lo and behold, it happened again. By this time a young man called José Maria Olazabal had arrived on the scene and there began a most wonderful partnership with Seve. At the end of it all Europe won by 2 clear points. Jacklin's reputation had soared. He was the one who had insisted on everything being first-class, cashmere jackets, Concorde travel, bring your own caddies, bring your girlfriend, your boyfriend, your partner, call them what you will. 'I, Jacklin, will handle all the press and off-course distractions, you just concentrate on the golf.' And he carried it off in fine style. There's no doubt the Americans were shell-shocked at losing for the first time on home ground. Rivero once more made the team and, with partner Gordon Brand, beat Crenshaw and Scott Simpson in the first day's fourballs. Although he played well, that was the only point he secured during that series of matches but he was a good solid team member.

The matches returned to the Belfry in 1989. Jacklin was still captain but Ray Floyd had been brought in to gee up the American team. Jacklin, by this time, was being carried along on a wave of adulation. It amuses me now to look back at my retirement when it was suggested that Peter Alliss should be the Ryder Cup Captain. 'No, No,' someone said. 'He will make too much out of it and become commercial.' I smile now when I see the enormous commercialism that has come over the last eighteen years. The flagging fortunes of Jacklin were rejuvenated on a grand scale and that was just the start of things. The result in '89 was a tied match, 14 points apiece, so the European team retained the trophy. It was slightly disappointing not to win, there were lots of very close matches; in fact, of all the twelve singles, eight of them came to the final hole at the Belfry. The format for the singles had changed in 1979 when all twelve players competed on the final day unless one was injured and then that match was declared a half. There was an interesting bit of side play here. Each captain was asked to put the name of a player in a secret place and then, if one of the other team should injure themselves, the person the captain had selected did not play and that match was deemed a half. Some strange injuries took place! But, at the end of the day, it was the same for everyone.

In 1991 the matches went to a new development in South Carolina called Kiawah Island, a wondrous place all very new but, in the kindest possible way, out in the sticks. The result was a win for the United States by 1 point – 14½ to 13½. Captained by Dave Stockton, they enjoyed their win enormously. Bernard Gallacher was captain of the European team. The contingent included Seve, José Maria and Bernhard Langer. Gallacher had placed David Gilford's name on the secret list just in case anyone was injured, and sure enough someone was – Steve Pate of the USA – so that game was halved, much to the chagrin of Gilford who felt rather left out of things and with good cause. A shy but determined man, he appeared very much on the sidelines. The Europeans went into the final day's singles trailing well behind but suddenly things began to go their way. Nick Faldo beat Floyd, David Feherty conquered Payne Stewart, Colin Montgomerie got a most unlikely half with Mark Calcavecchia. But then two losses, José Maria to Paul Azinger and Steven

Richardson to Corey Pavin. Seve beat Wayne Levi, Ian Woosnam lost to Chip Beck, who had been a mighty man in this series, playing some incredible shots when they were most needed. Paul Broadhurst beat Mark O'Meara but Sam Torrance and Mark James both lost their matches 3 and 2. So it was down to Langer and Irwin coming up the last. Irwin hooked wildly into the crowd. Many of us thought the ball was gone forever but somehow or other it appeared in a hittable position. They made their way towards the green and at the end of it all Langer had a putt of about six feet to retain the Ryder Cup. It wasn't to be. It slid away to the right and the Americans, who'd looked very down, were suddenly full of elation. Dave Stockton, their captain, was dunked into the Atlantic Ocean and later stated that he never had any doubts, they were always in complete control of the situation, which was of course absolute nonsense. But, on reflection, I think it's a good thing the result went the way it did. Our side had to lose sometime and there were enough people supporting both teams round that final green, many fuelled by alcohol, who might have created a nasty scene if Langer had holed the putt. There could have been too much triumphalism.

The matches returned to the Belfry in 1993. The European captain was again Bernard Gallacher; Tom Watson was given the honour of leading the Americans. There was much criticism here that the matches were being played too often at the Belfry. Well there was a good reason for that. The Belfry was the home of the Professional Golfers' Association who owned the title of the Ryder Cup. There was a 400-bedroom hotel available for both teams, huge practice facilities, the course was situated in the middle of the country, with a good network of roads, a substantial airport only six miles away and, one thing that had never entered the equation years ago, it was easier to handle security.

Here again the matches were very close going into the third day's singles. This time it was Peter Baker who played some staggering golf. He'd been kept back by Gallacher for the singles and he didn't disappoint, winning by two holes. Sam Torrance had been sleepwalking in the middle of the night and bumped into a chest of drawers, or whatever, and was withdrawn with bruised ribs. Strangely enough the magic name in the hat as far the US was concerned was Lanny Wadkins. They were both withdrawn at the start of the day. Costantino Rocca threw away a golden opportunity of beating Davis Love. He appeared to be overtaken by nerves at the *moment critique*, on the 17th green. José Maria, at the end of the day, lost by a couple of holes to Ray Floyd. Tom Kite was invincible against Langer and Faldo let a few chances slip away in his match against Paul Azinger.

So the Americans had now held the trophy four years and we were due to visit them again at Oak Hill in 1995. Lanny Wadkins was the US captain and Bernard Gallacher was given yet another opportunity to lead the Europeans to victory. Now here was a great turn up. Oak Hill is a fine course, America had a very formidable side. Once again David Gilford had qualified for the Europeans; how he'd grown in stature since his last appearance. Partnering Ballesteros, they beat Brad Faxon and Peter Jacobsen 4 and 3 in the first day's afternoon fourball; then on the second day in the foursomes alongside Bernhard Langer, he beat Corey Pavin and Tom Lehman but, when partnered by Seve, he lost to Jay Haas and Phil Mickelson. For the life of me, I couldn't understand Gallacher's thinking. The way he kept chopping and changing his fourball and foursome partnerships.

Seve led out the singles and lost 4 and 3 to Tom Lehman.

David Gilford beat Brad Faxon, the master putter, by one hole at the tail end of the field, Bernhard Langer lost to Cory Pavin and Per-Ulrik Johansson lost to Mickelson. But the European side won by 1 point. The play during those third day singles was memorable. As always in matchplay, mistakes magnify the situation but add to the excitement. Curtis Strange collapsed against Nick Faldo but Faldo had to keep going and play the shots to secure a win. The shot he played to the final hole and the five-foot putt to win the match were masterly. Irishman Philip Walton's victory over Jay Haas was no less superb, coming when everything was so finely balanced.

Over the years of the Ryder Cup competition I have never felt that our home side has ever had its strongest team, for a variety of reasons. And when we have secured victory, it's only happened because the 'lesser lights' have played their hearts out. Peter Baker, Paul Way, Philip Walton, David Gilford, Costantino Rocca, all of them having gone through some very iffy moments, suddenly managed an unlikely point that swayed the balance. How magnificent they all were.

In 1997 the matches left British shores for the first time. Valderrama in southern Spain was the venue and naturally a Spaniard had to captain the side and who better than Seve. The American captain was the vastly experienced Tom Kite. Going into the third day singles everything looked very rosy. The Europeans only needed a handful of points to secure victory. Although Ian Woosnam was annihilated by Fred Couples 8 and 7 in the top match, Per-Ulrik Johansson beat Davis Love 3 and 2 and, much against the run of opinion, Rocca beat Tiger Woods 4 and 2. Thomas Bjorn halved with Justin Leonard when, in all truth, he should have won but then a run of three losses began to look rather ominous. Langer steadied the ship by beating Brad Faxon but then Lee Westwood lost to Jeff Maggert. Colin Montgomerie could only halve with Scott Hoch and Nick Faldo lost a weird game 3 and 2 to Jim Furyk who holed chip shots, bunker shots and did the most extraordinary things over the last few holes while, at the end of the field, Ignacio Garrido lost heavily to Tom Lehman.

Incidentally, it was at this match that the Garridos joined the Alliss family as the only ones to have had father and son competing in Ryder Cup play. Suffice to say the Alliss family managed twelve appearances between us; I like to think it will be a long time before that record is passed.

Victory at last for Europe – what jubilation. I can see the crowd now running on to the 18th green hither and thither, matches conceded, nobody knew what was going on, complete disarray and Jaime Ortiz-Patino, the president and founder, desperately trying to keep the elegant ladies with their high-heeled shoes off his sacred 18th green.

Back in America in 1999, Ben Crenshaw was their captain this time, Mark James for the Europeans – what a strange contrast they were. Ben did some weird and wonderful things. He produced some incredible clothing for the Americans to wear and the amount of patriotism displayed by some of the players and, indeed, the gallery beggared belief. Contrary to what was said afterwards, it was not a happy atmosphere. Elements of the crowd were very rowdy and unsettling. Going into the singles everything was going Europe's way. Could they win yet again in the United States? The answer was no. The Americans came out with all guns blazing on that final day, the first six matches all going to the United States who played some magnificent golf, whereas some of the play by the Europeans was slapdash and nervy. The situation overtook them; it was not pleasant watching the over-partisan crowd, enjoying their triumphalism. I felt, if this was what the Ryder Cup was coming to, perhaps it was time to call it a day.

At the prize-giving ceremony Crenshaw pontificated as to how, once again, the game of golf was the winner and how everyone was delighted with the result, which was absolute nonsense. Looking back over the years there was a time when the matches created little or no interest in the United States. Being matchplay, it was difficult to get the timing right for the host television network. Suddenly the European side began to win. Interest was renewed and now the Ryder Cup has become one of the biggest events in the world of sport.

I found the 1999 matches unsavoury from the moment that Nick Faldo's good-luck message was binned by James. What the actual situation was there I'd like to have known. And then Mark James produced his book *Into the Bear Pit*, which was an interesting read but certainly did nothing to cement relations. And did things go 'missing' from the visiting team's locker room while the closing ceremonies were being performed? We never seemed to get to the bottom of that, did we?

The Ryder Cup was cancelled in 2001, due to the disasters at the twin towers in New York. The match was then moved to even years and we're told that it's going to continue that way; I thought that was the wrong thing to do. I believe they should have played the matches two years in a row to get back to an odd dated year, as happened in the Solheim Cup.

Back to the Belfry in 2002 – Captain Sam Torrance led the way and what a wonderful result it was, again very much against the run of play. Curtis Strange, the American captain, and Sam Torrance did everything except slash their wrists to let their blood mingle. They swore eternal love and friendship and, once again, the old hackneyed phrase came out that golf was the real winner. I don't think for a moment Curtis Strange ever envisaged his team would lose. He felt certain he had the men to do the job but they didn't come up trumps. He got a tremendous amount of criticism, some of it unjustified.

The Ryder Cup of 2004 continued to flow Europe's way. It really has been a remarkable run of form over the last twenty years. The popular German, Bernhard Langer, captained the side, becoming only the second European to be awarded that honour. He did a spectacular job, seemingly creating a wonderful feeling of camaraderie within his European team, which caused many Americans much consternation. Why? Well, they really find it hard to understand how such a hodgepodge of nations, all with very different characteristics, can come together every two years and play so brilliantly for each other. Every one of the European team was a hero, one or two slightly more than others, but to win by such a margin in the United States in front of their fanatical spectators was, indeed, a wondrous achievement.

The American captain, Hal Sutton, came in for much criticism. From the moment he stepped on to the tee sporting a huge Stetson he very quickly became the butt of many snide remarks. Some of his wounds were perhaps self-inflicted: for example pairing Tiger Woods and Phil Mickelson together for a couple of matches brought much ridicule, as these two great players don't always appear to see eye to eye; but just suppose they had jelled? If both of them had set out with a different mind-set, trying to make sure that their game matched or surpassed the other, it might have turned out to be a wonderfully bold experiment, which would have been heralded by one and all, and Captain Sutton would have been a hero.

It did appear as if the crowds, early on, took a shine to the Europeans. Why? Because they gave some of their time, signed autographs, caps, scarves, shirts, whereas the American team stuck to the tour policy of only signing in designated areas and for a limited amount of time. Not much, you might think, but it certainly created a better atmosphere for the Europeans than they had experienced on other occasions.

It was a glorious three days. Langer then announced that he had no desire to carry on and be captain again when the matches are played in Ireland in 2006. He has it in his mind to be a member of the team. I feel that unless he becomes a captain's 'pick', his chances of playing his way into the team are slight, much as I admire his tenacity and strength of thought.

I find vying for the captaincy rather vulgar – various people putting their names forward and information leaked out that so and so has more friends on the Ryder Cup Committee than so and so. Many big names and worthies have been passed over throughout the years, going back to Christy O'Connor Snr, John Panton, Max Faulkner, Ken Bousfield and, dare I say, yours truly. *They* say that to be a successful captain you have to be 'in the swim', know the players, have their respect. Well, I'm sure you can gain players' respect without necessarily being 'in the swim'. For example, high on my list of captains for the future would be Sandy Lyle, who won both our Open and the Masters, and is surely worthy of the captaincy. If you're looking for an Irishman, Christy O' Connor Jnr would make a good fist of it. He certainly has plenty of charisma.

Now, however, we know that the new captain for 2006 will be Ian Woosnam, a former stalwart of the Ryder Cup team, who was elected ahead of the other front-runner Nick Faldo, though Faldo has been chosen to take over in 2008. Ian Woosnam has knowledge and the respect of the players, and Sam Torrance, who captained the Ryder Cup team in 2002, had backed him. We *need* another victory in Ireland, and Woosnam will be most important to our chances of success.

As a curious footnote, I might add that in 1985 I had a letter from a friend, John Bowles, who had a jewellery and antique business based in Hatton Garden. He furnished me with some interesting information about the history of the Ryder Cup Trophy itself. The main body of the Cup was hallmarked in 1926. The lid was separately hallmarked and made in 1930. It is well documented there was an official match between the professionals of Great Britain and the United States in 1926 with the home side winning comfortably $13\frac{1}{2}$ to $1\frac{1}{2}$. It was such a success in terms of international friendship that a regular competition was established through Samuel Ryder, a seed merchant from St Albans who commissioned the trophy. It was made and the first event proper was played in 1927 so that makes sense of the 1926 hallmark. It's a known fact that Abe Mitchell, Sam Ryder's personal professional teacher, modelled for the golfer posing on top of the lid. Photographs with the lid prior to 1930 are in existence, so why was the present lid made four years after the Cup? There are no enlightening records in the PGA offices or the maker's workshop. The only man who could possibly have solved the mystery, apprenticed to the workshop at the time of manufacture, died in 1985. The only conclusion is that the original lid was lost or badly damaged and had to be replaced. It can very easily happen. The trophy triumphantly waved on high, the loose lid topples, the damage is done.

18

A GOLFER'S TRAVELS

'We got a sight of Everest on our way to Kathmandu, a tricky little course with dozens of monkeys everywhere'

Never did I, for a moment, contemplate when I first read that letter from Ray Lakeland of the BBC all those years ago, that the world of television would take me down so many paths and to so many countries doing golf commentary that has led on to so many other things, including *Pro-Celebrity Golf*, *Around with Alliss* and, perhaps the most spectacular of all, *A Golfer's Travels*. I find it hard to believe that last series happened eight years ago. It started so quietly with a letter from Sarah Dacre, the CEO of Clearwater Images, who wrote saying she was putting together an idea for a television series which will take us round the world to glamorous places, talking to famous people from various walks of life. It was an ambitious scheme, so much so that Roy Cooper, my accountant partner, and I wondered if it would truly ever get off the ground. But we hadn't realised the sheer doggedness of Sarah! She found a wonderful sponsor in the

Rover Car Group, which is now under the umbrella of MG-Rover, based at Longbridge near Birmingham. They were the most excellent of sponsors, plus the finished item appealed to them particularly as they'd entered an ocean-going yacht for the Round the World Race of that year.

We started off with Dame Kiri Te Kanawa at Loch Lomond. We had some great opening shots, not least of which were of the great lady herself arriving on the little mail boat that chugs up and down the Loch depositing mail for the various island-dwellers dotted around this wondrous stretch of water. Next came His Royal Highness the Duke of York, whom I first interviewed in the wonderful surrounds of Skibo Castle. We then played at Royal Dornoch in the foulest of weather. We even had the local minister, in fact the Right Reverend James Simpson, Moderator of the Church of Scotland (equivalent to an Archbishop), making up a three-ball. But he had no influence on the weather. Just shows you can't trust anybody! And then on to Durness, a picturesque little 9-hole golf course right at the top of Scotland (actually the most northerly course in Britain) where I played with Tattie, a fish porter in the local port and a real character.

Arizona was next. A great change from the rain and winds of Scotland. Here I met with Admiral Alan Shepard, one of the first Americans in space and leader of the 1971 Apollo XIV mission to the moon, and we played a few holes among the red rocks of Sedona. The Admiral showed off his golfing prowess by playing a golf shot on the moon, his ball is possibly still bouncing! It was then on to the Desert Mountain Golf Club near Scotsdale to play with Vice-President Dan Quayle, a gifted low-handicap golfer.

Las Campanas, in New Mexico, was our next stop. This was a

development under the banner of Lyle Anderson of Loch Lomond fame. Our guest here was Gene Hackman – what a delight he was! I'd been alerted to the fact that he could be rather uncommunicative but, in the event, he helped me enormously. We sat and chatted in a restaurant he part-owned at that time, overlooked by his paintings. I hadn't realised what a talented artist he is. In fact, he did a pencil drawing of yours truly which hangs proudly in my study.

I then flew to South Africa where, in Cape Town, I met up with Sir Garry Sobers, one of cricket's most famous sons. We played on a beautiful golf course, Steenberg, among the vines of one of the oldest wineries in South Africa, before I went on to meet Gary Player at the Lost City course, which he designed at Sun City. I played a couple of holes on that course with Andrew Mlangeni. He had been imprisoned with Nelson Mandela on Robbin Island for more than twenty-five years. Both men had poor eyesight, the result of many hours a day spent working in a limestone quarry. The glare of the sun had taken its toll, no designer sunglasses on offer there. Although well into his seventies, he appeared to be as strong as a lion. He'd done some caddying as a boy and had progressed to playing golf, good golf, too. I'm not sure he didn't get down to scratch. He was a remarkably calm man. He loved golf, was a good companion and cared about 'his Africa'. He loved his country and was desperate for things to work out. He thought they would but it needed much time, effort and goodwill to succeed.

I also played, on that trip, a few holes with F.W. de Klerk, an enthusiastic, if poor, golfer. During our few hours together he impressed me as a man who was determined that things should work out between the black and white communities; by now the genie was well and truly out of the bottle and, in some cases, out of control. It was shortly after this de Klerk's marital problems came to public notice and since then he's taken a back seat. I wish both him and Andrew Mlangeni well for, in my short time with them, they struck me as people who knew what was right and what was fair, but also knew how difficult it was to achieve their grand aims for South Africa.

Time to move on to Hawaii, that collection of extraordinary islands in the middle of the Pacific where on one side it never rains and on the other it never stops. I was privileged to play Mauna Lani with the Governor of the State of Hawaii, Ben Cayetano at Turtle Bay and then flew on to Koele Golf Club on the island of Lanai. Lanai is an extraordinary island with two spectacular golf courses, one at sea level and one up the mountain. The one up the mountain is called the Challenge at Manele. Our guest there was the incredible pop icon Alice Cooper, a man who had come through the dark days of alcoholism to resurrect his life, fame and fortune in the most splendid way. What a good companion he was.

On to Kapalua Maui, still in Hawaii, and the links at Kapalua for Hootie and the Blowfish, a pop group that had been together for years but had suddenly taken America by storm. All of them enjoyed a game of golf and organised their lives around the various Pro-Ams.

I've visited the Hawaiian islands a number of times over the years and am amazed that the pineapple industry, which used to be one of the largest in the world, has now sunk to virtually nothing. Why? The usual problems – cost. Its demise has brought about a whole new industry in Thailand and other parts of Asia. Seems ridiculous, doesn't it, because of lower wages you can harvest, box and ship fruit from an extra couple of thousand miles away and still put it into the shops and supermarkets cheaper than it can be grown in your own land.

Spain was next where I spent time with Jaime Ortiz-Patino at Valderrama. How he loves the club – his baby. On leaving the grandeur of Valderrama, I visited Rio Tinto, the first place where golf was played in Spain. This was the most basic of golf courses where youngsters learn their skills and try to emulate their Spanish heroes. Still in Spain, I played with Steve Redgrave, then holder of four Olympic Gold Medals who was going for a fifth in the Olympics in Sydney.

On to Thailand and the Blue Canyon Golf Club with Christopher Lee. Christopher and I are old friends. Many's the time he played in our *Pro-Celebrity* series and, once again, I found him interesting and entertaining. He'd brought along his charming wife, Gita, a statuesque Dane who, when they married, was one of the world's top models – a very sparky lady.

On to the beach resort of Hua Hin where I caught up with David Campese, one of Australia's greatest rugby union footballers. It was a remarkable place with a magnificent health spa nestling by the edge of the Indian Ocean, one of the best in the world. I couldn't resist the opportunity to make a journey to look at 'the bridge over the river Kwai', not at all as I imagined it, nor as it was portrayed in the great movie with Alec Guinness and William Holden. It felt very strange to stand on this narrow-gauge rail track imagining the terrible things that had gone on some fifty years before. There's a small museum which, although simple, portrays in vivid detail the horrors of the time. What an amazing trip that was.

The series was completed and appeared on BBC2, BSkyB and other satellite channels in the UK. It also appeared nearly everywhere else in the world and still runs to this day on airline in-flight entertainment through the Far East, eighteen international airlines screening the series on seat backs.

Sarah Dacre has high hopes that a new sponsor will be found for a further series. A lot was learnt from that first run. Any outdoor filming creates problems. There are the weather conditions, everything from rain to light, too much sun, not enough sun, too much noise. You know the sort of thing, just where you're in the middle of a key piece a helicopter appears out of the blue and ruins the shot. Then there's the cameraman's great fear, a hair in the gate – no I didn't know what it meant either but evidently a human hair somehow or other gets in the lens and when you take a shot it gives the impression of looking through a plate glass window with a huge crack running through the middle of it. If it's not that, it's battery change – all part of the great adventure of film and television.

The still photographs of this great expedition were taken by Brian Morgan, the Scottish photographer who's made a great reputation for himself producing coffee table books with the most splendid pictures of golf courses around the world.

Another remarkable trip began on 18 November 2000 and ended on 10 December. It had been organised by PrivatAir, a company based in Geneva, who had at their disposal a fleet of magnificent aircraft and, among other things, flew famous football teams around the world and did special assignments for the many sheikdoms in the Middle East. The idea was to get a group of golfers together, I would be the host and we would have the Millennium Golf Tour to end all golf tours.

We met at Stansted to be greeted by a fine crew and a splendid looking aircraft that could hold up to 150 people geared down to forty-two seats. It was a mixed bag of people, a number from the UK, some from Italy, half a dozen from Poland, who were then based in the United States – a very interesting collection indeed. I shall conceal the names to protect the innocent!

We set off and our first destination was Bermuda. The itinerary shows that we flew, whenever possible, during daylight hours, a great help. Wondrous hotels had been laid on for our route and golf of the highest quality had been arranged. We played eighteen holes at the Mid Ocean Club and, with the sun shining and a brisk wind blowing, it tested all of us. But it made a superb start to our magic carpet ride.

From there we went to Cancun on the northern tip of Mexico. It was an amazing sight, skyscrapers everywhere, golf courses popping up. I was told by the locals that fifteen years before there had hardly been anything there, rather like the early days of Miami Beach, La Manga or, nearer home, the Sandbanks Peninsula round Poole Harbour. It poured with rain so the golf was off and we spent a couple of hours in the clubhouse where I regaled my new friends with tales of wonder about golf yesterday and today. They were absolutely spellbound!

From there it was on to Las Vegas, one of the new Seven Wonders of the World. We played on that course which has a collection of replicas from the world's great holes, although I didn't think their idea of the 17th hole at St Andrews was anything like the real thing. But, the sun shone and the company was pleasant. Then it was up and on to the Monterey Peninsula where Spyglass Hill beckoned. The beauty of this particular plane was that the runway at Monterey was long enough to accommodate us so we were literally only a thousand yards away from the golf course, very handy. Monterey and its peninsula are very special but it was time to move on to Hawaii, to see the memorial to the carnage of Pearl Harbor and remember that day of infamy.

On to Fiji for fuel – no sign of Vijay, he must have been out practising! Off to Sydney. The Olympic Games had just taken place – and yes, Steve Redgrave had won a fifth gold medal. What a transformation had come over the city, new roads, highways, byways, hotels, all magnificent. We drove out to La Perouse, a splendid course right on the water at Botany Bay. We were almost round when the heavens opened and it was back to the clubhouse for another little lecture from 'Uncle Alliss'. Our Australian friends were delighted to see us and made us more than welcome.

It was time to strike out north. We got special dispensation to land at Ayers Rock. What an extraordinary sight that was; you couldn't imagine it hurtling through the sky and eventually crashing into our planet. It is seven or eight kilometres round and goodness knows how deep it is buried in the ground. It was round and very shiny and I'm told a lot of people have climbed up and fallen off! Very silly!

From there we flew north over Darwin and on to Bali, a sumptuous hotel and delightful people. Then it was Agra and a view of the Taj Mahal, amazing history and an amazing place. The locals could get in for the equivalent of 5p but visitors were charged about a tenner – well I suppose that helps the economy. To get in you had to run a gauntlet of beggars, some of them horrifically deformed. Vendors selling all sorts of junk reminded me of standing outside the Vatican years ago.

Time to move on and we got a sight of Everest on our way to Kathmandu. The sun was shining, the sky was blue and there was the familiar peak standing out so magnificently. I was amazed the Himalayan mountain range seemed to go on and on and on forever. Eventually a touchdown in Kathmandu and we were in another world. Hugh Scanlon would have described it as clean poverty. The amazing thing, there were no beggars but everything looked very impoverished. A new hotel had just opened, American-owned and very well run, not a million miles, would you believe, from the site of that 'Little Yellow Idol to the North of Kathmandu'. We wandered round one of the temples as night fell listening to the tinkling of the bells and the chanting of the monks. All in all, Kathmandu was an amazing experience. We played golf on the King's course, which was run by an ex-admiral from the Indian navy, a very attractive, tricky little course with dozens of monkeys everywhere. You had to have a fore caddy to make sure they didn't steal your golf balls. Wonder why they did that? I didn't see any of them playing.

Across the desert, leaving the mountain ranges behind, we touched down in Dubai, a place I'd never been before. I'm not too sure I wouldn't put that in my modern list of Great Wonders of the World. We stayed at the Burge Arab Hotel, a great edifice that looks like a dhow sail standing out in the ocean, hundreds of feet high. It boasts about seven stars of comfort and I'm not surprised. We were met by a fleet of white Rolls-Royces and Bentleys. We played at the Yacht Club and just stood about open-mouthed looking at this manmade creation in the middle of nowhere. Everything appeared to be very politically stable. Of course, there were many rules and regulations about what you could and could not do, how, what and where you could invest. But they're very mindful that, over the next twenty to thirty years, things may change dramatically. The government was already setting out its stall so that, in time, Dubai would be a major financial centre, an ideal stop-off between Europe and the Far East. They seem to have everything under control and it surely augurs well for their future.

It was time to leave and another day flight across Europe,

landing at Stansted at five o'clock in the afternoon. It was dark by then, but the journey across the deserts, Greece, the Alps and over France was something to remember. It was a privilege to be part of it. Good companions, never a cross word, some good golf, some nice friendships made, but not something you'd do every other year, it was certainly one of the greatest experiences of my life and looking back I feel sure that the short time I spent in Kathmandu was one of the most intriguing times of all.

Perhaps I should end this chapter with the 'Travellers' Ten Commandments', which we would all do well to remember.

1 Thou shalt not expect to find things as thou hast them at home, for thou hast left home to find things different.
2 Thou shalt not take anything too seriously for a carefree mind is the beginning of a fine holiday.
3 Thou shalt not let other tourists get on thy nerves for thou art paying out good money to enjoy thyself.
4 Remember to take only half the clothes thou thinkest thou needest.
5 Know at all times where thy passport is for a person without a passport is a person without a country.
6 Remember that if we had been expected to stay in one place we would have been created with roots.
7 Thou shalt not worry for he that worrieth hath no pleasure – few things are ever fatal.
8 When in Rome thou shalt be prepared to do somewhat as the Romans do.
9 Thou shalt not judge the people of a country by the one person who hast given thee trouble.
10 Remember thou art a guest in the other lands and he that treateth his host with respect shall be honoured.

19

THE BBC CREW

'The BBC's biggest outside event by far is the Open Championship or a royal funeral'

I've enjoyed my time enormously at the BBC and can't believe that more than forty years have slipped by since I first went up into that rather crude box on stilts halfway down the 18th fairway at Royal Birkdale.

In sport the BBC have been lucky: David Coleman, Harry Carpenter, both brilliant, Sue Barker, Clare Balding, Dougie Donnelly from Scotland and, of course, Steve Rider, who is outstanding. Over the last couple of years there have been several shake-ups within the sports hierarchy; Peter Salmon taking over as Head of Sport and a lot of very competent women entering the arena of television at the highest level. The golf team is brilliantly led by Barbara Slater whose father, Bill, played soccer for England and Wolverhampton Wanderers for many years.

It's interesting to look back and compare the personnel of 1985 with today. In 1985 the Controller of BBC1 was Michael

Grade, now back in the fold, and BBC2 was controlled by Graeme McDonald. The Director of Television was Bill Cotton. Their places were taken in 2003 by Lorraine Heggessy, Jane Root and Jana Bennett. Dick Francis was the big man in radio in 1985. By 2003 it was Jenny Abramsky. There's no doubt programmes have changed in personnel, content and style.

For Peter Salmon, it couldn't have been easy to follow in the footsteps of Jonathan Martin who reigned for so many years as Head of Sport in magnificent style, a small, wiry man whose devotion to sport was endless. The great thing about Jonathan was that for 98 per cent of the time you knew exactly where you stood with him. Perhaps on occasions he was a little slow to say 'well done' to the troops and maybe on others a shade too hasty to criticise but, on balance, his great strength was that he cared passionately. He was a keen negotiator and knew how important it was for the BBC to have top quality sport on its network, be it rugby, cricket, golf, the Boat Race, motor racing or other major sporting events. There were some who thought the BBC Sports bubble had burst. Well, it has not burst but you could argue that some of the air has escaped over the last few years. Although, when you look at the list of top sporting events that come under the BBC's umbrella, it is still very formidable, Auntie needs to be careful.

The BBC's biggest event by far is the Open Championship and it concerns me that a number of footballers, rugby players and the like have been brought in to do interviews, the idea being to produce a different view of what it's like being at this great event. Supposedly, a directive came from on high which read, 'I don't care what you do, just make it different and attract a younger audience if you can.' Well they're certainly trying to do that, not only here but on the ABC Network in the United

States where top golf producer Jack Graham has recently been 'let go'. Don't ask me why. Sometimes it's not easy for old dogs to learn new tricks. For many years the BBC Golf Department was produced and directed by John Shrewsbury and Alistair Scott, both of whom took the opportunity of early retirement, although they are still there to help out if needed.

When Jonathan Martin was Head of BBC Sport, he did like different sounding voices and accents – Scottish, English, female and, if possible, American. Alex Hay from Musselburgh was introduced to the BBC by David Coleman, one of the most famous sporting broadcasters Britain has ever produced. Alex's commentating career began in 1978 with the Open Championship at St Andrews, which Jack Nicklaus won. My wife, Jackie, clearly remembers the first time she ever met him. He introduced himself saying, 'Hello, my name's Alex Hay. I'm after your husband's job, ha ha ha.' Now Alex denies this vehemently. 'Only a joke – only a joke,' he cried *much* later!

Television certainly opened up a whole new world to Alex and, one could say, a different lifestyle. He'd been a golf professional for many years, coming up the hard way, building a reputation as an excellent teacher, aided and abetted to the full by his wife, Anne. I have great respect for him, not least for what he achieved at Woburn where he started life as the golf professional and ended up Managing Director. He became a very important cog in the Woburn Estates public persona. When Alex took over the club it was not making any money. Applying good commonsense and sound Scottish business instincts, he made a profit of some £30,000 for the club in the first year. The next year he doubled it and then it was trebled. Suddenly the accountants appeared out of the woodwork wanting to know what his projected figures were for the coming year.

He told them to hold on. 'Let me get on with it my own way and I'll do the best I can for you, the family and the members.' His best, although he had some detractors, was in my opinion magnificent. Now retired from the club, he and his wife are honorary members; Alex remains on the board as a consultant.

Oddly enough, I somehow suspected that all through his halcyon years there was a vein of insecurity running through him which was hard to pinpoint. He has a very fierce temper, which I've been fortunate to see on only two or three occasions over the twenty-five years of our friendship.

He's very careful with money, which is sensible, and he has a first-class business brain. He owns Galloways Restaurant in the heart of Woburn, which is run by his son, David, and his wife, Chantelle. His second son lives near Salisbury in Wiltshire and works for the local council as a surveyor connected, if memory serves me right, with the highways and byways department.

Unfortunately, some people at the BBC wanted him out. I say without fear or favour I fought tooth and nail to keep him in but that was one battle I lost, although there's a possibility he may substitute if someone falls ill, and he may participate in what's called 'interactive television' at the Open Championship in 2005.

There's no doubt there was a movement afoot for some time to relieve Alex of his duties. 'They' said he was getting too old and his voice sounded weary. It was rumoured that one of Britain's top management agencies complained to the BBC that Alex's analysis of one of their player's swings was not satisfactory – he was out of date, not keeping up with modern methods. They had no desire for Alex to comment on whether that particular player had a good swing or where his faults lay. Personally, I feel Alex Hay has one of the best analytical brains and is one of the best coaches/teachers I've ever come across, quite as good as Butch Harmon or David Leadbetter, and I've often wondered why he didn't continue his teaching career – then perhaps he's had enough. It's been a pleasure working with him over the years and I'd like to thank him for all the fun we've had. He was a good travelling companion and I know he will be missed by many.

Ken Brown is our man in the field. He tells us if the putt is uphill, in which case 'he'll have to give it a good rap' or downhill, in which case 'he'll just have to nudge it'. Then there's the putt that'll have to be 'laid off a bit to the right'. This refers to how wide of the target the player must aim if the ball is to follow an irresistible route to the hole. Ken also explains how this bunker or that has to be avoided, the wind's direction and strength, the quality of the lie, the length of the grass, which club he recommends the player to use and so on and so forth. Knowledgable and confident is our Ken, a Harpenden boy now in his mid forties with a good tournament record in the late seventies and eighties, perhaps the highlight of which was winning the Southern Open in the USA in 1987, along with four victories on the European Tour. When playing he had a very impressive short game and wielded an ancient rusty headed hickory shafted putter with devastating effect.

He began his TV commentary career with Sky but was snaffled by the BBC although he still works for a number of other networks (he does not have an exclusive contract with the BBC). When in partnership with Mark James (which has become more frequent over the last couple of years) their joint commentary can take them on flights of fancy.

Ken Brown is more of a complex character than you might think but sadly he seems to have lost his nerve for playing golf under prying eyes. I've asked him on a number of occasions if he'd come to the Grand Match, a splendid affair over two days played down at the Royal Cinque Ports Golf Course just north of Deal in Kent. Old Ryder Cuppers and, perhaps not so old, ex-Walker Cup players get together for a bit of fun and frolics, but he feels he is no longer able to perform in public. He tells me he knocks a ball around with his boys. They all adore fishing and every year he takes the family away. They find a cottage by a loch, fish all day and generally potter about, perhaps having a few holes of golf in the evening. Ken must have a very understanding wife but then perhaps she fishes as well. A good companion.

Julian Tutt is a relative newcomer to the TV golf team, having come to us from the radio. A good broadcaster with a beautifully modulated voice, he is a very handy single figure golfer and has aspirations of having a go on the European Senior circuit. He is another of our on-course operators; out there in all weathers, giving yardages to the flag and generally outlining the problems the players face, along with developing his good interviewing technique, which is far harder than a lot of people realise.

Beverly Lewis is our lady on the fairways and I have a high regard for her skills. At the time of writing she's vice captain of the Professional Golfers' Association and will be captain in 2005, the first woman to achieve that post and a great honour. It surely cannot be easy going into decidedly male bastions, making dozens of speeches. In her position it would be very easy to upset someone or for someone to upset her; there are plenty of silly people about who could well patronise her, perhaps unintentionally. Her husband, Ken, is a first-class artist specialising in golf scenes. I'm surprised that he has not become more famous, for his work is as good as any and better than most.

And what of the anchor men, the true professionals who get the golf programmes on and off the air? This is very critical, particularly in America. The first one I encountered was the BBC's Cliff Michelmore, a product of service broadcasting at the end of World War Two. We became great friends and now, although well advanced in years, Cliff still manages to play a few holes at the Petersfield Golf Club where, on a good day, he can still supplement his pension with a few net birdies! He taught me a great deal – a lovely man and Simon Alliss's godfather. Steve Rider, today's man in this all-important role, is a most accomplished broadcaster, unflappable and with a deep knowledge of golf and sport in general. He is a pleasure to work with.

Then there are the unsung heroes like Karen Williamson. She should have some grand title or other; she's in charge of the golf department so she answers the phone, does all the bits and pieces of admin, goes to every tournament. She just organises things and she's so brilliant I can't write about golf on the BBC without mentioning her name. Karen is retiring this year and going to live in York where she has relatives. She's been a tower of strength within the department, particularly for me – a godsend organising tickets and all sorts of things. I shall miss her greatly although a few may rejoice at her going!

At this point I must also mention special colleagues Dave Bowden, Jo McCusker, Sally Richardson and Chris White for their expertise and Peter Wright, engineering manager, responsible for all the lines and cables. He is a master technician.

Michael Hughesdon was another of our fairway warriors for many years. His father, Charles, was very prominent in the world of commerce and Florence Desmond, his mother, an outstanding actress in the thirties and forties, a real West End star. Mike matured late and developed into a first-class player.

Past captain of Sunningdale Golf Club and a member of various R&A committees, a good companion who would help anyone in need, he and his wife Carol are delightful characters. I was sorry when the BBC in their wisdom decided that they wanted a new voice on the fairways. I don't think Michael ever got the help and encouragement he needed but he still does interactive TV for the BBC at the Open Championship, so he's not entirely lost to us.

There are a number of others who flit in and out of our broadcasts. Maureen Madill, who does a lot of work for Radio 5 Live is a first-class coach. She has a great knowledge of the game of golf and a good turn of phrase. Laura Davies, one of the most influential figures in women's golf, has also appeared with us at the Open Championship – in her case, she's still so busy playing at the top level that I don't imagine we will see much of her over the immediate years ahead. John Hawksworth is occasionally on hand for the Open week and then sometimes we have Seve adding his special touch to the broadcast, plus Jean Van der Velde and Sam Torrance giving their own perspective.

I have not mentioned Peter Alliss as part of that close-knit BBC golf team, which I have been for so many years. Commentary on the game has been so much a part of my life that I should say something about my approach to that gentle art. Someone I admired greatly on television was Jack Hargreaves, who was a natural television broadcaster. I tried to work in his style. His show *Out of Town* for Southern TV, based in Southampton, was superb, so simple, informative and fun. He sat in his garden shed, a battered old hat on his head, a beard, rough clothes, smoking his pipe and talking about country matters. He'd take you ploughing, harvesting, fishing and walking through the countryside, and show you how to make things and tie knots, but it was his style that fascinated me. Some people insisted he was rather bogus because he didn't really know how to do all these things. I didn't care – I didn't care at all. I was captivated by the man.

Above all in my commentary, I try to suggest to the viewers that I'm sitting up in the grandstand with friends describing the scene below. It seems to work.

In preparation I try not to get to the course until about eleven, have a quick look around, watch a few players, 'feel' the pace of the greens, creep round the back of the gallery to see how things are progressing on the practice ground. I'm not one for barging into the practice area, parading up and down talking and shaking hands with one and all. I feel sorry for the paying customers because sometimes they can't see anybody practise for the gaggle of caddies, gurus, sport psychologists, psychiatrists, managers, trainers and general hangers-on all standing in the way.

I'm often asked why I don't socialise more with the players, spend time in the locker-room picking up bits of gossip. Well, that is not my style. Do theatre critics spend hours chatting with the various stars? Of course, they may have a friendship with one or two, but I don't think it's possible to give a fair appraisal if you're continually on a close social level. I agree, sometimes it would be nice if I had a few snippets of up-to-date information but is it life or death that he's changed his putter or caddie? I'm not in the business of promoting new golf clubs or other equipment. That's why I keep out of the way, observe from a distance, make my own judgments. I believe it can be tricky for a commentator to be too closely associated with the players.

As I explained in an earlier chapter, commenting on golf is not as straightforward as it may appear. This was brought home to me at the 2004 Masters where I thought we, in commentary, had done well. I thought Ken Brown and Australian Wayne Grady were in first-class form, Steve Rider was his usual out-standing self and everyone else had clicked into position, bearing in mind how difficult it is to follow someone else's pictures, in this case CBS TV, something of which the general public, and indeed the press, have no inkling. I was pleased with my own efforts and so it saddens me that almost my very last words were wrong.

I don't really know how it happened. I'd watched Phil Mickelson and Ernie Els battle it out over the last nine holes in magnificent style and I knew full well that Mickelson had a putt to win on the final hole but somehow or other my subconscious mind had geared itself into the strong possibility of a play-off. There were pictures of Ernie Els on the putting green talking to his various advisors, and there was Mickelson, no more than fifteen feet away with a putt to win . . . In all truth I thought the putt had missed, but it hadn't. And then I uttered the fateful words, 'It's not over yet . . .' Hands up – it happened and that was that.

Certain members of the press had a field day, although their main barbs came more than a week later. Fascinating how they made very pointed remarks that I was a 'veteran commentator', 'the seventy-three-year-old Peter Alliss' – I'm not saying that if I'd been thirty-five years of age they would not have been titillated; they would still have jumped up in the air but perhaps not quite so high. It was a good story for them and, boy, did some of them make a meal of it. Well, if you are a public figure, you are there to be shot at. Broadcasters age in the entertainment industry and I suppose that's show business.

20

CONSTELLATION

'Tall, dark and Latin-handsome with a flashing smile, Seve loped along the fairways . . . prowled around the greens'

I'm not one for comparing the skills of those who played before with the modern-day maestros. I think it's a total waste of time, like comparing winnings in golf or football wages or indeed the amounts of money films take over their life-time. I read, the other day, that Pierce Brosnan's Bond films have taken more than twice as much money as those of the most charismatic of all 007s, Sean Connery – about $780 million to $350 million. Well of course it would take more, you silly devils; when the Bond films started in the early sixties the best seat in the house was under 50p, now it's about £10 – pull yourselves together! But I digress . . .

My family and I have been involved in golf for the thick end of a hundred years and during that time much has happened. It would be difficult to make an ultimate list of which things have been the most important – was it the coming of the steel shaft, the rubber cored golf ball or cylindrical mowers so that greens could be cut with a machine rather than a few sheep, or an elderly gentleman with a very sharp scythe? Everyone has their own ideas of what is the most important, so I shall just concentrate on some players who, in my opinion, have made a tremendous impact in the world of golf, whether it be on or off the golf course.

I wrote in an earlier chapter my thoughts on those great men against whom I played in my own career. But there are more great men who have continued to grace the game in my career as a commentator.

Many people wise in the ways of golf, whose judgment is to be respected, believe that Jack Nicklaus has been the greatest golfer in the history of the game. That puts him into a pot that holds young Tom Morris, Harry Vardon, Walter Hagen, Bobby Jones, Bobby Locke, Peter Thomson, Byron Nelson, Ben Hogan and, of course, potentially Tiger Woods. If we were to shake that pot, who is to say that Nicklaus would not come out on top? As a player Nicklaus had a massive long game and was an outstanding, if deliberate, putter. He surely was one of the greatest for holing out from six to ten feet when it really mattered but I think his greatest single strength has been his mental capacity to think his way round the golf course. His concentration was immense. He could hold his form better than his fellow professionals and he once said that the greatest thrill in the game of golf was also one of his greatest challenges – three holes to play and a birdie to win.

In June of 1962, Nicklaus won the first of his four US Opens at Oakmont in a play-off with Arnold Palmer. Palmer was to impinge on Jack's life and vice versa with telling effect. When Jack arrived on the professional scene Arnold was king. Winner of the US Open in 1960 and the Masters in 1958, 1960, 1962, 1964 and our Open Championship in 1961 and 1962, he was a massive star. They were very different golfers, different personalities, different shapes, different looks. Palmer was the world's sweetheart. He would stop and talk to anyone, bores, hucksters, panhandlers, sycophants, drunks, old ladies, whether they were nice or not. Jack was different, he was not about to suffer fools gladly. He knew where he was going and nothing would divert him from that path. He was even known to keep such senior citizens as Hogan and Snead waiting on the first tee when going out for a practice round. Palmer was everyone's friend. Jack, when he started out, seemed rather, dare one say, 'slobbish'. He had a crew cut hairdo that really didn't suit him, was overweight, so much so he was dubbed 'Ohio Fats'.

Their swings too were very different. When Palmer swung lightning flashed; when Nicklaus swung thunder rolled. Palmer had blacksmith's hands, Jack's were small and delicate, he used an interlocking grip as his little finger wasn't long enough to give him enough power for the recognised Vardon grip. His swing was very upright, his right elbow was inclined to fly out at the top of the backswing. 'That'll never do,' they said.

Nicklaus marched on through a glorious career, his tally two US Amateur Championships, four US Opens, our Championship won on three occasions, the US PGA Championship five times and the US Masters six times, the first one in 1963 when he was just twenty-three years of age, the last when he was forty-six in 1986. There were six Australian Opens. He played in six Ryder Cup matches, including two as captain. He won seventy-one times in twenty-two years on the US PGA Tour between 1962 and 1984 and ten times on the US Senior Tour. He won the Byron Nelson, Ben Hogan and Walter Hagen Awards. He was the top money-winner eight times and he's an honorary member of the Royal & Ancient Golf Club of St Andrews. Only a handful of professionals have been awarded such an honour.

I asked him once what did he think was his main asset. He thought for a moment and then replied, 'I guess I could keep playing my game when they could no longer play theirs.'

Not for Tom Watson, Thomas Sturges Watson, the classic routes so many have taken into the world of tournament golf in America. No struggle from poverty or a deprived background through the caddy shed or as a dogsbody around the local driving range like a Hagen, Hogan or Trevino. Tom was more from the Jones-Nicklaus mould, prosperous family background, ample opportunities for play through the teenage years and, like Nicklaus, the act of turning professional 'when it pleased him'.

Tom went to Stanford University, the Harvard of the West, in San Francisco. He majored in business psychology, made the university golf team comfortably, won the State Amateur Championship more than once and turned professional at twenty-one. As a student at Stanford he had access to Pebble Beach where he would dream of playing in the US Open and needing three pars to win from Jack Nicklaus – 'and that dream came true' he was to say. As a professional he found the tournament game perplexing. He could rip off a 65 or 66 occasionally but he had to learn the essential trick of competing, the art of putting four acceptable rounds together, in other words – the art of winning. For a time he was considered a 'nearly man'. He led into the last round of one US Open and scored 79. But in 1975, at his first appearance in the Open Championship, Tom Watson's world was to be changed forever. He won. It was the beginning of eight golden years for Watson, eight years that brought him eight golden championships – eight majors.

Tom Watson stood around 5ft 9in, was trimly built with strong legs, powerful arms and hands, reddish-brown hair and an infectious smile with an irresistible gap in his teeth. On the course he was brisk, quick, businesslike, marching down the fairway optimistically. Nicklaus famously said of him, 'Tom knows where he is going.' In 1982 Tom Watson was champion of both the US and the UK. In 1983, at his fifth Open win, he produced yet another clinical finish. With a par-4 needed at Royal Birkdale's long and testing 18th, he hit an immense drive to the centre of the fairway, then a 2-iron 213 yards to the green. 'It was the best 2-iron of my life,' he said. Two putts and he was Open Champion for the fifth time. How that finish brought back memories of Peter Thomson's success – he played the hole identically for his victory in 1965.

In 2003 Watson made an evocative return to Turnberry and after a play-off with Carl Mason, won the British Seniors Open. One of golf's very best performers.

Seve Ballesteros – a sophisticated Arnold Palmer. Oh, the glorious period when Seve was the most charismatic player in the world – touch and feel; what skills and the ability to annoy all in equal measure. Strange how his career ended when Jack Nicklaus had his last hurrah at the Masters in 1986. Seve should have won that tournament. He had it in the palm of his hand and then dumped his second in the water at the 15th, Nicklaus holed a monster putt at the 17th, Seve was shaken – that was that. To me he never seemed quite the same again.

From the mid-seventies of the twentieth century to the mid-nineties Severiano Ballesteros was the most charismatic figure in world golf. He was a great champion with three victories in the Open Championship and two in the US Masters, not to mention an eventual career total of eighty-eight wins worldwide. He captivated the world of golf with his successes and a devil-may-care swashbuckling technique and with his presence and personality on the course.

Tall, dark and Latin-handsome with a flashing dazzling smile, Seve (pronounced 'Sebby' in Spanish!) loped along the fairways, prowled around the greens as though he couldn't wait to get to the next shot. Ballesteros took a cavalier attitude to the playing of the game. It was as though he accepted, and even rejoiced in, the philosophy of Walter Hagen (great champion of the 1920s) who insisted, 'Three bad shots and one good one still counts four.'

Seve was proud and stubborn, chippy with the game's establishment and often other players. He missed some Ryder Cup matches for one reason or another, then came back to inspire the European team and show its members that they were just as good as the Americans. He captained the winning team in 1997 at Valderrama in southern Spain, the first time it had been played outside the UK. Desperate for a victory in his homeland, and nervous, he rushed from match to match. Eventually the players had to tell him to calm down – politely to shut up!

Winning major championships had always been Seve's *raison d'être* but at the turn of the century, now advanced in his forties, perhaps he was to become one more victim of the game's old saying: 'very few win major championships in their forties.'

Nick Faldo, winner of six majors, was a driven man performing at the highest levels. What pleasure, joy and entertainment he brought to the British golfing scene. Now in his mid-forties, the glory days are probably behind him, but who knows?

A few years back the press suggested that Nick Faldo and I had a thing going. No, not *that* sort of thing – a feud, a feud that was no more than a slight tiff but one that saw certain newsmen seeking to make mountains where there were none. It hinged on Faldo making swing changes that I said I could not fully understand. As a young pro Nick had put some stunning scores together – 63s, 64s, 65s – on difficult courses, all played with a refreshing dash. He won a couple of tournaments and had an excellent Ryder Cup in 1977, winning all his matches, including a singles win over Tom Watson, the Open Champion. A tall (6ft 3in) strong lad, he had developed a wide rhythmic swing that gave him tremendous power through the ball but he seemed to lack consistency. He certainly thought so and found David Leadbetter, a tournament pro who had turned successfully to teaching. Between them they rebuilt Nick's swing.

I could not quite appreciate all this and wondered at its necessity, and said so. This was picked up and passed on to Nick who was quoted as saying, 'Well, anybody can climb a few steps up into a commentary box and immediately become an expert.' The writers came back at me and wanted to know what I thought. To and fro it went, the whole thing became silly. Innocent remarks were blown out of all proportion. There never was a vendetta, although certain journalists tried hard to make it so. I have the greatest admiration for Faldo and what he has achieved. Applying the yardstick of achievement only, three Open championships and three Masters championships make him the greatest British golfer of modern times, certainly over the past seventy-five years.

Greg Norman turns fifty next year and if he decides to joust with the Senior Tour, all the other silver-tops can look out. Of course, the big Australian may not have time for much more competitive golf, what with his other extensive and hugely profitable empire, but the fact remains that Greg was probably the most successful harvester of prize money in the last quarter of the twentieth century. He was leading money-winner in the US three times – in 1986, 1990 and 1995. In 1995 he was also US PGA Player of the Year.

Greg is the most prolific Australian winner of all time. Apart from anything else, he is one of the few players who have been leading money-winners in both Europe and the US and in eight successive years; through the 1980s he won at least two events each year, worldwide. He won two majors which reasonably should have been half a dozen. In 1986, for example, he led going into the final round of all four but won only one, the Open Championship at Turnberry. In his second Open win at Royal St George's in 1993 he set a record 267 which still stands. Bernhard Langer, his playing partner in the final round, in which Norman scored 64, said, 'In my entire life, I've never seen golf like that.'

Greg Norman, with his blond hair and magnificent physique, at 6ft a lean and muscular 13½ stone, was a delight to see marching along the world's fairways. He was a magnificent striker with a flowing, upright swing that generated fearsome clubhead speed. As a driver of the ball there were few better, with a trademark of his right foot sliding slightly to the left at impact and beyond. And his nickname 'the Great White Shark' proved a marvellous marketing tool, encouraging high-quality endorsements, which brought him the facility of developing substantial off-course interests in golf-course design and construction, property, golf equipment, clothing, automobiles, agronomy, wine-making and boat-building, to name but a few!

It would be difficult to imagine Ernie Els running for a bus. At 6ft 3in and 15 stone, they don't call him 'the Big Easy' for nothing. Ernie's processions along the world's fairways have a stately, bishop-like look to them. Serene is the word for the movement and body language of Ernest.

In his case, however, appearances cannot undermine the dynamics of his game and achievements – two US Open wins, victory in the Open Championship of 2002 at Muirfield, three successive World Matchplay titles in the 1990s and a total of five victories racked up in 2003 to equal the records of Seve Ballesteros and Gary Player. In the year 2000 Els finished second in three majors – the Masters, the US Open and the Open Championship – and in his first ten years as a professional he has checked in with around £7 million in prize money.

It all started in 1969 when he was born in Johannesburg. The young Els was particularly talented at cricket and rugby. He was a scratch golfer by the age of fourteen – gifted indeed. He turned professional in 1989 and in 1992 emulated the great South African Gary Player by winning the hat-trick of South African Open, PGA and Masters events.

Now, more than a decade into his professional career, he has won in Dubai, UK, USA, Japan and Hawaii, as well as his native South Africa, along with the $2 million Challenge in Sun City. Ernie has an immense presence on the course. He looks as though nothing could faze him with that big open smiling face and languid gait and flowing swing that makes striking a golf ball far and true look the easiest thing in the world. For at least ten more years Ernie will be a major player in the great championships of the game.

He was PGA Player of the Year in 2003 for the second year in succession and winner of the European Order of Merit for the first time. He and his family live in a splendid house alongside the 16th fairway on the West course at Wentworth, the home that once belonged to the Abrahams family, owners of Aquascutum (a famous name in the world of clothes and fashion, which still has its stately premises in Regent Street). Ernie is an honorary member of the Wentworth Club where he is always welcome.

It's very hard to believe but the name of Tiger Woods has been around for more than twenty-five years and he's not yet thirty. How can that be you ask? Well he was a child phenomenon. His father, who according to reports had a very distinguished war record, came away from the Asian wars physically unscarred. The way he drove his child on at a very early age to perfect his golf game reminded me of Shirley Temple, Judy Garland, Mickey Rooney, Elizabeth Taylor, even Bonnie Langford. Old black and white film portrays Tiger on stage with Bob Hope, hitting plastic golf balls into the audience. As soon as he could enter competitions he did and before he was into his teens he was winning them. He had an extraordinary record in amateur golf. Tiger won three successive US Amateur Championships, a staggering achievement.

Yes, there were one or two hiccups, he didn't win every battle. A memorable loss was to Gary Wolstenholme in the singles of the Walker Cup played at Royal Porthcawl in 1995. He played in just one Walker Cup match before he turned professional and started making and breaking all sorts of records. Woods is the complete golfer – rhythm, balance, power, timing, style, cool head, good nerves and, so far, apart from a ricked knee, he has suffered no injuries or been forced to have any operations, no appendectomy or tonsillitis. He has a presence.

My medical friends tell me that Tiger in body shape and structure is what's called an ectomorph. He is tall, slim with wide shoulders. His body shape and substance is a bold type, relatively thin but with a large covering of skin in comparison to weight. Since he started doing exercises in 1997 he has put on approximately twenty pounds of muscle. Ectomorphs have a very fast metabolic rate and lose weight rapidly. They need lots of training to maintain that muscle ratio. Incapacitated for seven or ten days, they could easily lose up to ten pounds.

In days gone by we would make a pilgrimage to watch Severiano Ballesteros hitting balls on the range; before him Jack Nicklaus and Arnold Palmer, perhaps Gary Player, and certainly Sam Snead. But you watch Woods open-mouthed. He can do extraordinary things with a golf ball. Whether he's just fooling around, bouncing a ball on the face of a 9-iron, playing high shots, low ones, chip shots, pitch shots, bunker shots, buried shots – the lot come pouring out of his enormous repertoire.

I remember long ago a vaudeville act called Rudy Horn. He was Dutch and rode a uni-cycle. While he was peddling around the stage he placed a saucer on one foot, threw it in the air and caught it on his head. He proceeded to catch six saucers and six cups, ending up with a knob of sugar in a spoon in the top one. It was one of the most remarkable acts I've ever seen in my life. Tiger Woods is in that category. Although you can see everything that happens, you marvel at how he does it, like one of the world's great illusionists doing things that seem impossible or those close-up magicians who baffle you although you're only a few inches away from their nimble fingers.

Fairly recently Woods got engaged. That brought outpourings of what would happen to him from the gossip writers; how he would cope with married life; what if 'babbies' came along, would they disturb his peace at night? They compared him to Jack and Barbara Nicklaus who travelled everywhere together, had babies and survived magnificently. And what of Gary Player bringing his family and delightful wife Vivienne thousands of miles from Johannesburg, trailing them round the circuits of the world, getting through it all, whether the kids were teething or had a touch of the runs. Unless Woods does something extraordinary – like buying his own rocket and disappearing to the moon – there's nothing else to say about him that hasn't been said before.

Many people get bored with Woods. 'He's too good,' they say. But that's like saying you're tired of hearing a wonderful musician or you're fed up with Frank Sinatra records. I've been privileged to see him play at close hand. He's been chased a bit of late but he's still the one to beat. I think we should all now just let the years ahead unfold to see where Tiger goes, what he does, how he plays, what he wins and not go delving round for some secret bits of nonsense just for the sake of making up a story. Hail to Tiger, he truly is the real article, but I don't think he will catch Jack Nicklaus.

Last on my list is a young lady who has certainly not yet earned the accolade of greatness, but who, one day, might. The sensation, if not of the age certainly of the moment, is Michelle Wie, aged fourteen, a lofty schoolgirl who in 2004 played in the Sony Hawaii Open, scored a second round 68 and got within a stroke of making the cut. The girl is 6ft tall and has the most gorgeous swing you can imagine and the American media immediately dubbed her a female Tiger Woods. I suspect someone along the way named her 'Tigress Wie', a shade premature, perhaps.

Michelle is very young, a child but potentially a very wealthy one. Having had all this publicity, it's a very sensitive matter for her to remain an amateur. For example, she's restricted in accepting expenses to those events confined to amateurs.

She's still got to finish school. Where will that be? I'm sure some of America's mightiest universities will be vying like mad to get her on the campus. She appears to be very bright so, who knows, perhaps she'll combine a golfing scholarship with proper tuition. It's a very interesting scenario. Wie would be a sensation on the regular LPGA Tour but she's got to wait four years for that to happen. But can you imagine all the matches that could be arranged, laid on especially for television. I wonder how far the LPGA would go in denying membership to someone under eighteen years of age.

Michelle Wie is a multi-millionairess in waiting. If she became a professional when she reached school-leaving age, she could sign a $30 million contract with consummate ease. All quite fascinating, so many people in high places pushing and shoving, trying to get a bit of the action. There's no doubt she is a very special talent. It's remarkable that a female should come along, out of the same mould as Tiger Woods, creating huge interest; it does have a touch of novelty about it.

Women competing in men's tournaments? I'm not quite sure what that proves, even if they should go forward and win an event. As for suggesting that one day she might win the Masters! Well, you never know. Over the last forty years women have moved forward and done extraordinary things as doctors, lawyers, airline pilots, bus drivers, truck drivers, fashion designers, comediennes, even as coal miners in Pennsylvania – now that's a hard life, much more testing than strolling round a golf course being paid about $25 for every step you take. We shall await with interest the future of Michelle Wie. Remember the great women who have gone before – Lady Heathcote Amory, Enid Wilson, Babe Zaharias, Patty Berg, Louise Suggs, Joanne Carner, Kathy Whitworth and, of course, Annika Sorenstam and Laura Davies – all with magical careers, but who knows, over the next thirty years this fourteen-year-old might surpass them all.

21

St Andrews
And The R&A

*'The course has stood the passing of time . . . I
am delighted there hasn't been too much major
surgery'*

I first set eyes on the Auld Grey Toon in 1948. I was there to
play in only my second professional golf tournament and was
being chaperoned by my brother Alec. We stayed at a modest
private hotel within 500 yards of the clubhouse.

It's extraordinary the things you remember. This was quite a
smart establishment as there was a bathroom on each floor.
How many of you remember that, when travelling years ago,
you always took a decent sized towel and a bar of soap in a little
aluminium box? This was long before plastic had been invented!
You'd try to get into that bathroom first, before too much mess
was made. Over the loo there would be a notice to the effect
'Please leave this bathroom as you would wish to find it' and
often you would go in to find it in a very distressed condition –

so much so that you'd spend five minutes cleaning the place up in case, when you opened the door, somebody was standing there who might think *you* were the one responsible for the mayhem inside.

Very few facilities existed round the course in those far-off days. A big heavy wooden scoreboard was carted around on the back of a small lorry and assembled and disassembled by one Eddie Carter, who worked for the PGA. A Londoner, chirpy, with odd false teeth, about forty-five years of age, he rolled his own cigarettes with very badly nicotine-stained fingers and was an absolute delight with a great sense of humour and a huge ability for hard work. It used to take him a couple of days to put up this gigantic scoreboard; he hand-painted all the names on pieces of wood that he could slide into the different slots. They were held together by wooden pegs, all tapped in alphabetical order. It really was a work of art. There was no tented village and no press room, although perhaps there might have been a very modest tent erected between the R&A clubhouse and the beach, which served as some sort of cover for the inky-fisted scribes. What an amazing collection of writers they were, too! Fred Pignon and Betty Debenham spring to mind. Betty was a small tubby rounded lady with hennaed hair and it was bandied about that she and Fred were lovers. I found it hard to believe. Fred's son, Laurie, went on to become a very respected reporter in the world of tennis. Henry Longhurst and Bernard Darwin were another two, and a short stocky raw Scot, Eddie Hamilton, who was a very good golfer, was another. Somebody called Robertson was usually there and Tom Scott, editor of *Golf Illustrated* for a thousand years, plus a number of others who flitted like grey figures across the scene.

I'd never seen a course like St Andrews. It took you a few

rounds to learn in which direction to hit your tee shots. You had to line up on a telegraph pole away in the distance, church spires, the window of a hotel, a gorse bush, anything. The greens were magnificent, all cut by hand, which took hours and hours.

Over the last sixty years the town has changed dramatically. There was a time, not too long ago, when it went dead. You could have bought Rusacks Hotel for under £100,000, hard to believe now. The university, one of the oldest in the world, seemed to be dragging its feet, but it was still golf for all. I'm not too sure it's any better or any worse now than in those unsophisticated days. Apart from the Golf Museum, built between the clubhouse and the beach, the buildings remain pretty well the same, which is all part of the magic. Behind the 18th green the old Atlantic Hotel with its sugar-shaker top, now student accommodation, looks as bold and proud today as it did then and the little shops down the side of the 18th green may be very different inside but the façade is the same as it was hundreds of years ago.

It's remarkable how everything has boomed over the last twenty-five years or so; half a dozen new golf courses have appeared. Who would ever have thought of that? A huge amount of publicity has been generated, along with some exaggerated claims by some of the new boys. Millions of pounds have been invested both south and north of the town. Somehow they seem to have forgotten that, at best, it's only a six-month season. Perhaps I'm exaggerating, but even if the new hotels have indoor spas and heated driving ranges, people have still got to be attracted to the area. It's a big gamble.

There's always an air of excitement when an event is played at St Andrews, particularly when it's the Open Championship. The course has stood the passing of time brilliantly although one or two bunkers have been added and some holes lengthened. I am delighted that there hasn't been too much major surgery. The course is a very different proposition when the ground is firm and the wind blowing. Then our modern gladiators cry like babies and declare how unfair it all is and they shouldn't be asked to play this great championship under these conditions. It's quirky – double greens, cross-over holes, a nightmare for spectators. Don't let anyone tell you that it's fun watching golf from the sidelines of St Andrews, it's not. Of course, you can get up in one of the grandstands. The R&A are very generous and provide well over 20,000 free seats for the wonderful collection of fee-paying customers who come every year to be told they can't do this and they can't do that. The officials do it all with smiley faces and the amazing thing is the crowds are kept in check with just a single strand of rope running down the side of each fairway.

Those who are lucky enough visit St Andrews at least twice, once when an Open is in full swing and again when all is cleared away and everything is naked and open with carefree families frolicking on the beach. Ah, that wonderful beach figured in the opening sequence of the film *Chariots of Fire*.

A splendid new clubhouse now nestles about 400 or 500 yards from the R&A building. Visitors had waited long enough for some sort of facility and at last the powers that be found some money and a site. It was built and it took off. The encouragement of golf for the young is going full bore in St Andrews – another feature that's helped to bring the town alive over the last few years.

The new Byre Theatre is up and running. What a huge bonus that must be when you think, many moons ago, there was only that little cinema in Market Street. Every time the Open Championship came around there was Glenn Ford portraying Ben Hogan with Anne Baxter as his wife Valerie in the old black and white movie *Follow the Sun*. I also seem to recall that a play featuring golfers always appeared at 'Open' time – you just had to see both.

I've grown more attached to St Andrews as the years have gone by and I can now understand why people would wish to retire there, particularly if you are a member of one of the clubs. Golf is readily available. Food and beverages are on tap at very advantageous prices. There's lots of camaraderie and free newspapers (that's a big saving). Afternoons may be spent in conversation with wonderful eccentrics such as Sandy Rutherford – what bliss – or playing a game of cards or walking the dog on the beach. Perhaps there would be a chance to get into conversation with one of the greatest champions ever, Peter Thomson, if he happens to be spending an autumn at St Andrews.

Will the town ever stop growing? I hope they save the harbour. Parts of the coastline are being eroded and there are some areas that need refurbishment. If it continues at this rate, who knows, they might even reinstate the railway.

That's how I arrived on my first visit. I remember that journey very well; it came as a bit of a surprise to me but not so much as Sam Snead's first visit in 1946 did to him. Rationing was still in operation, all was doom and gloom, and he looked out of the train on to a piece of property he called 'a raggedy bit of old land which looked like a disused golf course'. For the whole week Sam moaned, groaned, complained and virtually threw in the towel half a dozen times but with six or seven holes to go in the final round, things happened. He holed a putt here, played a good chip there and ended up the champion. He said the first prize was the equivalent of about $350 and it had cost him $1,500 to come over. He did not return until the millennium when he and all but a couple of the surviving champions came and played a few ceremonial holes at St Andrews. He even did a little tap dance on the Swilken Bridge. It was nice to see him and many other great past champions.

St Andrews with all its history, some of it fierce and bloody, has a unique place in the game of golf. When the R&A celebrated their 250th anniversary I was honoured to be asked to propose the toast at the dinner in June 2004. Shortly after the letter arrived I received a second one, from Lachlan McIntosh, the project secretary of the R&A. I thought, oh dear, they've changed their minds, they don't want an old golf pro saying a few words. But no, Peter Thomson, five times Open Champion, had also accepted an invitation to speak and the committee wished that wondrous man to propose the toast to the club and the game, and would I, they asked, respond to the toast proposed by David Pepper, Chairman of the Championship Committee, to the guests. Aaah yes, I felt as if a great weight had been lifted off my shoulders. So, two golf professionals speaking at the anniversary dinner – one, a lot more skilled than the other, to propose the toast to the club and the game of golf and the other, a fair player in his day, asked to respond for the guests. I was honoured indeed. I only wished it were possible for a link-up to them above, so mum, dad and all the other Allisses could look down and listen to their young lad speaking in front of such an august body, reminiscing about his first visit to St Andrews and the wonder and pain the game has brought. So in a rather masochistic way I looked forward to 2 June, the biggest tent ever erected in Scotland and the hope of getting through a speech without crying. Well, I can't help it, I'm emotional.

On my return from America in early March 2004 I opened my mail to find a letter dated 16 February from Peter Dawson, the Secretary of the Royal & Ancient Golf Club of St Andrews, which read:

On behalf of the General Committee of the Royal & Ancient Golf Club of St Andrews I have great pleasure in inviting you to accept our invitation to become an Honorary Member of the Club. As an honorary member you would not be required to pay an entrance fee or annual subscription. Please keep this confidential until after the business meeting at the Club on Wednesday 5th May.

WOW! My fellow honorary members are: the Duke of Edinburgh; the Duke of York; the Duke of Kent; President George Bush Snr; Tony Jacklin; Kel Nagle; Jack Nicklaus; Arnold Palmer; Gary Player; Peter Thomson; Lee Trevino; Roberto di Vicenzo; Tom Watson and, splendid news, John Jacobs, who received the accolade at the same time as I did. Just fancy, me an honorary member of the most famous golf club in the world, one of the proudest moments of my professional life.

22

HONOURS BOARD

*' "Doctor Alliss" – my mother would have been
tickled pink'*

In a long career in the game of golf other honours have come
my way. In November 2003 I went to Munich to receive the
Golf European Legend Award for 2003 and I am also a Captain
of Muirfield Village. There are twenty-four Captains of Muirfield Village, the Jack Nicklaus course in Ohio often dubbed the
Augusta of the North. Jack always sought to make his course
and club different from many in the United States. He has been
able to choose little bits and pieces from other golf clubs around
the world, which all go to make his complex very special. To
become a Captain, you have to be nominated by the other
Captains as someone who has contributed to the game either in
play or administration. With it goes honorary membership of
the club. Every year I'm invited to go back, provided with a first-
class ticket and accommodation, and attend a couple of meetings to decide who we're going to honour next year. There's
much pomp and circumstance. It's unique.

Muirfield Village is amazing, a place of long cold winters but what a wonderful tournament when the golf course is ready at the end of May and, by the way, they serve the best shrimp you've ever had in your life!

Selecting the 'honoree' each year takes place when the tournament is being played and in 2004, the main honoree will be Lee Trevino but they're also honouring Joyce Wethered. The MC in charge of that particular ceremony is dear Maureen Garrett, a life-long friend, former Curtis Cup player and captain and receiver of a Bobby Jones Trophy among many other things. I'm sure she's looking forward to her visit to Muirfield Village enormously.

I have been captain of the PGA twice and am now a life member. I was accorded the honorary life membership of the European Tour at the end of May 2003. Ken Schofield, the Executive Director of the European Tour, presented me with the Tour Silver Membership Card (of which I'm very proud) at a ceremony at the Tour's headquarters at the Wentworth Club, Virginia Water.

I was the first president of the European Women's PGA when it was formed. I told the members that if I could be of any help, either with their game or business dealings, they only had to call – no one ever did. I was also president of the Greenkeepers Association. I have always felt an affinity for greenkeepers, ever since my early days at Ferndown. I have tried in a small way to enhance their working conditions and perhaps made a few points that were acted upon, but I have no proof of that.

An honour of another kind, I suppose, is that I've been 'done' on *This is Your Life* – Eamonn Andrews was the man with the red book. I was over on the west coast of Ireland with Michael Hobbs, my collaborator on a book I was working on about various golf courses throughout the United Kingdom, when a call came through from John Simpson of IMG. He had someone he wished me to meet in London two days later; there was some big deal cooking that was going to make me (and IMG) a vast amount of money. Computers were really getting a foothold in society and the idea was to link up all the golf courses in the world so items such as handicapping and memberships could all be listed and at the touch of a button you'd get all the information you wanted on a huge variety of topics – all so easy and I was the man to lead the way.

I fought tooth and nail not to go. The weather was foul. I said there were no airplanes – 'Don't worry, he'll send one for you' – but much as I wriggled, I couldn't get out of it. I was driven to a small airfield near Shannon and took off in a horrendous storm heading for Fair Oaks, not far from Woking in Surrey. It was a nightmare journey but we arrived safe and sound, there was a car waiting with John Simpson in the back with a big smile on his face and we were whisked off to London. He then announced that this gentleman had some other engagements and we couldn't meet him until later on in the day so we'd go and have lunch.

I was looking rather rumpled, to say the least, and had brought my dirty washing home in a plastic bag. John had told me that after our meeting I would have twenty-four hours to kill before going back to Ireland to finish my work there, so I would be able to go home and collect one or two clean bits and pieces. We had a *very* good lunch and, looking back, I can see now why he got rather worried when I was into my fourth (or was it fifth?) glass of Sancerre! Afterwards, we climbed into a taxi, and were driving merrily along when suddenly the car stopped, I think it was outside the old Tottenham Court Road cinema where they used to record television programmes. The door was yanked open and there stood Eamonn Andrews surrounded by so many friends – Tony Jacklin, Cliff Michelmore, Henry Cotton, two of the old greenkeepers from Ferndown, Jimmy Tarbuck, Bruce Forsyth, many Ryder Cup players. What an array of talented people – I was thunderstruck and very proud they had taken the trouble to be part of the programme, not to mention Johnny Mathis and Arnold Palmer, who appeared on film.

I had no idea any of this was taking place. There was only one problem. The researchers had gone to my first wife, Joan, asking for various bits and pieces of information. She, rightly, sent them off with a flea in their ear, so at least fifteen years of my life were eliminated. My time at the Parkstone Golf Club, early days of the children's schooling, victories and defeat in tournaments and Ryder Cups were all obliterated. You have no idea what aggravation that caused. The number of people who wrote insulting letters afterwards saying how awful it was that I had not mentioned so-and-so and so-and-so who played such a big part in that period of my life. I was dumbstruck to think that people imagined *I* picked the people who came on the programme.

On reflection, it was one of the most unhappy times of my life; it ended up, after the show, with a group of us standing on the pavement, waiting for a taxi to pick us up, when I was attacked by my relatively new daughter-in-law Karen, telling me what a terrible mess I'd made of my relationship with son Gary and life in general. But all that was a long time ago. We've all passed a lot of water since then and I'm delighted to say my relationship with Karen, Gary and their children is loving and solid.

I have only golden memories of other awards. Back in the winter of 1993, Jackie and I went to the University of Humberside in Hull, my mother's home town, where I was given an honorary degree. We marvelled at all the new developments and how the dock area, once home to fleets of trawlers, had now been rejuvenated, although I don't know what my mother, grandmother and grandfather, Captain Rust, would have made of it all. I got dressed in fine robes and, with a mortar board set at a slightly nerdish angle, took my place on the stage. I was introduced, said a few words and then presented dozens of diplomas to the qualifying students. I wasn't sure quite what to say on such an occasion. You shake hands and say the customary 'Well done, good luck,' to which there were basically two replies from the students, who came in all shapes and sizes, 'Thanks' or 'Cheers' – interesting!

In 2001 I was contacted by Bournemouth University and asked, as someone who had been part of the town for so many years, if I would accept an Honorary Degree from them. Their Chancellor, by the way, is Lord Taylor of Warwick, the first black member of the House of Lords. I accepted with alacrity and, in time, made my way down to their magnificent campus, spread over many acres in an area where I used to live in my early married days. It was November and once more I donned my robes, this time of a different hue and said a few words extolling the virtue of good education, of going forward and being good citizens. I made one or two of them smile so I don't think I was a failure. I was, however, slightly surprised when I started to get mail from the university addressed to 'Dr Peter Alliss' and I enquired whether that was correct. 'Oh yes,' I was told, 'you have an honorary doctorate and you are perfectly entitled to call yourself doctor but you must, if asked, declare that this is what it is, and you don't have some exotic medical degree that entitles you to wander the world hither and thither doing extraordinary things with a stethoscope!'

'Doctor Alliss' – my mother would have been absolutely tickled pink.

I think I might claim a share at least of another honour, that of founding the Grand Match, a competition not quite matching that inspired by old Sam Ryder but nonetheless giving great pleasure to its participants. It all started with a conversation between me and Bruce Critchley. I was saying it seemed a pity that so many of the universities and grand old schools had various matches and competitions they could play in, e.g. the Oxford and Cambridge Golfing Society, the Halford Hewitt, the Grafton Morrish, and a number of others, but there was nothing for golf professionals once they'd got past the Ryder Cup stage, and so the Grand Match came to be – old Ryder Cuppers against Walker Cuppers. We were lucky at the time, our first sponsor was the John Laing company. Terry Fleming, one of the company's main board directors, thought it was a splendid idea. He also happened to be a member of the Royal Cinque Ports Golf Club. They found us a date, Critchley found a team of old Walkers and off we went. It won't be long before we've completed twenty years. It's been great fun, although my Ryders seem to be getting older and the Walkers younger. Critchley gave up the captaincy a few years ago, when his work with Sky and our date clashed; it coincided with the end of the Dunhill Cup played at St Andrews and getting down from there to Deal on Sunday night, ready to play on Monday, was more and more difficult, plus he was becoming very famous and rather busy, so the reins were passed over to Gary Wolstenholme and, latterly, Martin Christmas. John Laing went away. Touche Ross and later Deloitte-Touche and British Car Auctions held the fort; then after three years British Car Auctions pulled out and now it's solely sponsored by Deloitte-Touche. I do hope they will continue and, in the years ahead, who knows, I might be able to persuade some of the big boys to play – Sandy Lyle, Nick Faldo, Manuel Pinero, even Seve.

The teams, those who can, congregate at the Royal Hotel on the seafront at Deal on the Sunday afternoon. We have a fun get-together dinner that night with our sponsors, then on Monday it's Pro-Am day, eighty invited guests of the sponsors partnering Ryder Cuppers and Walker Cuppers – a shotgun start, 18 holes, then a black-tie dinner in the clubhouse with the prize presentation and a few speeches. The next day, Tuesday, 36 holes of foursomes golf but, if the weather is inclement, we are not averse to cutting the holes played to a sensible number. Most of the players don't mind getting wet once but twice is asking too much!

For a number of years I've had a caddy rejoicing in the name of Neil Coles. He works for the Channel Tunnel company, is married with a delightful family, and lives halfway between Deal and Dover. He's always there with a smile on his face and, bless him, he's kept smiling despite the fact he's seen my game deteriorate greatly since he first came on the scene! Deal have been very supportive and generous to us over the years. I had the honour of being made a member a few years ago. I only wish I lived nearer, so I could challenge Andrew Reynolds, the professional, or Jack Aisher, the president, to a few holes. However, I would be looking for some start!

23

FAMILY MATTERS

'Without being too maudlin, I ponder life and am disappointed with myself for not remembering more'

We left Leeds in 1980 to follow my fortunes in the Alliss Thomas Golf Construction business. We found a house in Hindhead, nestling between three small villages, Churt, Beacon Hill and Grayshott. We loved our new home but it needed a lot doing to it. It took two years to re-model and refit. It was in need of major modernisation.

Much of the credit for that of course is due to the lady I married more than thirty years ago. In every department Jackie has been an outstanding success but fulfilment for her has gone beyond that, the lady is an activist. She joined the Magistrates Association in 1982, proposed by her father – a Birmingham solicitor and a man of great stature – and seconded by a judge. In 1988 she wrote a cookery book with a difference – in between the recipes are stories from her life; she's currently working on a second edition, which will contain tales of travel, children, television and more recipes purloined from friends.

As if she needs any more interests, Jackie breeds Weimaraners. They've been part of the Alliss family now for over forty years. Our first one came from Newdigate in Surrey, when there were only about twenty registered at the Kennel Club. Now there are many hundreds and things have become much more sophisticated. They are beautiful animals and, if treated properly, make excellent pets/guard dogs/children's favourites – in fact, many things rolled into one.

In 1989 Jackie was asked to front an imaginative television series on cooking. This was before every TV company known to man was showing cookery programmes two or three times a day. Although she'd never stood in front of the camera before, she was very assured and did a superb job. The series started in Spain where they filmed Tony and Astrid Jacklin at home. Back in Buckinghamshire, Helen Wogan was her guest. Not only did Helen show viewers how to prepare her dish, before that she and Jackie were filmed at the local butcher's, selecting the joint. In Florida, at the Nicklaus household, a wonderfully comfortable home right on the water, Barbara was in tremendous form. Jack, who wasn't supposed to take part in the programme at all, couldn't resist the temptation to show off his fine array of fruit trees – oranges, avocados and grapefruits.

The guests were not confined to golfers' wives. Actress Michele Dotrice took part. She had recently married that fine actor Edward Woodward and they were living in Stratford-on-Avon. Kiri Te Kanawa was filmed in her delightful home in the middle of Leatherhead golf course and, finally, there was the great photographer, Norman Parkinson, who was living in the West Indies at the time. He was tall and white-haired, with a moustache and a twinkle in his eye. Meeting him was one of the highlights of the series for Jackie and at home there's a picture of them both on a beach in Barbados, no doubt talking about his wonderful Porkinson sausages, which I believe are still on sale today in many upmarket stores and supermarkets.

I was surprised she wasn't asked to do more shows because they went very well. Perhaps if she'd worn a baseball hat back-to-front or said 'y'know' every four seconds, she might have got a second series, but it was also at a time when strong regional accents were taking over. If you didn't have one, you felt you had to go away and learn one. It's the same today.

Jackie has also qualified as a pilot. She and a friend kept a delightful little French airplane called a Robin in a hangar near Frensham Pond. She once flew me down to Exeter when the Benson & Hedges tournament was being played at St Mellion. I had no qualms about being piloted by my wife. She was very good at landing, which is very important, although you only really need to bother about the last couple of feet!

In 1986 Jackie started an event management business, which has grown to almost thirty events a year. She's the chairman of governors of St Edmund's Primary School, situated on the main A3 just south of the dreaded Hindhead crossroads. She's a patron of GUTS (Guildford Undetected Tumour Screening) – a hugely successful local charity – and of the prostate cancer project. That then is 'My Fair Lady' – I've been blessed.

A man with a loving family is blessed. A man who has two such families is surely twice blessed. My first marriage with Joan produced Gary and Carol. It was surely pre-ordained that Gary would pursue a life in golf and for many years he was professional at the lovely Trevose Club near Padstow in Cornwall. Gary and his wife Karen worked long and hard in building up the business in the shop and Gary created a reputation for teaching that is second to none. Everywhere I went I'd meet people who had spent their holidays at Trevose and they all spoke in praise of Gary and his ability to be communicative with all age groups.

Their children are a delight, Craig now eighteen and Tara fifteen; both are keen on golf. In fact Craig, who's shot up over the last twelve months, is a very good young player indeed and might have dabbled with the idea of going into the profession but at this moment he's interested in geology. Tara has aspirations to be a physiotherapist.

When Gary left Trevose, he went to Hustyns, a spectacular hotel and golf facility on the outskirts of Wadebridge in North Cornwall. It was a big wrench to leave the club that held so many happy memories for the Alliss family but for various reasons, none of his making, it was time to move on. Someone once said 'a week is a long time in politics' but if that's so, three months covers a lot of ground in the world of sport – that's how long it took Gary and his family to pack up and go.

Carol has settled down near Chipping Norton in Oxfordshire with Brett Eeley and daughter Rebecca, who is an absolute charmer.

The children of my second family seem to have come to grips with life successfully as well. Simon went to Charterhouse, then Birmingham University where he took a sports and science degree, then a post-graduate law degree, which took him up to articled clerk level. He worked first for British Car Auctions but decided there was no future for him there. Like most graduates, he turned his hand to bar and building work until a chance remark by me to Ken Schofield led to him joining the staff of the PGA European Tour, where he is at time of writing. Henry went to Cranleigh and is at the University of East Anglia at Norwich, studying the history of art.

Sara was born in Leeds when I was the professional at the Moor Allerton Golf Club. She was a big baby, 10lb 4oz – a good size. She was always a bit of a tearaway. I think she could be the only toddler ever asked to leave nursery class. She was too adventurous, I fancy. She would disappear from the house, out and gone, over the road to the stables to look at the horses and farm animals. The postman used to bring her back. We learned to hide the door keys!

When we moved to Hindhead, she started school at the Grove, just off the A3, but that wasn't successful. She then progressed to the Royal Naval School in Haslemere, one of the oldest girls' schools in England. She was there for nine years and, although she didn't end up as head girl, she was a great character in the school. She had a huge passion for singing and sang in the school choir at the Seafarers Service at St Paul's Cathedral. From 1990–91 she went to Paris to stay with our friends the Decugis, ostensibly to learn French. It was during this time that she had classical singing lessons from Eric Tavelli who had worked with Placido Domingo.

She came home in 1991, and when no job came along she did a bit of nannying for nine months, looking after two little girls, very successfully I might add. Then, for three years, 1991–94, she was at Bedford College, which became part of De Montfort University. In her time there, she studied drama and English. She still continued her dream of singing and started a band with the original name 'Custard for Everyone', which just became 'Custard', doing the pubs and university gigs, supporting 'The Prodigy' and 'Doctor and the Medics'. You can see, they preferred sensible names!

In 1994–95 she took a year off but stayed in Bedford. She had a boyfriend at that time. We weren't sure how that would work out. To earn some money she worked in a nursery school and a pub, and sang in cabaret bands and working-men's clubs. She was enjoying life enormously. In 1995 she moved to London for one year, living near The Oval cricket ground. Then, with a little help from her friends, she bought a flat in Balham and got a job at the *Daily Telegraph*, starting in tele-sales, cold-calling, dealing with travel and gardening promotions. She did very well. She had a good telephone personality and worked up to the *Telegraph Magazine*, specialising in travel. Over the next five years she travelled extensively and was promoted to travel telephone sales manager with a team of eight, also dealing with recruitment and training. This was a good period for Sara. She travelled to Sydney, Melbourne, Las Vegas and all across Europe but eventually, after eight years, decided it was time for a change, if opportunity was to beckon.

In July 2003 it did. She met Kirsty Gallacher, Bernard's daughter, at a book awards lunch. Sara had gone there to collect a prize for my book *Alliss's Golfing Heroes*, which had won an award for best illustrated book of the year. Kirsty introduced her to Jane Morgan, of Jane Morgan Management, who was looking for someone to help manage a stable of clients that included Desmond Lynam, Clare Balding, Sir Bobby Robson and John Motson. The thought of a new challenge intrigued and excited her and so in August 2003 she handed in her notice at the *Telegraph* and in October started with Jane.

She's now got a serious boyfriend, Jonathan Bartle from Sheffield, my father's home town, who works in the motor industry, so who knows what the future holds for Sara Alliss. Hot news! Sara has just got engaged.

A Golfer's Travels was a series filmed for television in the mid nineties. I went to some spectacular places, including the Blue Canyon Golf Club near Phuket in Thailand, where I took tea with Christopher Lee, a charming man and prolific actor.

The bridge over the River Kwai turned out to be a single-track metal structure, nothing like in the film!

For the first programme, I travelled to the stunning Loch Lomond golf course where Dame Kiri Te Kanawa arrived on the Royal Mail boat, having delivered the morning post.

Above: Sean Connery got in on the picture when the BBC's Adam Cooper took this snapshot at Gleneagles.

Left: Loch Lomond, one of the most beautiful places in the world – when it's not raining.

Below: Terry Wogan and I attended the opening of the revamped St Edmund's School at Hindhead, together with Lesley Attwood and Ian Peacock from the Golf Foundation.

A wheelchair presentation at the Clubhouse Elie, a delightful course on the north bank of the Firth of Forth.

John Iles, chairman of Merlo, who are one of the country's largest distributors of heavy machinery for work on rough terrain, is a tremendous supporter of the Wheelchair Crusade.

Andrew Mlangeni, who spent twenty-five years in prison with Nelson Mandela, is pictured here at Sun City during my *Golfer's Travels* series.

Commentator at work – this pencil drawing was sent to me anonymously by the artist.

Nick Faldo – a dedicated and formidable golfer, Britain's finest.

Joanne Carner, or Big Momma, what a fabulous character.

For a number of years, Greg Norman lit up the game of golf as few others have been able to do.

The BBC team of the early nineties, *from left*: Dave Marr, Alastair Scott, John Shrewsbury, Clive Clark, Barbara Slater, Mike Hughesden and me.

Possibly the most charismatic athlete of all time – Arnold Palmer.

Michelle Wie – a young teenager. What does the world of golf hold for her?

Todd Hamilton (*left*) and Ernie Els at the 2004 Open at Royal Troon. From their expressions, it's hard to tell who won.

Honestly, I didn't pay him!

South Africa are indeed lucky to have two such giants in the game as Ernie Els and Retief Goosen, pictured here at the 2004 US Open at Shinnecock Hills. Long may they prosper.

My daughter Carol and granddaughter Rebecca, a real charmer.

Tiger strides out – so far not a great Ryder Cup record.

Our brood – and what a handsome lot they are – Simon, Sara and Henry Alliss.

Daughter-in-law Karen with husband Gary and their lovely children, Tara and Craig.

Sadly, the Alliss family have never been close. My brother died in his early seventies while living with his wife Joan on the island of Guernsey. He'd not enjoyed good health for a number of years and gradually succumbed to a blood disorder that quietly sapped his strength. The disparity in age and the war years may have been why we were not close. Although there are dozens of cousins dotted around North Derbyshire, South Yorkshire, South Wales and Western Australia, we've never had any great reunions. I've often wondered why when I compare our family to some others I've known who have been very much together. My conclusion is that it needs a good organiser with a little spare time as well as a sense of family. Joan, Alec's widow, still lives in Guernsey with her daughter Mandy but again it's just a question of Christmas cards.

Without being too maudlin, I ponder life and am disappointed with myself for not remembering more. People come up to me and say, 'Do you remember so and so?' OK, it was twenty or thirty years ago. 'Do you remember old Bill and Ben and do you remember Sally and Frieda?' In all truth, I don't. It's obviously such a vivid memory to them, I wonder how on earth it could have slipped through the honeycomb of my brain cells. I think of my family – distant cousins who over the years have never entered into the Alliss arena; friendships formed as a boy that have all passed into distant memory; the old boys at Ferndown who encouraged me so much; National Service, early marriage, times spent at Ferndown; my brother returning from what was then Northern Rhodesia; and taking over at Parkstone where I spent thirteen very happy years. I read somewhere that when you die, you will meet up with all the people you have loved in your life. It must be very crowded.

If I had my time again, what could I have done differently?

What *should* I have done differently? I thought long and hard but at the end of it all I thought I passed muster. Oh, there were some who might have thought that I hadn't done the right thing but on balance, I never set out to swindle anyone. I like to think my children have a good sense of what's right and fair, thinking of others, consideration. If it's instilled in you from birth, or early school days, it's not such a hard thing to do.

We've just had Henry's twenty-first birthday party at Buck-lands, which was a splendid affair. Just under seventy people came along. Even that number knocked a hole in my life savings but it was tremendous fun. The three godfathers were all there, two Scots, Jack Buchanan, our near neighbour, and Alastair Scott, who had worked his way up from being a cameraman on our first *Pro-Celebrity* series from Gleneagles in 1974 to being the director of television golf, football and swimming for the BBC. Terry and Helen Wogan were also present – Terry is a very good godfather. Sir Henry Cooper and his wife Albina were on hand, plus of course many of Henry's friends from university. I'm still trying to work out how sixty-eight people got through 108 bottles of wine; thirty-two of those were champagne, brought in supposedly just to toast Henry's coming of age! Discretion took the better part of valour with me and I tip-toed off to bed at about 4 a.m., only to discover that my dear wife finally locked the house up at 5.50 a.m. and had done a little bit of taxi-ing at 5.15 for one of Henry's friends who was just a little bit under the weather. What a good Samaritan she is!

I must mention here a lady who, over the years, became a part of my family. On 6 February 2004 my secretary Helen Cameron died after a very short illness. It's hard to believe that on 9 January she was here at our home arranging flowers for Henry Alliss's twenty-first. She was a caring, conscientious soul who has seen me in my blackest moods and heard language that I'm sure she didn't understand. At moments like that she pretended she was deaf – a gift bestowed on very few. She was given a splendid send-off by so many of her friends and relations.

Thank you, Helen, for all your hard work and help constructing articles for various golfing magazines and also for the major part you've played in putting this book together. It will be finished by Marilyn Cooper, my partner Roy's wife, whom I know will carry on the tradition of keeping me on the straight and narrow literary path.

God bless you, my darling Helen, and thank you for all your help over the years.

24

QUEEN'S COMMAND

*'There were figures in ceremonial dress
everywhere, some carrying swords, pikes, wearing
breastplates'*

Sunday, 28 September 2003 was a golden Sunday. I had been
watching the final day's play of the Dunhill Cup from St Andrews.
The Old Course was bathed in sunshine and I got to thinking how
lucky I had been in my life to be involved in the game of golf. Then
I opened some mail from the day before and discovered that Jackie
and I had an invitation from the Lord Steward to attend a State
Banquet at Buckingham Palace in honour of the President of the
United States of America and Mrs Bush.

All sorts of details were added – where to go, who to meet, if
you're bringing a chauffeur, present this voucher and he'll get a
packet of sandwiches. White tie and tails – I'd never ever worn
them! Where to get them? Was Moss Bros still operating? A
golden Sunday indeed, tinged with a little panic. How long had
we got – how long?

I was slightly apprehensive as we set out for Buckingham Palace on 19 November. With the possibility of demos against President Bush, security was formidable and the time schedule was tight and precise; we were asked to arrive between 7.50 and 8.10 p.m. As it turned out, I needn't have worried. Everything went smoothly.

We pulled up in front of the Palace, police and anti-terrorist officers examined the car and waved us into the quadrangle. Out we got and progressed up the red-carpeted steps and through the entrance. Figures in ceremonial dress were everywhere, some carrying swords, some carrying pikes and wearing breast-plates. It was rather overwhelming. Then it was up the grand staircase and into a big room where we met the Mistress of the Robes, a very handsome lady. Some thirty or forty people were there already, enjoying a pre-dinner drink, and many familiar faces were on view – the Prime Minister and Mrs Blair, Colin Powell (the American Secretary of State), the Archbishop of Canterbury, the Chief Rabbi, David Blunkett and his faithful guide dog among many others. Ewan Baird from Aberdeen was there. Together with a group of friends, he is developing what they all hope will become the finest golf club in Denmark. With the golfing success of Thomas Bjorn, I see no reason why the course should not become a reality.

Ian MacLaurin, now Lord MacLaurin, and his charming wife came up to say hello. He looked years younger having shed the responsibility of trying to introduce new ideas to the hierarchy of the cricketing world. Lord Vestey came over and was very complimentary about the way golf was presented on television. His presence seemed to attract others who also expressed their interest and pleasure in watching the modern golfing gladiators.

My dinner companion was Lady Branson, Richard's wife. What a delight! A down-to-earth Glaswegian who has been with the *enfant terrible* for more than twenty years. On my left was

Mrs Roberts, wife of Major General Sebastian Roberts of the Irish Guards. Immediately opposite was Princess Alexandra, the Honourable Lady Ogilvy, but since the table was getting on for six feet across, there was no possibility of conversation in that direction, so my evening was spent in bright conversation with the two ladies left and right.

Musicians of the Scots Guard band played light music in the Minstrels' Gallery. The programme finished with the march 'Good Old Vienna' but, hold on, here was Pipe Major Rowan of the Argyll and Sutherland Highlanders with a dozen stout pipers who paraded majestically round the great room making the rafters ring and the chandeliers dance. Who would dare to suggest that a true Scottish gentleman is one who can play the bagpipes but doesn't?

The Queen spoke, making, I was told, the longest speech anyone had ever heard her make. How eloquent she was. Her voice seems to have grown stronger. This was followed by a toast to the President of the United States and his great country. Then the President was on his feet. The man, sentiments and politics apart, spoke succinctly and with great sincerity. His toast was to the Queen and all she stands for.

We moved to an anteroom for after-dinner drinks and coffee – here was some time for social intercourse. We were fortunate to spend a few moments with the Duke of York who insisted upon using his new title 'Mr Captain' (of the Royal & Ancient Golf Club, that is). Princess Anne looked spectacularly well and the Duke of Edinburgh looked as fit as a fiddle and still with a saucy twinkle in his eye. We spoke with the Duke of Abercorn, the Lord Steward and then, believe it or not, came a conversation with the President of the United States, who rather threw me by saying how much he'd enjoyed listening to ABC's commentary the week before from Kiawah Island where the World Cup had just been played. Like his father, he was very keen on the game, although he didn't get out to play as often as he would like.

It was time to go. We had had a memorable evening, one I doubt we will ever repeat. One person, however, was not impressed by the occasion. Godfrey Smith of *The Times* wrote an article, headlined 'Dinner Dunces at the Palace', which I found patronising and critical, especially when he pointed out that the President's drinking habits – he is teetotal – meant Mr Bush could not appreciate the fine wine that was served. He posed the question, 'Isn't it time that she [the Queen] was spared the absurdity of state banquets altogether?' It seems the Queen can't win – if she has breakfast at a modest table with a toaster and Tupperware box on view, she is criticised; if it's all pomp and circumstance, she is still criticised. I don't think Mr Smith deserves the lady.

Later, I reflected on my life in golf and how I came to represent that royal and ancient game among the great and the good. We had been told that President Bush had also hired his outfit for the white-tie dinner – heigh ho!

I wondered what Jackie made of the evening and here are her memories of that very special occasion.

'BIRD'S EYE VIEW'
State Banquet by Jackie Alliss

When an invitation dropped through the post requesting our attendance at the state banquet at Buckingham Palace for President Bush on Wednesday, 19 November 2003, 'Why,' I asked Peter, 'have we been invited?' 'Not sure,' said he. 'Something to do with golf I expect.' Wow, I thought, what a great excuse to go and buy a new frock.

The great day arrived. There were tight arrangements for guests' arrival and due to the very vigilant security, we queued up on the forecourt of the Palace while the car was thoroughly examined. Then it was into the inner courtyard and up the marble stairs – take a deep breath and *don't trip*! The Palace is magnificent, spacious and elegant with a sweeping staircase carpeted in red leading you to the State Rooms, where we were greeted by the Mistress of the Robes. We then went into the reception area where we bumped into Ian MacLaurin and his wife – lovely to see familiar faces.

In a short time we were in the line-up to meet the Queen, the President, the Duke of Edinburgh and Mrs Bush. Foremost thought? Please let me not wobble on my curtsy. Then we went in to dinner. Again, I had a moment of panic when I realised to my horror that Peter and I were on different tables. 'Please don't leave me until one of my dinner neighbours has arrived,' I whispered and, bless him, he didn't. The table was glorious – two long leaves, the top table linking them, decorated with tall flower arrangements in deep pink and red with shades of green trailing down from the high pedestals.

Dinner was a clear soup followed by a delicious délice de flétan, which is halibut with herbs and a subtle sauce, then suprême de poulet fermier au bazilica (chicken with a herby stuffing) with finely chopped savoy cabbage, sauté potatoes and perfectly cooked root vegetables, all served in the most beautiful casserole dishes in solid gold. The table itself was set in gold – gold plates, gold cutlery, gold cruet, gold everything. It was very different. Pudding followed, to my surprise – a bombe glacée coppelia, which is a coffee ice-cream bombe with fresh fruits – and then a programme of music by the Argyll and Sutherland Pipers with their Highland Salute to the Queen. They do it so well – every kilt swung in unison, every foot tapped in time. It was stunning to listen to and wonderful to watch.

We retired for coffee and Peter and I were fortunate enough to be presented to President Bush. The President is a golfer and he and Peter have many friends in common, so there was much to talk about. Then the royal family departed and we made our way back down the sweeping red staircase to be met by our car. It had been quite a night. We'd had conversations with everyone except the Queen and Prince Charles. Prince Philip continues to amaze me, although he does seem to be getting a little shorter, but the twinkle in his eye and the sharpness of mind is there for all to see. It was a truly memorable evening, and we felt privileged to have been a part of it.

My overriding memories are of the red-clad Guardsmen lining the corridors and whispering 'Evening Mr Alliss' – golfers obviously – the sheer opulence of the State Banquet Hall, the elegance of the ladies of the Queen's Household, all of whom looked wonderful, and the Queen, of course, who was tinier than she appears when you see her in the press or on the television. I also remember the beautiful dresses of all the members of the royal family. My dinner partner, Lord Abercorn, the Lord Steward, made me feel totally at ease and was informative and charming. The menu/guest list booklet, bound in gold with a red, white and blue ribbon, is a souvenir to keep for my grandchildren.

Peter says his overriding memories are the sheer scale of the operation and, in a way, the simplicity of the service, the food service that is. I'm not sure how many stars Egon Ronay would have given some parts of the presentation but, for me, it was an occasion of a lifetime.

25

OH, ISLAND IN THE SUN

*'Mauritius is a lovely island and the people are
very kindly but they should be wary about
overdoing things'*

We discovered Mauritius and the Belle Mare Plage resort and
golf course some years ago. Before that we used to go to
Antigua and before that it was Tobago. Our holidays really
began through golf in the early seventies. David Thomas
returned from a pro-am in Tobago saying how glorious it
had all been, so in 1972 Jackie and I, together with a group
of friends from Moor Allerton, went off to sample the island's
delights. Ronnie Sumrie, our dear friend from Leeds, came
along, as did Don Fryer, a small, lively, property developer, John
Greenwood, a member of Moortown and Ganton and, for a
long time, the youngest winner of the Yorkshire Amateur
Championship, and Martin Curtis, a member from my Parkstone days, who made his living cutting grass. Now that may

sound strange but he had a number of contracts to make sure the grass at airfields up and down the country did not get too long. It was rather like painting the Forth Bridge but he did get a little respite during the winter!

Over the years, many friends came and went but Ronnie Sumrie was ever present, and what fun he was to be with. The Mount Irvine Bay Hotel was the venue. The course had been designed by the late Commander John Harris and cut out of a coconut plantation. It was an absolute delight even though the humidity could be monstrously high. We went there for ten or twelve years, until the prize money started getting bigger and bigger and players started arriving with bogus handicaps in an effort to win the $10/15/20,000 first prize. I'd spent too many years trying to hole four-foot putts to make a living, I certainly wasn't going to sweat over them when on holiday.

So we found another wonderful Caribbean island – Antigua. At that time there were three places to play golf. The Half Moon Bay Hotel had a modest 9-hole layout at the southeast end of the island. Mill Reef was a wondrous development with hundreds of acres of prime land and just fifty houses dotted about. The 9-hole course had a couple of holes that would have fitted into anyone's best eighteen in the world. Absolutely stunning, it was very élitist and private. Then there was Cedar Valley, an 18-hole course where we played much of our golf and where Jackie and I met the late Viscount Portman and his wife. A mad keen golfer, jazz enthusiast and reformed smoker, Eddie Portman was good company but he could go berserk if anyone lit up within 500 yards of his nose!

It was here that my deal with the PowaKaddy company was cut, sitting on a fallen tree on a lonely beach. The principals involved were John Martin and Joe Catford, who had started

PowaKaddy. Joe was the inventor and John the marketing man. Between them they created a great business. My connection ended at Christmas 2003 but what a long and happy association it was, thanks to Joe and John and latterly John de Graft Johnson and David Wells.

Con and Barbara Collins were another two great friends we teamed up with in Antigua. Con was then one of Ireland's foremost racehorse trainers, living on the Curragh, and Barbara had modelled for Balenciaga with Helen Wogan – two statuesque beauties, and both great fun. I enjoyed Antigua, the smiling faces, the rather antiquated cricket ground right next to the prison where, in those days, they still hanged criminals who did very bad things. Inmates could watch the cricket through the bars of their cells, freedom so near and yet so far away.

After Antigua we moved on to Mauritius and the Belle Mare Plage, which is run by the Constance Hotel Group, owners of the Prince Maurice and Le Muria resort in the Seychelles. A wonderful character called Adolphe Vallet, a man of high energy and foresight, is the company chairman. His family have been on the island for many generations and played a large part in the island's growth. Another of our new-found friends is retired judge Peter Rountree, whose family have a large plantation on the southern end of the island. They are contemplating applying for permission to build a golf course and hotel but this costs a great deal of money, so a rich partner, say a Ritz Carlton, Four Seasons or a Marriott Hotel Group, is needed to shoulder the expense. I have been involved in designing another new course, the Links, which is also owned by the Constance Group. It's settled in well and is an added attraction for the island.

Mauritius is a lovely island and the people are very kindly but they should be wary about overdoing things. The infrastructure is frail and when you think about what happened along the Costa del Sol, I wonder if things may overtake them, particularly if there is a shortage of rain for two or three years – that could seriously damage the economy and environment.

Judge Rountree is a big man, well over 6ft tall, a lover of golf and good whisky. He's just bought a house alongside the 18th fairway at the Belle Mare Plage course and intends to spend a couple of months a year on the island to get away from the dreariness of British winters.

We go for two weeks at the end of November, beginning of December. It's a long flight, twelve hours, but we've collected a nucleus of good friends who don't mind taking their holidays with us. In 2003 the whole of the Alliss brood went – three children, mum and dad. We arrived on the morning of the rugby World Cup final, Australia v. England. A large TV screen had been set up in one of the conference rooms and, after a quick wash and brush-up, we all went down to watch the match, along with sixty or seventy other people. There were a couple of Australians and some French but the majority were English. When the final whistle blew and England had won, the joy was overwhelming. I thought it was rather amusing a few weeks later when the French President was visiting London. He said how wonderful it had been for northern Europe that England had won the World Cup. I wonder if he would have used exactly those words if France had won? I think not, it would have been solely France's joy and, as for the rest of northern Europe, they could paddle their own canoe.

The Australians present took defeat in good spirit, as indeed did David Campese. Before the tournament he'd been slagging off England, saying effectively that they were a load of old poofters and had no chance of winning the championship and,

God forbid, if they were to win the World Cup, he would walk up and down Oxford Street with a sandwich board extolling that fact. Well, England won, and he did. On 15 December 2003 there he was, walking up and down Oxford Street as he had promised. I suppose it says a lot for the man, but it was under the banner of Ladbrokes the bookies. He took plenty of stick but he's got broad shoulders.

The Campese incident reminded me of how dangerous predictions can be, specifically in sport. I remember a time at the delightful Lindrick Club near Worksop on the borders of Nottinghamshire, Yorkshire and Derbyshire. The occasion was the 1957 Ryder Cup. After the foursomes we were 3–1 down and Desmond Hackett, the premier sports columnist with the *Daily Express*, wrote, 'If Britain and Ireland manage to win, I'll eat my hat.' Now Hackett was famed for wearing a brown derby, or bowler as it's better known in our circles. Well, we won and, bless him, he did – but he cheated a bit. He had one made out of cake mixture, not a large one I hasten to add, but he got it all down.

Another journalist of the day, Jack Wood, a great character and former bomber pilot from World War Two, was one of the first writers to start writing articles with a bite to them, bordering on the vitriolic. He wrote that if the home team won, you could bury him underneath two tons of compost. This piece appeared in the *News of the World* and I suppose, being the *News of the World*, they were very constrained in using the word 'compost'. Anyway, I'm not quite sure what happened after our amazing and unexpected victory. Perhaps he compromised by putting on a pair of Wellington boots and standing in a cow pat for five minutes. All in all, it shows how careful you have to be when speaking of the chances of underdogs.

Our holiday was enjoyed by all although I could have done with another few days. I was just beginning to switch off when it was time to come home. Simon Clough is the professional and does a fine job along with his American wife, Karen. They fit into the island life very well and make everyone most welcome.

Another course opened while we were there, at the Tousserok Hotel, designed by Bernhard Langer and under the wing of the IMG organisation. The hotel itself is owned by the Sun Group, who created the famous Sun City complex some hundred miles north of Johannesburg. The course is interesting to say the least, built on a very difficult piece of ground, much of it a mangrove swamp. I try never to criticise other people's work because you never know what restrictions have been put on them by the terrain, the environmentalists or the size of the budget, but, for what it's worth, I think the majority of the greens are too small. Some of the short holes are perched up in the air like thimbles – miss the green at your peril! There's lots and lots of water. The course is on an island so a little boat runs from the hotel jetty half a mile or so to another jetty where you're picked up in a smart golf cart and taken up to the clubhouse where you are greeted by David Marsh, who has spent most of his life setting up golf courses in various parts of the world, a lot of them under the banner of IMG. He has built up a very fine reputation and makes everyone feel at home. Considering the course had been grassed/seeded some five months before, the quality of the fairways and tees was amazing. The greens were a little new but after another few months they should improve dramatically. Evidently, they are trying out a new seed combination that can be sustained with brackish, salty water, and I'm told you don't need much of it. If successful, that could revolutionise golf in hot countries. I wish them well.

Just a few yards up the road from the Belle Mare Plage, another grand hotel, the Saint Geran, has a splendid 9-hole, Gary Player designed golf course, which hardly seems to get used at all. That's very surprising, although there's a good deal of snobbery in golf, which I find rather tedious. I've heard people who don't play very well say, 'Oh, it's just a little nine-hole course, can't be much good, hardly worthy of my steel,' when in reality the course is probably much beyond their meagre skills. The course runs right along the edge of the beach, stopping at the edge of the Belle Mare Plage property, so, if you do get tired a couple of holes from home, you can just step along the beach and call in at the new Belle Mare Plage Italian restaurant, which is an absolute delight.

During that holiday, I had the opportunity to play quite a bit of golf with my sons Simon and Henry. On our final day we had nine holes with Simon Clough, Adolphe Vallet and Ian Poulter, who was holidaying on the island with his family before taking part in the Mauritius Open. Believe it or not, I felt slightly nervous stepping on to the 1st tee with Ian. I didn't want him to think I couldn't play now, and perhaps never could, but apart from a couple of holes where I put balls in the water, my golf was relatively good and I came away with happy memories of our nine holes and high hopes for Ian, who has a huge talent – needs a bit more rounding off, a touch of polishing here and there, and to slow down a whisker, but if he doesn't become a giant star over the next five years, I'll be very surprised. Of course, much depends on temperament and nerves.

When we returned from Mauritius we drove more or less straight to the wedding of Katherine Helen Bernadette Wogan, Terry and Helen's daughter, and what a splendid affair it was. The church of St Nicholas, a beautiful building in the fair village of Taplow, was filled with the most wondrous flowers, and the service was very different. Father Brian D'Arcy, a regular on Terry's 'Wake up to Wogan' breakfast show, was officiating together with the local vicar, Alan Dibden – a dual wedding, Anglican and Catholic. Katherine had been brought up in the Catholic faith and Henry Cripps, the bridegroom (a distant relation of the politician Sir Stafford Cripps) in the Church of England. They had a choir. If I had a magic wand, everyone getting married, and indeed everyone being seen off to the great country club in the sky, should have a choir, and a trumpet or two to enhance the various hymns. The trumpeter's rendition of the 'Bridal March' from Lohengrin added a touch of magic. It wasn't a long service and afterwards we all made our way to Wogan Towers, a large, majestic, late Victorian house. Over 200 guests spilled on to the terrace and out into an absolute village of marquees, which Mr Wogan referred to in his speech as only the second man-made object that could be seen from outer space, the other being the Great Wall of China!

The flowers and table decorations were exquisite. The bride and groom, and many of the rest of us, got quite emotional. The father of the bride spoke and once or twice I thought I detected a catch in his voice. Father D'Arcy eulogised about the joys of marriage and how wonderful it was to see young people so much in love. I looked round at the wondrous scene and hoped they would see each other through to old age but my silly mind wandered to thoughts of pre-nuptial agreements. Dear old Father D'Arcy did go on a bit and, at the end of it all, I wondered, listening to him, how anyone could ever contemplate divorce – but, as I well know, it happens. As my grandma used to say, 'You've got to live closer than next door to know what people are really like.'

The meal was splendid, the wine flowed, and around 9.30 p.m. the curtains behind the top table were drawn back and there was yet another marquee, about half the size of a tennis court. A six-piece band was primed and ready to go and they were being led by the new singing sensation Jamie Cullum. What a grand surprise! Suddenly everyone was up and dancing, leppin like banshees; I wouldn't have been at all surprised if there had been a woman upstairs in bed getting double helpings of porter!

After our long flight, and a sixteen-hour delay, we were beginning to flag, plus I was the only person in a lounge suit. Well, there had been no indication on the invitation that it was morning dress and, dammit, we had four hours only to get from Heathrow home, powdered, shaved and back to Taplow. Strangely enough, I didn't feel all that awkward. I think my dear wife was slightly worried for me but I managed to carry it off reasonably well due to a mixture of extreme arrogance and stupidity! We tip-toed away at about 10.15 p.m. – the last carriages left about one o'clock after bacon butties and fish and chips at the end of a glorious day. Wogan probably had used up his entire salary for a year or two to cover the cost but how worthwhile it had all been and, you know what – I didn't see a photographer from any one of those magazines that splash out half a million quid for the privilege of showing people signing on the registrar's dotted line.

This fine occasion brought back memories of another wedding we attended a few years ago when Joanna Leschallas married Edward Berry, a first cousin of Princess Diana. Jackie and I met the Leschallas family in 1969. Anthony was then the managing director of Mentzendorff, the wine importer whose flagship was the Bollinger Champagne marque, and we met him and his wife Lindy when the company decided they would have a modest tent at the Open championship to see if they could introduce people to the idea of having a glass of champagne on a hot day or, for that matter, a cold, wet and dreary one. That was the year Tony Jacklin won at Royal Lytham & St Annes and it was the start of a custom that has gone on ever since. Every year the familiar red and white tent is set up close to the action. It's very different from those early days when no profits were made – they must have wondered whether this champagne thing was a sensible idea. I'm glad they persevered. Today Simon Leschallas is at the helm, continuing his father's great tradition.

Joanna and Edward were married in the late eighties at the Cranbrook parish church, known as the Cathedral of the Weald because of its size and beauty. It was a beautiful sunny day, the service simple and elegant. The two princes, William and Harry, acted as pages. Princess Diana fussed around like all good mums do, and was delightful. The guests were served superb canapés and, of course, Bollinger. A beautiful cake arrived – a piece for you and a piece for you – then it was time to go. Some said it was an 'old-fashioned wedding'; I thought it wonderful in its simplicity. Sadly, Joanna and Edward are now divorced but I'm told it's all very civilised. Well, that seems to be the modern way. They speak to each other on a weekly basis, still care very much for each other but just decided they no longer wished to be married. Three beautiful children were the result of their liaison.

And now we come to the end of the adventures of Alliss. Most recently I've been down to Wadebridge in North Cornwall to participate in the opening of the new Gary Alliss Golf Academy at the Hustyns Hotel and Spa, some three or four miles south of the town. What a wonderful oasis, although it's not the easiest place to find – oh yes, there are plenty of signposts but the way gets narrower and narrower, rather like the road down to the splendid Gidleigh Park Hotel near Chagford in Devon. It's a superb facility. Others may be larger but I doubt whether there are any with more sophisticated appliances on view to help a golfer improve. It's a whole new challenge for Gary but with his love and understanding of the game, and the huge input and enthusiasm from the owner, Terry Johnson, this will, I'm sure, become a very special place for those looking for a peaceful holiday or a cure for their socket!

I hope to go on for a few more years yet, enjoying the delights and frustrations of this marvellous game of golf. I know a number of people think that I am well past my 'sell by date' and wish I was more technical in my commentaries. I honestly don't think I need to add my sixpen'orth to that argument – there are certainly enough at the moment who seem to know the reason for every shot that doesn't go as straight as an arrow.

Over my life in golf, which is now well over fifty years, I have met and enjoyed the company of so many people it would be totally impossible to mention them all here. I would be bound to forget somebody who played, if not a great role in my life, someone who stimulated me, created situations and introduced ideas and ideals that have stood me in good stead over the years; friends and acquaintances who had no involvement in the game of golf, who have, through their good fellowship, afforded me advice, friendship and, above all, set standards that in many cases I have tried to follow.

As you get older, you realise the stupidity of war. It intrigues me that we are a country going on for 60 million people. I read somewhere that there are approximately 75,000 to 80,000 in jail. Some are there, perhaps, who shouldn't be, but let's double it, no let's treble it and add another 100,000 for good measure, so now we are up to 400,000 people who are either dangerous, dishonest or just plain nasty and yet not very much seems to be being done to control, eliminate, dispense, train – whatever you wish to call it – that number and it's continually 'the rest' who are pummelled and punished. The latest example is the possibility of an increase in death duties. I've always considered that tax to be grossly unfair, particularly for those who have started modestly, scrimped and saved, worked hard and paid their taxes. Just because they have been frugal and saved a goodly sum of money, the government decides it wants a further donation. It is quite ridiculous with the amount that is totally wasted in the affairs of this country and, indeed, throughout the world. But there I go, pontificating again but, oh dear me, I do wish somebody would grasp the reins and do something instead of trying to please the wrong end of the spectrum.

Thank you for your support, your friendship, your encouragement over the years. I have indeed been fortunate in surrounding myself with so many good friends and wonderful acquaintances, and a special word to the women in my life whom I've loved and from whom received much love in return. You are always in my thoughts.

Appendix 1

LEND A HAND

The Wheelchair Crusade was instigated by George Makey MBE in 1975 when he had the idea of generating money for powered wheelchairs for young people who were suffering from spina bifida, muscular dystrophy and the like. Towards the end of the seventies he asked me if I would participate, which I was more than happy to do. But back in those early days, never did I think it would reach out to so many people or influence so many lives. Since we began, we are approaching £5 million in monies donated and pretty well every penny has gone towards wheelchairs which, when we first started the programme, cost £600 or £700. Now the most expensive ones can go up to £10,000–£12,000.

Over the years there has been tremendous support by a number of golf clubs up and down the UK and in Ireland and also small groups of people who have clubbed together in an effort to generate funds that go towards buying a wheelchair. It's always difficult to pick out any particular club but one is very special. It's the Helsby Golf Club in Cheshire. It is a remarkable club with an amazing group of members who have followed our Crusade for many years and have collected enough money to provide a staggering number of wheelchairs. They have been led by Bert Dyson who has never flagged in his enthusiasm for helping these unfortunate young people. Their efforts have seen the count of powered wheelchairs given to local children, to the end of 2003, reach 174 – that's right, one hundred and seventy-four – over twenty years! In addition, thirty manual wheelchairs were bought and sent to Iraq to help children who had been hurt in the recent conflict.

The Helsby Golf Club Powered Wheelchair Appeal is affiliated to the Sunrise Medical–Peter Alliss Masters Charity, a CAF Registered Charity, account number T/50219819.

Helsby is an unassuming club sited about a mile from the M56 at Junction 14 in Cheshire and has a pretty woodland course running to around 6,200 yards. It is not Wentworth, Muirfield or Loch Lomond. It doesn't pretend to be, but its achievements have been remarkable and typical of the support of several other clubs.

Helsby's main fundraiser is the Helsby Golf Club Powered Wheelchair Classic, a golf day held in June in which some 230 golfers participate. In the first year, a cheese and wine party, a raffle and a golf competition raised £540, not quite enough for a powered chair but Marley Tile Ltd donated the balance. Marley at that time were sponsoring a nationwide appeal known as the Marley Wheelchair Classic. Helsby has had various celebrities attending their golf day, including Cyril Smith MP, the Duke of Westminster, Roger Hunt, 1966 World Cup team member, and many other Everton and Liverpool footballers. Not one of them has asked for a penny appearance fee.

The club's involvement began in 1983. Alan Lee, Chairman of the appeal, tells the history:

The idea was formed when a club member, who attended the Open Championship at Royal Birkdale in 1983, saw Lee Trevino and Seve Ballesteros presenting a number of powered chairs to handicapped children. Seeing the faces of these youngsters as they received their wheelchairs was unforgettable and he felt Helsby Golf Club could do something. They now involve local companies, in addition to the club members, in supporting in many ways. Bert Dyson has been the Appeal Secretary since its conception. Without his dedication we would not be where we are today. We have a wonderful committee who work hard and give their services free and we are well supported by our club's management and members.

Incidentally, the 2003 accounts showed an income of £33,068.80. Bert Dyson, announcing that the expenses for the year were £321.22, warned they may have to be higher in 2004! In all, the appeal has raised more than £300,000.

My father's old club at Ferndown has also contributed to a wealth of wheelchairs, particularly in the south of England. Ferndown is located some six miles north of Bournemouth and every year, for the last fifteen or sixteen, I have joined forces with John Iles and his company Merlo to stage a Pro-Am on a Monday in September. That particular year's captain and I split the profits, his share going towards local charities, which have covered an amazing range of activities. Mine, as always, goes towards powered wheelchairs. The club and local supporters have been wonderful over that long period. The Dormy Hotel at Ferndown also played a great part in this event, along with the then manager, Derek Silk, who worked tirelessly on behalf of our golf day.

Early in October we have the Alliss Masters, a grand-sounding title! It's basically for those who have contributed to the Crusade during the year and over the years it has worked very well. Off we go to the Elie Golf Club and stay at the Craw's Nest Hotel at Anstruther. Again, both these institutions have looked after us brilliantly. The most players we've ever had at Elie in any one year was about 110. Depending on how much a golf club raises, they get a place in the tournament, which is an 18-hole Stableford affair played on this delightful golf course directly opposite the mighty Honourable Company of Edinburgh Golfers across the Firth of Forth. Should you ever find yourself in that part of the world, or you're thinking of a golfing holiday in Scotland, do explore the south coast of Fife. There are so many delightful courses and, of course, your base must be the Craw's Nest, providing you only need three or four hours sleep a night and have the constitution of a lion!

Dr Hamish McLeod, another stalwart of our Wheelchair Crusade, practised medicine in Moffat for many years and was one of the first doctors on the scene at the Lockerbie disaster. A remarkable man, able to build his own aeroplane, he even constructed a motor car. He was semi-retired when he saw a medical position advertised for the Carnival cruise line, based in Florida. He ended up being their chief medical officer, revitalising and revolutionising the facilities on board their fleet of giant cruise ships.

Another huge contributor has been the Turkey Federation. Each year they have a golf day, a big gathering and huge auction; they are totally committed. It still staggers me when a cheque for £20–30,000 arrives, which they suggest we 'put into the kitty for people less fortunate than ourselves'. There's Tony Endersby, a stalwart at the Chestfield Golf Club in Thanet, and John Roper, one of the kings of the Turkey Breeders' Association. A wonderful character, he farms near Cromer and has an amazing collection of friends who, year after year, contribute in one way or another to our funds. Danny Rowe comes readily to mind. How often I've enjoyed his company for a game at Swinley Forest; and there's Roger Cooke, one of the finest fundraisers and all-round good eggs I've ever met. George Makey continued to play a big part well into his eighties but sadly he died in July 2004, aged eighty-nine.

My other charitable interest is in DEBRA. This is a research organisation, which is also a support charity, for those suffering from Epidermolysis Bullosa, a fearful inherited disease that at the moment cannot be cured. When a child is born with EB, the proteins that normally hold the skin together do not function. That means that outer skin and internal linings do not fuse and can be so fragile that any knock or rub, even a parent's hug, can cause astonishing blistering, tearing and permanent damage. A child with this condition may have to face three hours of preparation each morning before he or she can face the day. Sufferers will have slept trussed in bandages, which nevertheless often fail to protect from blisters and broken skin. These bandages have to be delicately removed, blisters lanced and a complete body-covering of fresh bandages applied. The child is never without paddings or dressings. Apart from this appalling daily trauma for the child, mum and dad have to cope with their own trauma, knowing that, at the moment, there is no cure.

In 1978 a group of parents of EB children, frustrated by the lack of both medical and social support, decided to band together as a self-help association to share experiences and to provide support for one another – hence DEBRA, Dystrophic Epidermolysis Bullosa Research Association. The leader of the group was Phyllis Hilton whose daughter Debra suffered from the dystrophic form of this condition. Despite lack of funds, the group survived and grew. Now DEBRA funds vital research and development, supports families living with EB and funds specialist teams of nurses and advisors and educates the medical profession, acting nationally and internationally on behalf of EB sufferers.

This EB condition is almost beyond belief. Could there ever be a more worthy cause than helping these suffering children? If you would like to help, contact John Taylorson, a giant contributor to the cause, at:

DEBRA House, 13 Wellington Business Park, Dukes Ride, Crowthorne, Berks RG45 6LS. Telephone: 01344 771961.

In March 2004 Channel 4 showed a most extraordinary programme about Jonny Kennedy who suffered from EB. It was a very harrowing programme but dealt with his enormous courage and tenacity. You can't say too much about someone like Jonny Kennedy or, indeed, his parents who were magnificent, and the small number of people whose children suffer from this terrible, terrible illness. I was privileged to meet Jonny on a couple of occasions, the last when he came to a fundraising dinner at the Wentworth Club where he lifted everyone's hearts with his wonderful spirit.

Sadly, there comes a time when you feel you've spread yourself as thinly as you can in the quest for funds for worthwhile charities. Personally, I reached that stage some years ago, although Jackie is involved in a number of charities to which I add some weight (well I've got a little to give!). When you see how some charities are run, how much money is collected and how little actually reaches the end destination, it can be very off-putting, so caution has been my friend. It's amazing how many people give so willingly with no thought of any reward or mentions in despatches.

FOOD FOR THOUGHT

If a child lives with criticism he learns to condemn
If a child lives with hostility he learns to fight
If a child lives with ridicule he learns to be shy
If a child lives with shame he learns to be guilty
If a child lives with tolerance he learns to be patient
If a child lives with encouragement he learns to be confident
If a child lives with praise he learns to appreciate
If a child lives with fairness he learns justice
If a child lives with security he learns to have faith
If a child lives with approval he learns to like himself
If a child lives with acceptance and friendship he learns to find
love in the world.

These words were read at the funeral of Andrew Hughes-Onslow, an old friend of mine.

I would be true for there are those who trust me
I would be pure for there are those who care
I would be strong for there is much to suffer
I would be brave for there is much to dare
I would be friend of all, the foe the friendless
I would be giving and forget the gift
I would be humble and know my weakness
I would look up and laugh and love and live.

Appendix 2

MY GOLF CAREER

I covered my Ryder Cup record earlier but the following statistics cover my overall career.

Represented England in what was the Canada Cup, which in 1966 became the World Cup, on ten occasions. Played at Laval-sur-Lac in Montreal in 1954 and again in 1955 when the matches were played in Washington DC. Then on to Tokyo in 1957; Mexico City in 1958 and Australia in 1959; 1961 Puerto Rico; 1962 in Buenos Aires; 1964 Maui in Hawaii; 1966 again in Tokyo and my final appearance was in 1967 when the matches were played in Mexico City. Best performance was runner-up in 1962 in the individual, tying with Arnold Palmer.

Tournament wins
The Spanish Open Championship in 1956 and 1958; the Italian in 1958; the Portuguese in 1958. The 1958 wins were in three consecutive weeks. The Brazilian in 1961.

Other victories
Daks in 1954 at Little Aston
The Dunlop in 1955 and 1959
The PGA Championship in 1957, 1962 and 1965
The Sprite, tied in 1960
Swallow, Penfold in 1964
The Esso Golden at Moor Park in 1964
The Jeyes in 1965
Martini, tied in 1966
Rediffusion in 1966, Channel Islands
Agfa Gevaert at Stoke Poges, now known as Stoke Park, in 1967
Final victory was the Piccadilly in 1969 at Prince's in Kent

The West of England Championship four times in 1956, 1958, 1962 and 1966
Sunningdale Foursomes in 1958 and 1961
Wentworth Pro-Am Foursomes in 1959 and the Assistants Championship in 1952

The Home Internationals in 1967
United Kingdom v. Europe for the Joy Cup in 1954, 1955 and 1956

Played for England once as an amateur in the Boys Championship at Bruntsfield Golf Club on the west side of Edinburgh in 1946.

Miscellaneous
PGA Captain twice in 1962 and 1987
Vardon Trophy winner in 1964 and 1966
Inaugural President of the Women's European Professional Tour
President of the British Greenkeepers Association

Honorary memberships

The PGA

The European PGA Tour

The Royal & Ancient Golf Club of St Andrews

Auchterader

Letham Grange

Peel

Guildford

Ferndown

Parkstone

Trevose

Beaconsfield

Royal Cinque Ports Deal

Coombe Hill

Moor Allerton

Wentworth

Stoke Park

Chestfield

Lelant West Cornwall

Broadstone

Lahinch

Hindhead

Whitburn

Loch Lomond

Old Thorns

Royal Porthcawl

Muirfield Village

Kemper Lakes in Illinois

Appendix 3

A Propos Nothing – My Cars

In the early fifties when I was getting into my stride as a tournament golfer, the motor car, which is now commonplace, was (a) a necessity for my work and (b) a status symbol. But when a fetish becomes an obsession, a man can consider himself well and truly hooked and that has been me and the motor car. It's been one of my great extravagances.

The first car I bought was an open-topped Morris Minor circa 1949, it cost £675 and the number was DPR 725. My brother had ordered it on his return from service in the Royal Navy at the end of the war. It arrived, costing £550, he didn't have the money so my father took it off him, ran it for four years and then, being a good businessman, sold it to me for a profit! Yes, dear old DPR 725, funny how you always remember your first car and your service number, mine in the RAF Regiment was 2435517. But, back to my cars, that was the first, black of course and a very good little runner.

It was round about that time I made friends with John Lee.

His family had an old established motor business in Bourne-mouth and for many years were the main Rover and Vauxhall dealers. John was married to a very vivacious lady called Vivi-enne who staged many of the Bournemouth ice-rink extrava-ganzas. She was a very good contact lady. Another pal was Bill Forman, who was married to a delightful Danish lady. They had a garage business exactly where the Bournemouth Conference Centre stands today. He was the agent for Sunbeam. So over a number of years I fluctuated between Vauxhalls, which ranged from Wyvern to Velox to Cresta. The last one was a fine American-looking car with a wrap around windscreen and a full bench front seat in rather an exotic colour, and my friends called it nipple pink and grey. I also had a full range of Rovers, 2000TC, V8, all wonderful cars. In all those years the only thing that ever went wrong was an alternator.

David Thomas and I had a couple of jazzed up Sunbeam Rapiers fitted with a Jack Brabham conversion, which gave them seven forward gears operated by a little switch on the steering column. My number plate was 4343 EL, Dave's was 4344 EL, so I was one up after four! His was grey and red, mine was dark green and light grey, very smart, wonderful little cars.

For a time I had a Lotus Cortina. Many of you will be familiar with that white car with the distinctive green flash down the side and the Lotus badges on the rear wings. A Sunbeam Alpine was very nice and a good bird puller, but you needed to do a Charles Atlas course to put the hood up. Then I had a smart 2.4 Jaguar with red upholstery, oooh what a magnificent looking machine but totally under-powered with a horrible gearbox. Then on to a Riley Healey shooting brake, a special car, possibly a one-off. It was very distinctive, the sort of thing that Princess Anne might have driven twenty-five years ago. But sadly I was going a bit fast across Salisbury plain and put a piston straight through the engine!

I then found an R Type Bentley – you remember the one I mentioned earlier with the big lift-up boot lid and which caused some consternation at Parkstone Golf Club.

By this time my home life was in disarray and I moved to Leeds with a Rover V8, dark blue in colour, and an overdraft of about £6,000. But that car kept going for another couple of years by which time I'd saved up enough money to purchase a BMW Coupé bought from the British Car Auctions establishment at Brighouse, just off the M62 near Bradford. In fact, I had two. One was in two shades of brown and had an aluminium body and was a real flying machine, the other aquamarine. Both were superb, handled beautifully and created much interest although there was just room for two people, a set of golf clubs and a toothbrush.

I remember going to Ganton in 1975 to watch play in the British Masters that Bernard Gallacher won. On the way over I picked up a couple of friends, Ronnie Sumrie and Don Fryer, who was a bit of a jazzer and also a member at Moor Allerton. My BMW was greatly admired by Don, who had a Rolls-Royce, which he assured me was in magnificent condition. The only person to have owned it before him was an elderly lady who drove it carefully and she convinced him it had never been raced or rallied. To cut a long story short, we did a straight swap. Yep, suddenly I was the proud possessor of a 1968, remember the year was 1975, maroon, or garnet as they liked to call it, Rolls-Royce.

A year later I acquired the number plate 'PUT 3'. It was advertised in *The Sunday Times*, a Leicestershire number. The advert read: 'Golfers look, PUT 3, on a 1971 yellow V12 Jaguar

2+2.' The price was £2,500. I thought this was all too good to be true. I didn't want 'PUT 1', that would be ridiculous, 'PUT 2', well that was a bit ordinary, 'PUT 4', no, although I had done it twice in my life! 'PUT 3' struck the right sort of chord with my sense of humour. I phoned my dear friend David Wickins, the chairman of British Car Auctions – well, if you want a bit of information always go to the top man. I asked him the price of a V12 2+2 1971, 18,000 miles on the clock, with the number plate PUT 3. He thought at £2,500 it was a good buy. So off I went down the M1 to rendezvous with the V12's owner at the Leicester Forest service station. We must have been very trusting in those days. We exchanged log books and cheques, at least I think that's how the deal was done, and I drove off only to discover a few hundred miles later that the radiator was absolutely knackered. It looked as if someone had fired a couple of rounds of 12-bore pellets into it.

So the 'Primrose Flyer' had to go but I retained 'PUT 3', which I have to this very day, although there was a hiccup along the way. I bought a Rolls-Royce from a doctor who also had his own personal number plate. Somewhere along the line the paperwork got mixed up and his number was 'lost' so he wouldn't give mine back. I said, 'Look, what's the use of "PUT 3" to you?' But no, he wouldn't have it unless I paid him several hundred pounds, which annoyed me greatly, but then I'd gone through far too much with dear old 'PUT 3' to lose it to some bad-tempered doctor.

By now I was seriously into Bentleys and Rolls-Royces. Almost all the deals were done through British Car Auctions. I was lucky on a number of occasions to have someone with me who understood the auction business. You can strike lucky particularly if you're selling a car on a day when two people are after the same machine, but beware, dealers are always mindful of a car's retail value. They won't go mad.

My first couple of sorties into the world of car auctions were wonderful. I'd kept both cars for over a year and sold them for a thousand or two pounds more than I'd paid. Then I got a bit carried away, paying £18,000 for an absolute beauty but two years later I was very lucky to get £11,500 for it. But, on the whole, they've been great fun to drive even though the old Rolls did wallow a bit.

What have I got now? Well, it's my last extravagance, it's a Continental T Bentley circa 2001, dark pewter in colour, almost black in fact, with black upholstery, an aluminium dashboard, a huge single exhaust pipe sticking out of the back, a good-sized boot, two very comfortable front seats and, if pushed, you could get two five year olds in the back, as long as the journey wasn't going to be for more than five miles. Yes, I know, an extravagance, but it's sensational, so beautiful in fact, I hate taking it out when the weather is inclement. But I've got to be careful it doesn't carry me away, particularly when I'm driving through the night, the moon full, the road dry, the motorways empty . . . suddenly you glance down and, horror upon horror, you're just a wee bit over the speed limit!

INDEX